FAMILIES in
PERPETUAL CRISIS

FAMILIES in PERPETUAL CRISIS

Richard Kagan
Shirley Schlosberg

PARSONS CHILD AND FAMILY CENTER
ALBANY, NEW YORK

W. W. Norton & Company, Inc • *New York* • *London*

Copyright © 1989 by Richard Kagan and Shirley Schlosberg

Published simultaneously in Canada by Penguin Books Canada Ltd.,
2801 John Street, Markham, Ontario L3R 1B4.

Printed in the United States of America.

First Edition

Library of Congress Cataloging-in-Publication Data

Kagan, Richard.
  Families in perpetual crisis / Richard Kagan, Shirley Schlosberg.
— 1st ed.
    p.   cm.
  "A Norton professional book."
  Bibliography: p.
  ISBN 0-393-70066-6
  1. Family social work—United States. 2. Problem families—
Counseling of —United States. 3. Foster home care—United States.
I. Schlosberg, Shirley. II. Title.
HV699.K34 1989
362.8'2'0973—dc19

ISBN 0-393-70066-6

W. W. Norton & Company, Inc., 500 Fifth Avenue, New York, N. Y. 10110
W. W. Norton & Company Ltd., 37 Great Russell Street, London WC1B 3NU

1 2 3 4 5 6 7 8 9 0

CONTENTS

To Laura, Michael, Joshua, Michelle,
and Al, Susan, Claudia, and Adrienne

PREFACE

FAMILIES REFERRED TO CHILD welfare agencies are often fearful, angry, and untrusting. They expect to be blamed. Most have had a history of long involvement and placements with multiple agencies, courts, hospitals, and child protective services. Professionals are often seen by families as intimidating parent figures who are insensitive in many ways to the family's primary needs and inadvertently threaten the integrity and stability of the family.

Referral sources often seek help for severe problems such as recurrent incidents of abuse, neglect, family violence, and delinquent behavior. However, these families usually do not come to agencies asking for help. Instead they feel victimized by interventions from family courts, educators, and social services staff (Kaplan, 1986). Intensive interventions may be resisted as an intrusion into the family. And services of limited duration (e.g., under four months) may have little long-term impact on members of these chronically troubled families (Compton, 1979). In general, chronically dysfunctional families have been perceived as unresponsive to traditional family or individual therapies (Riessman, 1973; Weitzman, 1985). The most striking thing about these families is their resistance to change despite the orders, pleas, exhortations, and the combined efforts of multiple community agencies. Accordingly, placement is often utilized to remove the pain for both the family and the community of acting-out parents or children who are often dangerous to themselves or others.

Working with families who have long histories of severe problems can be overwhelming. Family workers experience hostility and rejection from these families and often become frustrated and feel the same despair experienced by their "clients." The helplessness, depression, and repetition of serious problems encountered can exhaust the most energetic practitioner.

This book is based on a model of family work we developed in the Prevention Program of Parsons Child and Family Center after 11 years of experience working with more than 1,000 families with children at high risk of imminent institutional placement. This model reflects both traditional approaches to family therapy and the need to be innovative in order to engage crisis-oriented families. Use of this model has prevented placement of children in 88 percent of families served*; moreover, high satisfaction with services has been reported by families involved in the program (Frawley, 1986; Reid, Kagan, & Schlosberg, 1988).

This is, of course, just one of many home-based family counseling programs which have been developed in the United States in recent years (Kaplan, 1986; Maluccio, Fein, & Olmstead, 1986; Norman, 1985; Zigler, Weiss, & Kagan, undated). Parsons' Prevention Program differed from other prevention of placement services by providing extended family counseling on an outreach basis for chronic multiproblem families and by accepting referrals of "children in placement" where "diligent efforts" were required to reunite children with their families or, if that was not possible, to work towards an adoptive placement. The Prevention Program was based on collaborative work with county departments of social services, county departments of probation, and family courts. Parsons' Prevention Program operated with two primary assumptions: (1) that major "permanency" issues existed in all cases of children referred, and (2) that families needed one family worker with whom they could form a strong relationship over time and who could respect and help families with dilemmas stemming from past traumas, losses, and lack of trust over generations. Families with severe multiproblem crises were assumed to have chronic problems requiring intensive and lengthy efforts to improve each family's ability to cope and lessen individual problems. Given the acting-out tendencies of these families and their overt resistance to past and current therapeutic programs, primary efforts were made to engage families and referral sources in a working relationship with staff. Prevention workers had to have the ability to develop intensive rela-

---

*This figure does not include surrendered children, wherein the goal of placement was to develop reattachments to an adoptive family. Total N for this study was 288 and based on work between 1981 and 1985.

tionships with chaotic families characterized by chronic and severe problems, e.g., physical or sexual abuse, neglect, or violence.

The Prevention Program worked with many families who had refused to work with other family counseling services or placement agency staff or who had dropped out of other treatment programs after only a few sessions. The Prevention Program focused on helping families to interrupt dysfunctional family patterns from generation to generation as well as to cope with immediate problems. In short, the Prevention Program provided an alternative to traditional outpatient services, crisis counseling, day treatment school placements, or institutional placement for children.

This book is written for family workers* in public and private social services agencies, mental health clinics, psychiatric hospitals, and other facilities who have committed their time and energy to helping families in severe and chronic difficulty. In this book, we will examine the need for permanence for children in families and the impact of loss, trauma, and abuse across generations and over time. We will share techniques for "getting in the door," engaging resistant clients, and working with patterns of resistance. We will also discuss the "how-to's" of doing home-based family assessments. A family systems approach for helping children in placement will be presented. We will examine how professionals can help a family at the point of placement to plan for change using time as a catalyst. Strategies for helping families who demand that, "You change Johnny" or demur that, "We just can't make it this weekend . . . " will be presented. Assessment approaches and treatment interventions will be discussed for children "in limbo" (after Finkelstein, 1980) where attachments and relationships—the context of crazy or dangerous behaviors—are unknown. We will look at how to help a family reconstitute when a member returns or leaves permanently. Finally, we will examine critical issues and survival strategies for practitioners.

Our hope is that practitioners can build on the theories and interventions described in this book to develop a better understanding and more effective approaches for helping children and families referred to agencies, clinics, and hospitals for chronic and severe problems.

---

*Throughout this book we will be referring to family workers to represent caseworkers, social workers, psychiatrists, and psychologists in public and private agencies.

ACKNOWLEDGMENTS

THIS BOOK IS BASED ON our work with families referred for chronic and severe problems to Parsons Child and Family Center's Prevention Program. We are very grateful to John Carswell and Nadia Finkelstein for their support of our writing and for establishing an environment at Parsons which promotes professional development. We would like to extend special thanks to Drs. Wander de C. Braga, Margaret Griffel, Carl Mindel, John Myers, and Lenore Sportsman for their insights, creative interpretations, and consultations, to Prevention supervisors (Diane Aman, Harvey Baines, Julie Maher, Kathleen Pratt, Steven Roberts, Timothy Selby, Robin Sorriento, Cynthia Szypulski, Dorothy Tristman, Mary Wolf), who helped build this program (currently serving four counties), to Teresa Kennedy and Cheryl O'Henesian who helped introduce the program to neighboring counties, and to the Prevention Staff whose sensitivity, caring, long hours and mileage have made Parsons' Prevention Program a success.

We are heavily indebted to the families who shared so much of their lives with us and to the staff of Albany, Schenectady, Rensselaer, and Schoharie Departments of Social Services. In particular, we would like to thank Andrea Burger, Director of Children and Family Services, and Sharon Clancy,

Supervisor of the Permanency Unit, Albany County Department of Social Services; Jane Whamer, Schenectady County Department of Social Services; Jack Craney, Rensselaer County Department of Social Services; and Gilbert Chichester, Commissioner, Department of Social Services, Schoharie County. We would also like to commend and thank the New York State legislature for enacting the *Child Welfare Reform Act* which mandates preventive services work on permanency for children.

We want to thank Ellen Flynn for her patience and dedication in typing endless revisions of this manuscript and for her editorial assistance. We are indebted to Michael Nichols, Ph.D., for his thoughtful, encouraging, and validating critique and editing of this manuscript, and to Nadia Finkelstein for her encouragement and helpful editorial advice from the inception of this book to its completion. Susan Barrows has contributed greatly to the clarity and strength of this book. We thank her for seeing promise in our work, for her help in editing this book, and for guiding it through publication.

Most of all we want to thank our parents, spouses, children, and grandchildren for teaching us what it really means to have a family. This book would not have been possible without the patience and fortitude of our spouses and children who put up with our preoccupation with "the book" and supported our effort.

FAMILIES in
PERPETUAL CRISIS

Perhaps we are now ready to shift from our historical focus on *saving children from their families* to a more vital focus *on saving families*. This requires a willingness to change — societally, institutionally, and professionally — an awesome task, but the least we should expect for the millions of children touched by the child welfare system.

— A. Maluccio et al., 1986, p. 301

To a worm in horseradish, the whole world is horseradish.

— Old yiddish saying cited in Kushner, 1981

CHAPTER 1

Families in Perpetual Crisis

THE D. FAMILY* DID NOT request help. In fact, they did not want it. Mrs. D. canceled her first meeting with the family worker, was not available for a third, and, when we arrived for a scheduled family consultation and intake conference, said she was not expecting us. A tall, husky 30-year-old woman, Mrs. D. immediately began complaining about her 10-year-old son who was not doing his work at school and often refusing to go at all. She went on to say that she was concerned because Anthony, her eight-year-old son, was talking about joining his deceased grandparent and also wanted to "drop out" of school — second grade.

Mrs. D. said that ever since she had become pregnant at age 16 her life had revolved around a series of violent relationships, including one where she had thrown an abusive husband through a window. She had been physi-

*The case examples used in this book are based upon real families. Names and identifying information have been disguised and some cases reflect composites of more than one family with similar dynamics.

1

cally abused by two of her husbands, and her 13-year-old daughter had been sexually abused by a relative of one of her boyfriends. Mrs. D. momentarily shocked us when she said that she had tried to poison one of her abusive husbands but that her mother had stopped her.

Twenty minutes into this session one of the managers of her apartment complex delivered an eviction notice. Mrs. D. appeared unconcerned about this notice and went on without hesitation to describe her numerous and severe medical problems. "I'm not gonna be here long." Once again, we became alarmed enough to ask, "Are you thinking of taking your life?" She denied being suicidal and blamed herself for not taking better care of her children and allowing them to be abused. At the same time she was enraged at the school official who had reported her to Child Protective Services for neglect. Mrs. D. said she had no one whom she could truly rely on. She said that she couldn't ask for help from her mother, as her mother had suffered a series of nervous breakdowns and had been chronically abused by Mrs. D.'s father. Her current problems included fear of losing her job and mechanical breakdowns with her car, which she needed for her job.

As Mrs. D. talked on and on about her difficulties, her eight-year-old son sat close by, with his arm on her side. When Mrs. D. appeared most upset, he began talking about his own wishes to join his deceased grandparent. The other three children sat on the floor playing with a few toys and occasionally glancing at their mother. Mrs. D. ignored the children and went on to detail how her mother had left her with an older relative who had sexually abused her for four years. Through all this, Mrs. D. maintained an engaging smile.

The D. family, like many others referred for abuse or neglect, appeared stuck in generations of repetitive crises, which had led to concern by the children's school, monitoring by the county child protective services department, and threats of placement of the children for their own safety. The D. family members had experienced traumatic events and chronic losses so painful that to deal with them would risk the disintegration of the family and a terror so immense that survival depended upon tolerating what had happened and continued to happen from generation to generation: beatings, sexual abuse, assaults, chronic neglect, etc. Despite assistance and services from the children's school, social services workers, and mental health professionals, nothing had changed.

CRISIS-ORIENTED FAMILIES

Ongoing abuse and violence in families like the D.'s stimulate intense excitement, shock, terror, and thrills, all of which divert from the family's problems. Living in a crisis-oriented family is like riding a roller coaster 24 hours a day: terrifying, energizing, and addicting. Families in crisis manage to flirt with disaster and avoid feelings of emptiness and despair. If you have grown up feeling cold, worthless, powerless, and depressed, crises make you feel alive.

Growing up in a crisis-filled family means knowing no other way of life. With the threat of the collapse or dissolution of your family hovering over you, any diversion, however dangerous, provides some relief.

Real, rather than perpetual crisis, puts us into acute grief. Families experiencing intense stress, e.g., the death of a loved one, are facing a loss which contains within it the possibility of change. As in the Chinese definition, real crisis involves both opportunity and risk. It means becoming vulnerable. Real crisis precipitates a process of grief and mourning leading to an acceptance of the loss and new attachments through definable stages, including denial, idealization of the lost person/object, rage, bargaining, despair, denigration of the loss, detachment, withdrawal, and reattachment (Bowlby, 1973, 1983; Parad, 1965; Thomas, 1967).

The normal course of life triggers automatic crises that individuals and families must face as they move through each stage of individual and family development (McGoldrick & Carter, 1982). For example, pregnancy, the baby being weaned, children going to school, adolescence, children leaving home, sexual activity, marriage, middle age, menopause, old age, and death are all stresses which families will eventually experience. These are stages of life which provoke real crises and challenge family members to grow and further develop themselves or stagnate for fear of change.

For families in "perpetual crisis," the grief process is blocked. After countless experiences of loss and trauma, family members have experienced too much pain to risk feeling once again the loss and emptiness of grief. Instead they remain stuck in the stages of denial and rage (after Steinhauer, 1974). Crises become a way of life. Instead of becoming vulnerable and facing change, crisis-oriented families protect themselves from facing difficult issues. The roller coaster has started and there is no getting off. It is exciting and dangerous but paradoxically comforting: When there appears to be nothing anyone can do to stop or change the direction of the car, all you can do is to hold on.

Crises also serve to get other people involved, including school officials, child protective services, and probation workers. This, in itself, can be comforting, as it brings in outside forces of control and provides relief from loneliness. Families in chronic crises are seeking in many ways to be controlled. When they fear loss of control, they bring people into their lives through abuse, neglect, delinquency, or other acting-out. To outsiders coming into the family, the family may appear mired in terrible, shameful tragedies. But to the family, these serial tragedies may seem more comfortable than real change or true confrontation of the painful dilemmas in their lives.

Crisis-oriented families typically act out themes which have never been resolved. The mother who was raped, brutalized, and betrayed by her family at age 13 finds her own daughters sexually abused at the same age in a seemingly unstoppable cycle of multigenerational trauma. The parent who was sent to an institution as an adolescent may find herself petitioning the court for placement of a delinquent son at the same age.

Who are the parents typically referred to child welfare agencies? In training sessions, we ask child welfare staff to identify behaviors they have experienced in work with crisis-oriented families. These typically include:

- not keeping appointments but calling "constantly"
- having no sense of time (the day, the week, or month) or consequences
- inviting friends to be present during the meeting
- keeping the television or radio on during sessions
- making dinner or doing housework while you're sitting there
- pulling the shades down and locking the door to give the impression that no one is home
- not being at home for scheduled sessions or not having an important family member present
- unable to say no to themselves or to others
- moving frequently from apartment to apartment
- moving frequently during sessions
- fighting with their friends

A profile of common characteristics would include: untrusting, suspicious, denying, impulsive, impatient, needy, often overwhelmed, easily frustrated, sometimes lacking in knowledge, lacking in basic skills, unreliable, inconsistent, and often angry and prone to periodic outbursts (tantrums) involving violence, substance abuse, and injury.

In many ways, a description of parents referred for services resembles that of children at an early developmental age—one to three years old. Some parents may be withdrawn, immobilized, and depressed to the point of seeming only partially alive. These parents resemble young children who have been hurt so much that they have given up. In terms of emotional and social development, parents in crisis-oriented families appear stuck in the developmental stage where they experienced unresolved loss and severe trauma.

Much of this is the legacy of growing up with chronic abuse and neglect from an early age. Studies of children who have experienced abuse or maltreatment have documented a cumulative effect of abuse over time, with a significant decline in competence over their first years of life (Farber & Egeland, 1987). A child's resilience to abuse is strengthened by having an early strong and secure attachment with a parent who is emotionally responsive to the needs of the child. However, a lack of emotional support by the child's parents has "devastating consequences" and " . . . no one has presented data indicating that there are children who function competently despite an ongoing exposure to abuse" (Farber & Egeland, 1987, pp. 283–284).

LOSS, TRAUMA, AND ABUSE:
A MULTIGENERATIONAL LEGACY

To understand families in perpetual crisis, the practitioner must appreciate the impact of abandonment, abuse, and despair over generations. Family members who have lived with the terror of being vulnerable to assault, rape, death, and repeated separations have typically learned to rely on denial in order to cope with their anxiety. The family worker needs to appreciate the power and necessity of a family's problems in protecting and balancing the family. Understanding why the family needs to stay the same helps to avoid becoming locked into a struggle to change the family.

Typically, parents in crisis-oriented families are blamed for not giving their children the love, nurturance, and discipline they need. The practitioner, however, needs to see not only what parents are not doing but also how they have learned to use their energy. For parents who have experienced neglect and abuse themselves as young children, most of their energy is devoted to the next trauma: assault by a husband, rape by a neighbor or boyfriend, placement of a child into foster care, rejection by the family.

Families in perpetual crisis appear to be dancing around a pit of emptiness. One false move and they can fall. One false move and we can be kicked out. We sense danger and fragility. We feel anxious and tense in working with these families. We walk on eggshells worrying about whether we too will be abandoned by the family as we work to prevent the next disaster.

Families in perpetual crisis have lost resources over time. They often have few reliable connections to relatives and friends or with churches, neighborhood organizations, schools, clubs, recreational groups.

The narrowing of resources from without made the J. family vulnerable to placement and prolonged separations. Marcy and Cindy, ages six and seven, had been in placement for two years, with little likelihood that they would return home in the near future. Their mother, Barbara, had visited them once each week and remained isolated at home. She had a succession of short-term boyfriends who gave her little support. Her family lived in a nearby city but had not been in contact with her for many years. Barbara had grown up as the "bad girl" in the family.

Marcy was withdrawn and masturbated excessively in public. Cindy was oppositional to staff. Both girls remained isolated in their foster home and showed vitality only when visiting their mother.

Under the stress and strain of traumatic experiences, individuals learn to constrict their own abilities to think and act. This becomes a necessity in order to protect and balance the family. Again, visualizing the family as dancing around a pit of emptiness, there simply is no room for considering new thoughts or behaviors. The risk is too great. Each individual must continue the intricate moves (roles) that balance the family, even if these moves entail great harm to others, risk to oneself, and separation over time.

This is the legacy of generations of trauma. The harm caused by past abuse, neglect, and violence is not limited to the traumatic acts; rather, it also includes ongoing patterns of family and social relationships. The context of trauma necessitates that family members deny feelings and facts, alter their affective responses, and change the meaning of what happened to them (Rieker & Carmen, 1986).

Individuals in crisis-oriented families, like two- or three-year-olds, can only see their parents as "good and loving" or "evil." This reflects the intensity of feelings of abandonment and annihilation that would ensue if individuals allowed themselves to deal with the separation, loss, and cruelty they have actually experienced. To repress and deny trauma becomes imperative for survival and continuance of basic connections in the family. The result, however, is often tremendous damage to each individual's identity and well-being. Individuals become locked into positions where they lack nurturing attachments and yet are still caught in overwhelming responsibilities to their families. They have known (and can see) no other way. Denial must continue to protect the family and its fragile bonds. This is the context that results in chronic and severe problems.

Individuals who have lived with inconsistent, immature, and erratic parenting are not able to grieve their losses (Rutter, 1981; Vaillant, 1986). Instead, because of a lack of nurturing attachments that would have allowed them to deal with traumas they have experienced, they are mired in their rage.

BEHAVIORS AS METAPHORS

Realizing that family members' behaviors protect them against tremendous pain, balance family dysfunction, and prevent feared changes, the family worker looks at the presenting behaviors in the initial crisis as metaphors for needs and dilemmas in the family. A youth's stealing food often reflects unmet basic needs for sustenance and nurturance in the family. Another youth's throwing rocks at girls represents his fears and anger over rejection and beatings by his mother. A mother's neglect of her child reflects the unmet needs and neglect she experienced as a child.

John, age 14, was arrested for shoplifting a pair of $250 sunglasses and had previously been brought to court as a "person in need of supervision" (PINS) after running away from home many times. At the family assessment, John, an only child, sat across from his mother wearing the "hot" *sunglasses. The sunglasses kept us from seeing John, helped John keep his feelings secret from everyone, and protected any secrets John had with his mother—the very secrets which led to John's needing to escape from the family.*

Families repeat themes of trauma, abuse, and neglect experienced from the past. If we as clinicians miss an important issue, clients will hit us over the head with that issue time and time again until we begin to recognize its full impact. Thus, a family's concerns about an adolescent daughter's sexuality may later be magnified as fears of pregnancy, allegations of sexual abuse, reports of another child's sexual acting-out, hotline calls reporting parents being involved in sexual behavior with children, etc. The underlying themes—in this case sexual abuse—will be played out with increasingly dangerous behavior until the family can be calmed down through outside controls and/or the underlying issues and dilemmas are addressed.

A family's real trauma and fears are hidden by the acting-out behavior of family members, as well as myths, ghosts, and rules that serve to balance the family. Crisis-oriented families are like alcoholic families. They have an enabler, a scapegoat, a hero, a lost child, and a mascot (after Wegscheider, 1981). However, in crisis-oriented families these roles can shift rapidly, leaving practitioners and helping professionals feeling a sense of chaos. Moreover, each role may be played by multiple parties, in direct proportion to the intensity of the family's stress. Different family members may be in serious trouble in the community ("scapegoats") at a given time or sequentially over many years, as one after another is placed in institutions or foster care. At the same time, "heroes" may be maintained at a mythological or fantasy level in crisis-oriented families, e.g., the husband who will rescue the family after he gets out of prison in five to ten years, the mother "*falsely*" accused of chronic neglect and abuse, etc.

"Lost children," on the other hand, are very real and stimulate helping professionals to initiate rescue missions. The waif-like child wearing ragged clothes sitting in the corner, hiding behind the couch during a family visit, or asking to sit on the practitioner's lap, reflects the emptiness, neediness, and despair in the family. Neglect implies both physical and emotional hunger, as well as a stifling of autonomy and a vulnerability to anyone who might offer attention or caring. "Lost children" can also be the parents who having been neglected, sit waiting to be fed, and are often criticized for not feeding their children.

The "mascot" provides the family with humor, distraction and, in short, relief. The pressures of this role, however, may be enormous. While the pranks and childish behavior of the favored adult or child may seem like fun, the "mascot" role carries a price. "Mascots," according to Wegscheider, fear going crazy and may be seen as psychotic, class clowns, or suffering from a variety of somatic illnesses. Individuals in this role are often under medical care and reflect the craziness experienced in the family.

The role of "enabler" is often overlooked with crisis-oriented families, as it is frequently played by professionals and community authorities, who may be seen at different times as either "heroes" or "scapegoats." We have worked with some families referred for prevention-of-placement services where 10 other professionals and agencies were already involved. As the family members appeared more and more in danger of violence or harm, the professionals involved requested more and more services (homemakers, vocational training, individual and family therapists, probation officers, child protective workers, childcare workers, teachers, physicians, and foster parents).

Often professionals working with families in perpetual crisis feel greater pain and worry more than the families. Feelings of over-responsibility and guilt are common, as things inevitably go wrong. Some professionals in the enabler role work hard to bottle up their feelings of anger and to manage their fears and despair by working harder and harder to save families in their caseload from impending destruction. The intensity of this task and the overwhelming responsibilities transferred from families to family workers lead to exhaustion and resentment. Leaving the agency may be seen as the only solution. Or, much worse, practitioners may remain in their positions, feel stuck, build up resentments, and "burn out."

Professionals caught up in "enabling" roles often miss the context of a family's behaviors and their own roles in an ongoing cycle of crises. The conflicts of crisis-oriented families may then be played out by helping professionals.

Moving In and Out of Crisis

Crisis-oriented families show the world a cycle of going in and out of periods of violence, abusive behavior, etc. This is the external manifestation of a family's anger and avoidance of pain. On the surface, there may appear to be little rhyme or reason for phases of "out-of-control behavior" (after Fossum & Mason, 1986); instead, one senses that the family needs ongoing monitoring, supervision, and the application of outside controls, i.e., police, child protective services, probation, or periodic placement over time.

As practitioners working with families, however, we can use ourselves to assess not just the content of the family crisis, but also the underlying emotional process. Figure 1.1 illustrates how this process typically works in crisis-oriented families. Every family has a limit of tolerable pain and energy. For families that have experienced multigenerational trauma, this threshold is fairly low. In addition, a family's tolerance is influenced by the extent of resources that family members can utilize for help; the fewer the resources, both internally and externally, the greater the need for dysfunctional behavior to balance stress both from within and from without. Stress from within can result from transitions within the family as the family evolves over time, e.g., a child going off to school or leaving home. External

Figure 1.1

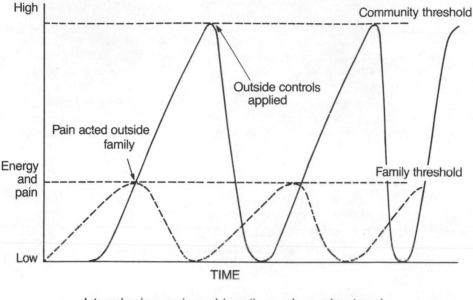

---------- Internal pain experienced (emptiness, depression, terror)
———— Pain acted out externally (crises, violence)

stresses include loss of a job, a child's difficulty with a current teacher, threats of eviction, attacks on the children by neighbors, etc.

The true pain of emptiness, depression, and terror experienced in the family must never be felt. Rather, as the internal pain experienced by a family mounts, it crosses the individual threshold and triggers a desperate need to "act out," resulting in out-of-control behavior, e.g., violence, intoxication. When this out-of-control behavior becomes a threat to society, controls are applied from outside through the police, child protective services, school authorities, etc. (after Ausloos, 1981). The family's pain subsides and is often replaced by anger at community authorities. Neither the family's true dilemmas, rules, and conflicts nor each individual's needs for support and nurturance are addressed. These unmet needs again lead to vulnerability and internal feelings of pain, stimulating once again a phase of out-of-control behaviors, crisis, and so on.

We have used the image of a family dancing rapidly around a pit of emptiness—a black hole. This pit holds the ghosts and horrors of hidden traumas (past and present) which the family cannot face or resolve. Therapy involves slowing the family down and building safety nets, ladders, and other supports to reduce the family's terror in facing its dilemmas.

Another way to view this cycle of behavior is shown in Figure 1.2 (after Ausloos, 1981). The recurrent experience of abuse, trauma, and violence

Figure 1.2

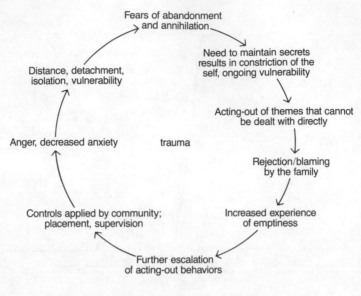

After Ausloos, 1981

leads to more primitive terrors of abandonment and fears of annihilation. The child growing up in such a family learns that traumas and abuse/neglect are unavoidable experiences which must be kept secret. This leads to vague feelings of emptiness and unease and an inability to deal with reality. If it can't be talked about, it can't be dealt with.

When these feelings of abandonment, annihilation, and tension reach a threshold, someone in the family will act out tensions in the family, typically through behaviors which are metaphorical to the pain experienced in the family. As illustrated in Figure 1.1, controls are applied by authorities when the family's problems threaten the community. This stabilizes the system and reinforces the family members' feeling that everyone is against them. This is accompanied by increased distance and a greater sense of detachment among family members, particularly if a child, youth, or adult ends up in placement, e.g., in a residential treatment facility, foster home, alcoholic treatment center, or jail. The ability of family members to deal with the family's pain remains at a minimal level as anxiety and pressures decrease.

THE MEANING OF TIME: RIGID VERSUS CHAOTIC FAMILIES

Crisis-oriented families run in place with seemingly no thought of either the future or the past. This orientation to the present — to current crises — differentiates crisis-oriented families from other families. Guy Ausloos has described chaotic families as families where "time's rhythm is dictated by events coming either from within the family or from the outside, so that everything is continuously changing; time is eventful" (1986, p. 551). The family worker working with chaotic families tends to feel overwhelmed and is easily caught adrift in the current of chaotic and disorderly sessions. At the end of such sessions, family workers often say that they can recall only a succession of events with little coherence or meaning. Interventions appear pointless and work with the family appears doomed to repetitive crises. This will eventually exhaust the practitioner.

In contrast, in families characterized by rigid transactions (often schizophrenic families), "time slips away imperturbably without any changes taking place, time is arrested" (Ausloos, 1986, p. 551). Family workers working with these families tend to feel confused and to hold overlong sessions, entranced by the illusion that if they gather just one more piece of vital information they will hold the key to the family's dilemma. At the end of such sessions, family workers may find that they have forgotten a great deal of the content because of the tremendous emotional overload.

Families' differing orientations to time lead to different therapeutic strategies. For rigid families, it may be essential to mobilize time *and* events by stimulating a crisis or prescribing "no change" (Ausloos, 1986). In contrast, for families with chaotic transactions, it may be necessary to use techniques to slow the number of events that occur within a certain time, to develop clear contracts with time limits, to help the family recover the past and plan for their future. Prescribing "no change" to chaotic families typically has little effect (Ausloos, 1986). For anxious and obsessive families, it may be important to work on developing a new awareness of the past, which can help them to understand and work on relationships and connections in the present.

With families in perpetual crisis, we focus the family on clear but limited issues, e.g., what must happen to get a child home from foster care. This forces the family members to hold onto their crises and redefines eventful acting-out (Ausloos, 1986) within a clear contract with consequences, e.g., continued placement of the children. We help the family members to work on limited goals within a broadened perspective which includes the events of their past and choices for their future. Wherever possible, slowing down events allows the family to take charge of the present.

Mr. M. and his son, Raymond, age eight, were referred for possible placement of Raymond because of his uncontrollable behavior in school and at home. Raymond often wandered out of the classroom and looked dazed and fearful when teachers tried to bring him back to his room. Mrs. M. had recently died after a long illness. Mr. M., who had been absent from the home, came back to care for Raymond. Even though he had been estranged from his wife, he now kept her ashes on a shelf in the living room. Raymond and his mother had had an especially close relationship, which left no room for outsiders.

*It was necessary to focus Mr. M. and Raymond on a limited but signifi-
cant change in order to prevent a developing pattern of chronic crises. The
family worker asked them to set a time limit within which to bury Mrs. M.'s
remains. This forced them to address their loss within a certain time frame
and to move beyond the preoccupation with each day's crisis around Raymond's behavior. Raymond and Mr. M. had to deal with their past relationships with Raymond's mother, the need to let her go, and lastly, their new
father and son relationship.*

Focusing on limited but significant changes can also help to generate
anxiety in a family that has become accustomed to living with chronic
violence and instability.

*Five children in the R. family had been sexually abused by their moth-
er's boyfriend. The children were placed in three different foster homes.
The mother denied all knowledge of the sexual abuse and refused to
believe her children's reports that it had happened. The children, fearful of
losing their mother but ambivalent about returning home, refused to talk
about the abuse and yet misbehaved wildly during each visit at the family's
home with the family worker present. Over a period of two months, one by
one they agreed with their mother that nothing had happened. Despite
the physical evidence of sexual abuse, the family remained in complete
denial. Crisis after crisis occurred around the children's placement, mother's housing, and her relationships with her boyfriend.*

*In order to engage Mrs. R. in the process, we explored with her events
in her life, her history, and whether she wanted her children to return
home. She had been sexually abused as a child and needed to get in touch
with that experience before she and the children could confront the denial
of the present sexual abuse.*

*The family worker focused her efforts on helping family members
achieve their stated goal of reuniting. This meant taking a risk by increasing the length of visitations. This increased anxiety which in turn led to a
crisis. The children, fearing repeated sexual abuse, broke through the denial and shared with the county and family worker that mother's boyfriend
was secretly in the home and had abused them in the past. Disclosure led
to mother, boyfriend, and children together addressing the sexual abuse
and the reasons for placement. The family could then begin more productive efforts toward reuniting.*

HISTORICAL FACTORS IN CHILD WELFARE

Crisis-oriented families have typically been too passive or too disorganized to respond to the approaches and requirements of outpatient clinics and
have been referred to child welfare agencies. Often children have been placed
in group care institutions or foster homes. Historically, foster care in the

United States was developed as a means of caring for orphans or rescuing children from impoverished and sometimes abusive or neglectful parents and raising them to become productive members of society (Fein, Maluccio, & Kulger, 1986). In the nineteenth century, orphan asylums were established where destitute children could receive an education and live until they could be reunited with their families. By the turn of the century, large asylums were seen as inappropriate for the needs of children. Many orphanages were converted into "homes for children," which provided smaller cottages and more staff to work with the children, in contrast to the large dormitories and regimentation of the orphan asylums (Dulberger, 1988). Later the needs of these children were seen as better met through temporary placement in substitute "foster" families until their own family or relatives could take them back. However, by the 1960s and early 1970s it was realized that short-term or crisis-oriented foster care had, in most cases, become long-term placements (Gruber, 1978) with children often shifted through multiple foster families and feeling like second-class citizens who could be moved again at any time. Few organized efforts were provided to maintain and strengthen biological families or prevent out-of-home placements (Fein et al., 1986).

Children in foster homes often grew up wondering why they were never adopted and not feeling equal to their foster parents' biological children or friends. Even more devastating than being an orphan is knowing that your parents had you "placed" — gave you away — and not knowing why (Simpson, 1987). Nevertheless, a foster home can be the most consistent, nurturing setting for a child who can neither return to his or her biological parents nor be adopted. In such cases, the challenge is to maintain the child in the foster home over time. Foster parents need to be resources to the child after the child grows up, as well as to help the child's biological parents.

In the mental health system, hospitalization was developed in the 1800s as a humane breakthrough in the treatment of serious psychopathology. State hospitals provided a safe haven for both children and adults, often in the countryside and at a distance from their families. At the same time, the hospitals reassured communities that they would be safe from those hospitalized.

Residential treatment programs were developed in the 1950s with the hope of providing a much more therapeutic environment for children than was possible in hospitals, orphanages, or homes for children. It was hoped that, with support and guidance from warm and caring staff, children could develop social and behavioral skills, work through early traumas, and change maladaptive behaviors. Residential treatment centers worked to provide a caring and educational milieu 24 hours a day for children having difficulties in their families and communities. Yet, shifts changed two or three times a day. Staff left for promotions or better paying jobs. Children in residence always knew that staff went home to their own families. Youngsters also came and went. Residential programs, despite the best and most intensive of efforts, could not provide consistent, caring relationships which could endure over time.

Some children's behavior improved in residential programs. However, without change in the family, the children returned home only to act out again. Other children in residence would expect and often provoke the traumatic experiences which initially led to their placement — typically chronic abuse and neglect. Children who became too aggressive or defiant would find their fears of abandonment confirmed with their transfer to another facility and the loss of staff with whom they had begun to develop a trusting relationship.

Tragically, children generally left residential programs with few connections or resources to help them cope with future stresses. Often children past the cutoff age for child welfare services came back to their agency looking for their childcare worker or former teacher, but found no one who remembered them. For such young adults, it was almost as if their past had been erased.

Child welfare facilities are not responsible for individuals 21 or older, while adult services in most states require that individuals pursue help on their own and are often conditional on acceptable behavior — quite unlike the structure, guidance, and commitment of the group care agencies where the young adults grew up. For many youths growing up in an institutional setting, there are few adult institutions that can provide similar levels of structure. The armed services is a substitute for some. More often, jails and hospitals offer the only equivalent resources for them as adults. In California, 33 percent of children at the California Youth Authority and 69 percent of the inmates of the prison system have been in foster care or institutional placements (Stark, 1985). Nationally, over 58% of youth sentenced to long-term, state-operated juvenile institutions have had one or more prior admissions to correctional facilities (Beck, Kline, and Greenfield, 1988).

Between a quarter and a half million American children are estimated to be currently living in foster homes, group homes, and residential treatment centers (Norman, 1985). Over one-quarter of all foster children move through three or more consecutive placements and approximately 20 percent return to foster placements within one year of discharge (Norman, 1985). Nationally, foster children average just under three years in placement, with a large number of children remaining in placement throughout childhood (U.S. Department of Health and Human Services, 1983).

The process of placing children in and out of foster homes and institutions has created serious problems. Child welfare practitioners have come to realize that foster care and mental health services can only provide temporary relief, safety, and nurturance and that the ideal goal for all children is to have a family that they can call their own. Children who lack the stability of permanent relationships with adults and don't know with whom and where they are to grow up often become so anxious that they are not able to master the skills needed to be competent and stable adults. For these youngsters, planned interventions to achieve "permanency" are essential (Goldstein, Freud, & Solnit, 1973).

In the 1970s the federal government funded several demonstration projects designed to prevent *long-term* foster placement. The Oregon Project, for example, demonstrated the efficacy of "permanency planning" in moving children out of foster placements to biological or adoptive families and preventing the breakup of families (Lahti et al., 1978). In New York State, the Child Welfare Reform Act (1979) mandated prevention services to families with children at risk of placement and mandated that children be in placement no longer than one year. Similarly, the Adoption Assistance and Child Welfare Act (Public Law 96–272) passed by Congress in 1980, mandated efforts to prevent placements and to promote permanency for children at risk of placement or currently in placement.

Child welfare agencies are aware of the need for permanency planning (Kaplan, 1986; Maluccio et al., 1986; Norman, 1985). What has become more and more apparent is that accomplishing such an enormous task requires a strong philosophical commitment, self-awareness, a knowledge of laws and regulations, the ability to engage the most change-resistant systems, and skills in assessment and intervention with "resistant" families. Practitioners in community and group care programs must have the ability to experience the anxiety, rage, and pain of families with chronic and severe problems and the skills and energy to work with a multitude of helpers, regulatory agencies, and family members.

PERMANENCY: A DEFINITION

It is our basic premise that if children are to reach their potential as adults they need a predictable, dependable, nurturing, safe environment in which to grow and which will be a resource to them as adults. This definition of permanence is assumed by most people to be nothing more than their just due; it is a given for those of us who have had the good fortune of growing up in reasonably stable families. A safe, consistent, and nurturing environment permits the development of attachments between children and parent-figures, attachments which represent affective bonds that can endure over time. Even when our parents are no longer available to us, there remains within us a sense of roots; this ensures a modicum of security and enables us to face the inestimable number of losses and acquisitions that we experience throughout our lives.

For many of the families referred to child welfare agencies, a predictable, dependable, nurturing, and safe environment is an unknown experience and a seemingly impossible goal. Children, parents, grandparents, and even great-grandparents have experienced immense pain through repeated separations, physical or sexual abuse, neglect, deaths, and violence. Family members appear mired in repetitive cycles of denial and of aggressive or self-destructive behaviors which perpetuate conflicts, crises, and vulnerabilities to trauma. Over and over we have seen families repeating transgenerational cycles of loss, abandonment, crises, and trauma.

The essence of "permanency work" is to help the next generation avoid the terrors of abandonment, annihilation, or engulfment experienced by those in previous generations, who grew up with no one they could count on for ongoing nurturance, safety, and caring.

WORKING ASSUMPTIONS

1. Zebras don't belong in zoos. The problems and "psychopathology" we see in a child or parent fits into the context of primary family patterns, family traits, and the impact of abandonment, loss, and trauma from generation to generation. To view a child's or adult's behavior in isolation from his or her primary family or history is like looking at a zebra in the artificial setting of a zoo, labeling its stripes as psychopathology, and failing to appreciate how they help the zebra survive in its natural habitat.

2. Traumatic incidents often lead to involuntary recurring thoughts, feelings, and behavioral reenactments of the trauma in hopes of mastering it — being active and in control instead of a passive victim. This is often experienced with denial, numbing, and a constriction of perception, behaviors, memories, and relationships (Horowitz, 1976; Krystal, 1976, 1978, 1984). Parents and children become trapped at the developmental stage where they experienced *both* the most nurturance and the most trauma. In effect, children and adults use behaviors (e.g., tantrums, running away) typical of an earlier age — the age at which they lost the love and caring of their primary parent. For example, the 12-year-old who is running away, bedwetting, oppositional, and fighting with peers is acting behaviorally and emotionally like a two-year-old.

3. The most important need of such children and parents is to avoid the terror of abandonment. Emptiness feels like dying (Maltsberger, 1985), like falling into a void, or a black hole. Some clients are like drowning victims ready to grab hard onto anyone who comes near — no matter what happens to them. Others seem to be floating in the eye of a storm while all hell breaks loose around them.

4. For such families, the past is the present. The present is the future. Life goes in circles around an inner void of nothingness. What cannot be said is acted out. Secrets of sexual abuse may be replayed with promiscuity as an adolescent girl repeatedly places herself in situations where she is vulnerable to experiencing what has happened in the family but has not been addressed. Or a mother may demonstrate the same violence she experienced as an abused child. This leads to endless reenactments of traumatic incidents from generation to generation.

5. Professionals who try to help a child or an adolescent without working with the child's family are trying to rescue the child. Ignoring parents, siblings, aunts, uncles, cousins, and grandparents who have relationships with the child, as well as behavior patterns which have evolved over genera-

tions, can provide only temporary relief. By itself placement often reduces pain and anxiety in the family—the anxiety that families need to change.

6. It is not just the experience of trauma that maintains dangerous behaviors and cycles of crisis in families but also the inability to deal with painful feelings and conflictual relationships (Rieker & Carmen, 1986). Crises in families are metaphors for the child's and parent's desperate need to avoid—to avoid facing the intolerable challenge of growing up and to remain emotionally like a two- or three-year-old.

7. Crisis, in and of itself, is addictive. Addictions to behaviors like sex abuse, promiscuity, gambling, etc., are similar to addictions to alcohol and other substances. Families in perpetual crisis and families with passive addictions are avoiding painful dilemmas (Fossum & Mason, 1986). All reflect a desire for escape, an outlet for expressing anger and vulnerability, a drive to be out of control, and an inability to face critical issues.

FAMILIES WITH CHRONIC AND SEVERE PROBLEMS

Major theories of family therapy have been based on work with essentially competent families who are experiencing sufficient anxiety to seek help from a family therapist. In contrast, chronically dysfunctional families typically show little or no anxiety and have been perceived as unresponsive to traditional family or individual therapies (Weitzman, 1985). Such families have often become accustomed to living with serious crises. Their lack of motivation for change fuels a corresponding increase in the anxiety levels of school officials, social services departments, courts, mental health professionals, and other community agents who feel responsible for a child's or parent's safety and well-being. This anxiety in turn leads to increased pressures on practitioners in child welfare agencies to resolve problems quickly and prevent their recurrence. Yet, family workers often lack a solid framework for dealing with the chaotic and frightening environments they experience during home visits or find reflected in the aggressive and self-destructive behavior of parents and children referred for help.

Families with multiple crises and a history of chronic and severe problems often appear determined to defy practitioners who try to help them and to prove, "You don't understand. No one can help. And in the end, you, too, will blame, hate, and reject me." With such massive resistance to services, it is easy to dismiss such families as unresponsive to therapy, to watch their children move in and out of foster homes or group care facilities, and to rely on the criminal justice system (the police, courts, and jails) to provide controls when their behavior becomes a threat to the community.

Yet, these families cannot simply be accepted as tragic, doomed, or bad. Crises can be seen as a powerful form of resistance to change which can be used from a positive perspective to gain insight and leverage in working with chronically troubled families. Our challenge is to utilize a family's orientation to crises as a clue to the family's emotional process, traumatic experiences, resources, current stresses, beliefs, and fears. The meaning of crises in these families can help us to understand where a family is emotionally, how to engage families in a working relationship, how to empower families to improve their lives, and how to interrupt the cycle of crises so that the next generation can put an end to the addiction.

Children who are growing up in the worst families are not identified as patients and are not brought in for therapy.

—Frank Pittman, 1987, p. 165

Therapeutic responsibility begins with seeing your own position in the system.

—Gianfranco Cecchin, 1987

CHAPTER 2

Home-based Family Assessments: "You Don't Have to Tell Us Anything"

W E USE A TEAM APPROACH for home-based assessments. Initially, the family worker who will work with the family members visits them with the referring worker. This family worker may meet with the family several times to explain the agency's role and how we work. The family worker begins the assessment process utilizing a framework for home-based family assessment (see Appendix A) and a genogram (see McGoldrick & Gerson, 1985). The family members are prepared to meet the worker's supervisor and consultant. In addition, the family is asked to sign releases so that significant others working with the family can be invited to the assessment conference.

The family members are always told that they will be in control of the process and can share as little or as much as they want. When the consul-

19

tant, supervisor, and family worker meet with the family, additional layers of information are shared by all present. A conference is then held involving the family, family worker, supervisor, consultant, referring agency, and all significant service providers to establish an initial working contract.

After the consultant and caseplanner have talked with the family, we usually have a brief meeting for the consultant, caseplanner, supervisor, and referral source to consider: (1) how to organize the conference, (2) issues to be addressed, (3) coordination between practitioners, and (4) recommendations. In the following session with the family, it is important that the consultant and caseplanner tie together the family's strengths, pain, problems and dilemmas. Family workers need to show both respect and understanding for a system that may be moving out of control and heading toward greater problems, but at the same time contains resources for change.

We also write an initial working contract that is agreed upon by the family and all other helpers. Families in perpetual crisis need goals. The assessment and intake conference can be used to set initial goals and a time limit.

In this chapter, we look at the first contact with the family, the home-based visit, and ongoing team assessment. The success of our efforts will depend on our ability to engage, assess, and contract with the family.

CONFLICTING AGENDAS

People seldom want to change longstanding habits, behaviors, and ways of life. Even self-referred clients come into therapy not to change but to seek relief from stress (Pittman, 1984). We look for a fast and effective solution to our problems: a pill, a word of advice, a court order, etc., something which requires little effort from us and almost magically makes the pain go away, solutions which are as quick and easy in time and energy as America's fast-food restaurants and the action in television dramas. Real change involves taking risks, exposing vulnerabilities, and persistence over time.

At the time of referral, most crisis-oriented families demonstrate a desire: to reduce pain, to hide secrets that could threaten the family's balance, to remain loyal to the family, to get someone to control them, and to utilize all possible resources and energy to maintain a "no change" position in defiance of outside controlling forces.

Family workers going out to meet with families in their homes typically begin with opposite (but complementary) goals (see Table 2.1). They want and expect to promote change, in even the most impossible situations. In addition, family workers may also feel an inherent pressure from funding sources to prove that they are successful in achieving the goals of the funding source, e.g., preventing placements or reducing the costs of psychiatric hospitalization.

Table 2.1

CONFLICTING AGENDAS

Clients' Goals	*Therapist's Goals*
1. To reduce pain	1. To get into serious issues, thus often creating pain
2. To hide secrets that could threaten the family's balance	2. To help family members share secrets
3. To act out and avoid painful issues	3. To help families gain insight
4. To remain loyal to the family's rules, beliefs, and patterns of interaction, despite hardships for the individual	4. To help individuals grow and change for their personal good while maintaining positive connections to the family.
5. To get someone to control them when they are out of control	5. To not control clients and instead have them learn to control themselves
6. To utilize all possible resources and energy to maintain a "no change" position	6. To promote change

UNDERSTANDING OUR ROLE

The first step in home-based family assessments is to understand our role. Do we have power or are we powerless? Child protective services workers have a great deal of power over the family. Probation officers also have power. Consulting psychologists and psychiatrists who will be writing reports for the court are also imbued with power; their reports can convince a judge or child protective worker to make an intervention. Outreach family workers, on the other hand, have little or no power with families. It is important to recognize our own position and to address the implicit power issues in our relationships with clients. Recognizing our powerlessness gives us an opportunity to offer clients, who feel powerless as well, a choice of working or not working with us.

We need to recognize the impact of our race, sex, and age in working with families. The young, white, single woman going to visit a middle-aged black grandmother can in no way be seen as fully understanding the grandmother's situation and dilemma. It is important to be honest from the beginning, recognizing differences and our limitations.

Understanding the conflicting agendas and roles of clients and practitioners sets the framework for our approach to home-based family assessments. The assessment process is designed to begin to engage "resistant" families and at the same time to help the practitioner develop an initial hypothesis and an initial contract for working with the family. This process involves looking at: (1) the referral, (2) the family's home, (3) the presenting crisis and present individual and family problems, (4) family expectations and goals, (5) patterns of response, (6) the past, (7) past and current helpers, (8) the impact of past placements, and (9) family-worker dynamics.

The Referral

Referrals of families with chronic and severe problems typically come with a sense of urgency and despair. "We need you to work with the Smith family. How soon can you start?" "Mr. Paxton threatened suicide yesterday. When could you get a worker out there?" "We need an assessment for court by Friday on the Vanck family. Can you do it?"

We need to respect the urgency felt by the referral source and at the same time avoid becoming so caught up in the current crisis that we cannot gain a perspective on how the family interacts with professionals and, more specifically, what patterns and roles we are being drawn into.

We begin by looking at how the family was referred to us. We ask the family or the referral source for a history leading up to the presenting crisis. What has been done? What are they doing and what do they plan to do? We need to know what attachment the referring person has to the family. What does the family understand about the referral? Will we be seen as interlopers? Will the referral be a loss to the referring person? Why is the family being referred *now*?

If a worker has been loved by family members but is no longer able to continue with them, the current referral to us may represent a massive loss. This needs to be recognized, respected, and dealt with by talking about what that worker meant to the family and the extent of his or her future involvement. Opportunities may be created for the family and the referring person to share their feelings of loss, including natural feelings of denial, anger, and emptiness. Crisis families often have attachments to authority figures, including the child protective worker who has visited regularly but has been a thorn in the family's side. "Hated" persons can often be neglected losses. Families can be helped to talk about what life will be like when a former worker no longer comes to visit.

Crisis-oriented families have typically been plagued by losses and have been unable to deal with them. The referral process frequently gives us a glimpse of how the family deals with loss. Our sensitivity to this loss shows family members that we are not afraid to touch some of their pain.

Another useful question is: How many people have been brought in as helpers for the family? The more people involved, the more powerless everyone in the system feels. In some cases, ten or more professionals may be involved at any given moment, working on all aspects of a family situation—from medical crises to household management to supervision of one child by a probation officer. Often there is an illusion of power (with so many professionals involved) and yet a predominant sense of powerlessness to make changes and prevent disaster.

With such families it is useful to recognize the family's persistence in keeping so many helpers engaged in managing multiple crises. The family is in a powerful position. Every new crisis upsets more people; the number of professionals involved reflects both the family's tenacity and helplessness. In such cases, our inclination is to reduce the number of people working with the family. Yet we need to work cautiously and recognize that each departing helper—no matter how powerless or impotent—may represent a loss. With several agencies involved, a clear hierarchy is needed to establish who does what with the family. The agency that is working with the parents and engaging the family as whole needs to be in charge of coordination and treatment planning.

The Family's Home

When we go out to a family's home we put ourselves on our clients' turf. Since their home is their "castle," we need their permission to enter. This gives control to clients and communicates our concern. It also allows person-to-person contacts which would be impossible in an office setting.

Working in the family's home allows family members to share clues to problems without verbally betraying family secrets. For example, one family's apartment was dark, with shades drawn and only a small light focused on mother's many medication bottles, indicating her feelings of disability and dependence on drugs to cope with each day. In another family, the empty whiskey bottle on the mantel symbolized the family's unspoken struggle with alcohol. An eight-year-old girl led us into an unfinished house, which corresponded to the unfinished nature of her grandparents' marriage and the uncertain status of the girl in her grandparents' house. In another family's apartment, a three-year-old boy repeatedly went in and out through the screen door, saying, "Going home, coming back...going home, coming back." This boy was visiting his mother but living in a foster home. His moving in and out of the house symbolized the issues for him—moving back and forth between the foster mother he had grown to love and the biological mother who wanted him back. Another family had no bed or bedroom for a boy in a residential treatment program, reflecting the family's ambivalence about taking the boy back.

Assessing the home requires tuning in to our own feelings. Do we feel unsafe? Do we worry about stairs cracking beneath us or about slipping and falling on a darkened stairway? Do we want to leave at the sight of bugs crawling on tables and people?

Is this a home we would want to live in? Is the furniture comfortable? Are there decorations on the wall that signify warmth and a sense that this is a home? Or is the house "too neat" and "sterile"? Is disorder overwhelming? Are there smells that are overpowering or repugnant? Are the blinds drawn and the house dark? Are there neighbors coming in and out at will or sleeping in the family's bedrooms? Can other people listen to intimate fami-

ly discussions? Are there doors to give people a sense of privacy and security? Can the outer doors be locked? Is the radio or TV blasting while we
attempt to speak? Are a room, bed, toys, and the necessary furniture and
equipment ready for the child which the parents say they want to bring home
from foster care?

It is useful to notice photos, especially of missing people, as well as
decorations, paintings, and ornaments that a family values. These can help
us examine whether the family members have resources and connections and
where they look for comfort and guidance. In one family's apartment, the
walls were covered with religious artifacts, and the family was actively corresponding with TV evangelists, but had no involvement with local churches.
Another family had pictures of only lost or deceased members on the man-
telpiece. Another prominently displayed an ornate urn containing ashes of a
beloved (although formerly abusive) father, whose death marked the collapse of the family. Some families live with bare walls and tightly drawn
shades. A mother in one family, cited for neglect of her child, was able to
raise and maintain beautiful plants in her living room.

We look for strengths in the past and the present. For example, a picture
of a mother proudly holding a trophy may contrast sharply with the same
woman ten years later, overweight and sitting forlornly in a chair complaining about her son's running away. A broken-down farm house may once
have been the center of a thriving and well-run farm. Looking through
photo albums and pictures can be very valuable methods of joining with
families and learning about their history, strengths, and past connections,
that is, who and what were important.

It is also valuable to assess the family's broader environment. What is
the neighborhood like? Is it dangerous for family members? Is the house in
keeping with the surrounding neighborhood? Is the neighborhood run-
down and impoverished? What are the neighborhood resources? Are they
too far away for families to utilize? Are there safe places for the children to
play? Does the house stand apart, with the family representing an era gone
by? Are the children able to fit in with neighbors or do they stand apart
because of their race or background—teased, picked on, and alone?

Families cannot work without a roof over their head. If a family has no
home or is threatened with eviction, this is the first issue that must be
addressed. The family members' identity and security depend upon having a
home. No therapy can coexist with homelessness.

The Presenting Crisis

Assessment begins by engaging clients "where they are." For families in
perpetual crisis this means assessing the presenting crisis—the reason for
referral. The family worker needs to validate and respond to family concerns
about the presenting crisis and current problems, such as losing their present
home, fights with neighbors, hassles from child protective services, fears
that their daughter might become pregnant.

The family worker visits the home with the referring person, e.g., the child protective worker, probation worker, school psychologist, or mental health therapist. The family worker is introduced, outlines how the program works, and differentiates him or herself from investigative child protective services, probation, the court, etc. "You don't have to meet with us." Initial meetings are held to see if the family would be interested in working with us and whether our services would be useful for the family.

Asking the family's permission to enter the home is more than just a verbal formality; it is crucial as a concrete sign of respect for the family. The practitioner must consider what it would be like to have a group of professionals visit his or her home. Accordingly, we thank the family for welcoming us into the home. We stand until we are told where to sit. After all, it is the family's "castle" and we need to demonstrate that family members are in control.

These families feel powerless. We begin to empower them with the question, "Where should we sit?" Radios and TVs are often on at the time of the home visit and often represent a passive battle for control. We ask family members to lower the volume, stressing our need to hear rather than their need to listen.

With the referral source present, we share that we have talked with _____ or have read information from _____. This tells family members that we are not keeping secrets from them. It is important that we describe who we are, why we're there, and our purpose, e.g., to help the family stay together. Then we ask about the crisis that generated the referral, exploring different members' perceptions of the problem. For example, mother may see the child as a "monster," but how do others, including the child, view the child's behavior? At the same time we need to recognize that children feed into their roles and take care not to rescue the child. To interfere too soon with a child's position as a scapegoat, distractor, etc., would strip the child of an accustomed role. It is a serious mistake to form coalitions with children against their parents. This would risk destroying the child's identity within the family and immediately challenge the family to prove us wrong.

Respect for the family means recognizing the mutuality and interdependence of roles played by family members. Our objective may be to help an adolescent girl stop acting (and being seen) as the wayward troublemaker in the family, but this will require shifts in the positions of several family members and involve family members' taking great risks. Our job in the assessment is simply to be respectful, to be curious, and to learn with the family what has happened and how the family functions.

What actually happened that led to the referral? The family worker asks for every detail. What did they say? What did they do? This is done from a stance of "you don't have to tell us anything." Stressing that family members are respected and can control what they share, we pursue the details: "I tend to get very nosy, so I need to ask you to please tell me when I am getting too nosy and asking about things you don't want to talk about." Acknowledging the need to keep secrets and the tension around what to share may have the paradoxical effect of increasing family members' willingness to talk about difficult issues.

If a child has been abused or neglected, we are curious about the abusive act and the particular neglectful behaviors. What was happening in the family, with the child, and in the community? What were the pressures on the family at that time? Has the crisis occurred before? Have there been abuse complaints or hotline reports before? How do family members perceive the crisis? Do they agree with the child protective worker or probation worker about the reason for referral?

We look at acting-out behaviors as symbolic of what cannot be addressed directly within the family. For instance, if a child is blamed for running away, clues to traumas will be uncovered through asking when the child ran, with whom, and where did she go? Were other relatives, neighbors, authorities involved? How did the child's behavior affect the family? Who else might be running away?

A mother complained about her daughter's running away from home nightly and filed a PINS (person in need of supervision) petition in court. Asking questions like where and when did she run elicited that her daughter was running to her paternal grandmother's house in order to catch a glimpse of her father.

Thefts may be seen as a reflection of unmet needs in a family member or a reaction to issues which cannot be addressed directly. Stolen food may represent a child's desperate need for nurturance. A daughter's repeated thefts from a parent may represent unspoken rage at what the daughter feels the parent took away in the past, e.g., a mother sending the father away, becoming absorbed in work, etc.

We want to learn how serious the problems which led to the referral actually were (and currently are) for the family. What were the pressures that led up to the presenting crisis? We know that variations of this crisis will be repeated unless the cycle is interrupted.

We want to understand and reflect the feelings of family members about their presenting problems. Circular questions (after Selvini Palazzoli, Boscolo, Cecchin, & Prata, 1978, 1980) enable family members to share their perceptions in a neutral, nonthreatening manner and open up the flow of information in the family (Cecchin, 1987). The worker can ask a family member how her mother, father, grandmother, etc., would have handled a problem or what advice she would give to a parent, a child, etc. Here questions involving "least," "most," and "if" are very helpful: "Who was most upset?" "Who is most worried?" "Who is most hurt?" "What would

John say was upsetting him the most, if he could really share his feelings?" "How does Dad see the problem?" "What does Grandma think needs to change in the family?" "If John went to school, what would grandpa do?"

If people do not talk, there is no point to getting into a battle to force them to talk or participate. Other family members may be asked to speak for silent (or absent) individuals, "If she could talk, what would she say?" Such questions help to clarify differences in perceptions and uncover interactional processes in the family, family rules, and family beliefs. First visits and consultations may deal only with the current pressures on the family. In some families, the rage is so intense that anger and hostility are the only issues dealt with in sessions. To probe further would only exacerbate the family's feelings of outrage. For instance, parents may exclaim, "We don't know what we are accused of . . . " Or an angry father may make threatening gestures and refuse to sit down. We must respect family members' need to ventilate and express anger or we will be fighting them, repeating their experiences with other helpers.

With family members who are intensely angry, we verbally recognize how angry they are but nevertheless ask to stay and try to help. They may be implicitly testing to see whether we will: (1) respect the full extent of their anger, (2) be scared away by their rage, or (3) try to control them as so many authorities/professionals have done before. We can respond from a position of (1) respect for the stress experienced by the family, (2) a refusal to take control, and (3) persistence in asking to return and to help.

It is important to hear the family's message and to recognize key words. If a family talks about "accidents," we use the word "accidents," while continuing to confront the seriousness of these "accidents."

A child had been placed in foster care with bruises and a broken arm. The child protective worker believed the father was responsible. The father and mother insisted that they didn't know how the child was hurt: "It was an accident."

We avoided pushing through their denial too fast. Denial protected the family, and if the parents ended up feeling too much shame in our sessions, they would not allow us to come back. Our goal was to help them decrease pressures that could cause such "accidents." We engaged the parents by saying that "accidents happen when under pressure" and then worked to understand the pressures they experienced.

We need to stop family members if they share too much too soon. Such families may become so frightened that they will not let us return. When a family is revealing too much, it is useful to say, "You know, you have shared so much already today. We would like to come back later and meet with you again." This "go slow" message respects a family's pain, conveys a message of concern, and implies a need to develop a long-term relationship before the most sensitive issues are addressed. This contrasts dramatically with many families' experience with professionals who expect them to share painful issues immediately but soon disappear, leaving them feeling exposed and shamed once again.

The practitioner needs to keep track of time in assessing crisis-oriented families. Assessment sessions should be time-limited. This permits the family worker to end a session with a message, "There is too much to learn at one time. Can we talk about this when we return next week?" Some families may use an assessment session to make a major decision, e.g., surrendering a child or having a child placed on a long-term basis. When such major changes are proposed, it's a good idea to ask them to slow down and avoid making rushed decisions. Families can be advised that rushing ahead may lead later to "second thoughts" and to blaming themselves or others (including us) for whatever happens. Such families may want to "dump" a problem and thereby avoid the pain of actually facing issues. For instance, a stepfather may encourage his wife and stepchildren to become involved in family therapy so that he can feel more comfortable leaving the family. A mother may use an assessment session to announce that she does not want her 16-year-old daughter back home and wants the county to care for her. The practitioner needs to recognize "dumping." Hasty decision-making is a way of avoiding pain. Family workers can focus instead on the painful pressures facing family members, letting them know that we are there to help them to "slow down" on making critical decisions. We want to give a message of hope to hopeless families.

Families suspected of abuse and neglect cannot trust. And why should they? In fact, we caution them to *not* trust us. "You don't have to trust us and you shouldn't . . . we are here to help, but there is no reason you should believe that after all you've been through. And after all, we are mandated reporters as well—just like all doctors, teachers, nurses, etc. The law says that we have to report abuse and neglect." Family members and family workers know this already, but leaving it unspoken may create the illusion that the family worker will keep family secrets that involve danger or harm to people.

The abusive family may go on to tell us of a past incident which resulted in a hotline call, e.g., their child exposed a cigarette burn to a teacher. Talking about this incident gives the family worker an opportunity to say that, "We too would have to report them if that should happen in the future." Messages of "don't trust," "go slow," and "there's nothing you have to share," deflect efforts to get the family worker to take on the role of a child protective worker and also fit within a model of dealing openly with relationship issues. The "don't trust" message also works well for child protective workers who build helping relationships with clients, but at the same time must set strong limits.

Family Expectations and Goals

Our goal is to empower the family. This means avoiding the "one-up" position and adversarial relationship almost inevitable in relationships between families and agencies working with involuntary clients.

Most families start with the expectation of being attacked and are prepared to defend their integrity by taking a stand of "You can't make me!" Families expect to be blamed or diagnosed as sick or bad. We need to make it clear that we are not there to force changes, nor will we take over the parents' responsibilities or make choices for them. Instead we want to stress options, including the right of parents to make choices about helpers. Even when a family has been court-mandated to receive family counseling, choices exist: "You have every right to go back to court and appeal the order mandating counseling, go to another agency, or ask for a referral to another agency. Also, we as practitioners are not bound by a court order to work with you. We are interested in helping only those families who want to work with us and who choose to work with us after learning how we work."

We ask family members what *they* think the agency can do and what *they* would like to see happen. What are the expectations of both parents (if present), "significant others," and children? Do these match or conflict with the stated expectations of professional helpers, authorities, etc.? If expectations are incongruent, we attempt to establish what the reality is and to clearly identify the limits of help the family can receive and the kind of work the family needs to do.

A father brought his 12-year-old son to a residential treatment center through a school district referral. The father stated that he wanted treatment for his son because of his multiple behavioral problems, which were "driving (him) nuts." The father was asking implicitly for a three-year placement which would take care of his son to age 16. This corresponded to the father's own placement for three years at the same age. In this case, the incongruence between the father's desire (for a three-year+ placement for his son) and the state mandate (for the father to make a decision within one year on whether his son would return home) had to be recognized and addressed before admission.

If family members say they "want nothing," it is useful to probe further about pressures within and stresses on the family. Typically families will say that all they want is to get "child protective services off (their) backs!" This can be a legitimate goal and leads to a discussion with child protective services workers of what specifically needs to be done for monitoring to be discontinued.

Other families may clearly blame their adolescent son (or daughter) for current problems. Here again, it is not productive to rush in to rescue the child—however needy he may seem on the surface. Instead, we accept the family's goals, as long as they are reasonable, and very gradually explore the pressures within and stresses on a family that are associated with the youth's behavioral problems.

By asking what the family wants, we are implicitly giving the family a message that we will listen. The family's present definition of the problem can be viewed as a symbol of current issues with the realization that as the family develops more trust and begins to develop more competence, this symbolic definition will probably change.

We also want to check on the family's expectations over time. How will the family be doing in one year, five years, ten years, or when the son (or daughter) is 25, 35, or 45 years old (after Minuchin & Fishman, 1981)? Since most crisis-oriented families have only a vague sense of the future, questions of this nature help to widen their perspective. In addition, they help us differentiate families that are stuck in the past, in the present, or in anxious contemplation of the future.

As mentioned earlier, the family's definition of a problem can be seen as a metaphor for family issues which cannot be discussed.

One family's concern focused on the 12-year-old son's use of drugs. Everything else seemed irrelevant, including the mother's addictions.

In another family, the 12-year-old son of a recently separated mother had vandalized a neighboring apartment. The boy's father had left the family and rarely visited. When he did, he devoted his attention to his daughter, paying little heed to his son. At the assessment, the workers sensed an emptiness in this newly broken home. Nothing was on the walls, and furniture was missing. The family had defined the problem as the son's destroying property. His behaviors seemed to be a metaphor for the emptiness and breakup of the family.

We avoid becoming locked into a rigid and specific focus on any one problem or pushing a family to define a specific and concrete problem as the primary concern. Most families will comply with requests to identify a specific problem which they want to change. Nevertheless, families will often cite relatively minor issues while ignoring deeper conflicts. The worker, when listening respectfully and carefully, will "hear" underlying problems.

The parents in a family referred for physical abuse and suspected sexual abuse defined their primary problem as their son's telling fabricated stories in the car. Such a definition pointed toward salient issues in the family, such as telling lies and the son's distracting the parents from their conflicts. These conflicts could only be addressed after a relationship had been formed with the therapist. Telling lies in the car was a metaphor for the family's need to hide other issues rather than a burning problem that the family was determined to resolve. If the family worker were to become preoccupied with any one specific problem, e.g., "the son's lies," the child with the "problem" would feel that therapy was missing the point and that the family worker was not able to deal with other more critical issues. On the other hand, if the worker were to brush off "lying" as "not the real problem," all hope of establishing a therapeutic relationship would be lost.

Patterns of Response

By focusing on family members' reactions to the presenting crisis and what happened before the crisis (and afterwards), we can begin to see a pattern of behavior that has developed and recurred over time.

One family's history revealed that both the grandmother and the mother had each surrendered three children and now, the teenage daughter was being pressured to give up her first child.

In another family, concern was expressed about an attempted rape of the 13-year-old daughter. The maternal and paternal grandmothers had been raped at the same age, and the mother was sexually abused as a young adolescent. The 13-year-old daughter was dressing provocatively and complaining of threats by several boys.

Looking for patterns helps to keep us curious and at the same time respectful of the complexity and powerful forces involved in a family.

In one family referred for services, a boy had been bruised and the school authorities had reported the family to child protective services as a case of physical abuse. The father and stepmother, on the other hand, expressed concern about the boy's behavior and said the child had thrown an enormous tantrum, upsetting the father and leading to the father's hitting the boy several times with a belt. Looking at these behaviors sequentially and in context revealed that this incident occurred at the same time that paternal grandfather was dying and the father was very depressed. At the time of the child's tantrum, the father was threatening to kill himself. The father was desperately trying (and failing) to find a suicide hotline until he was distracted by his son's tantrum. The resulting bruises led to the family's being reported to child protective services the next day.

This sequential pattern of the boy's throwing tantrums and getting into trouble whenever his father was deeply upset (violent or suicidal) was found to have occurred many times, leading to the boy's repeated placement with the paternal grandmother. The process symbolized the boy's position as protector of his father. He was caught between loyalties to his father and grandmother (who had raised him for many years), and had taken on the role of both protecting his father and expressing the rage and resentment in the family.

In addition to piecing together the patterns of traumatic response, we assess the family's pattern of responding during the family assessment and the interactional roles played by family members. We look at relationships between parents and children, among the children, parents and their relatives, and between the family and the community (the school, religious organizations, and referral sources). Seating arrangements and choices tell us about family coalitions and triangles. We note who talks for the family, who responds to whom, who gives eye contact to whom, and who cares and acts for whom. Who expresses pain in the family or is everyone silent? Who is absent? Is there a rule setter? Who in the family has power? Do the parents have power?

The observations we ignore come back to haunt us. The four-year-old child in foster care visiting her mother at the agency offices who goes immediately to the toy box rather than to her mother is telling us about bonding. If we ignore working with mother and child on the need to bond, we will be forcing an artificial reunion.

Members of the crisis-oriented family have developed an intricate dance which helps them avoid facing fears and shame. The meaning of isolated behaviors (e.g., a child's tantrum or a father's striking his son) can be understood only within the entire sequence of events that frames the context for each person's behavior. In some way each member's behavior helps to balance the family and protect against vulnerabilities. Specifics of the pattern may vary, but the essential themes and roles repeat over and over again.

The Past

In looking at the past, we focus on losses and attachments for each family member. Constructing a time line and a genogram from the family's sharing of significant events in its history (losses, acquisitions, marriages, deaths, births) helps the worker to develop hypotheses in early sessions. In later sessions, these tools can enable the family members to see patterns and link the past to the present and future. Such structured techniques should not, however, be used during initial sessions with families. Families might feel that the practitioner is putting them in little boxes or other rigid categories, e.g., diagnostic frameworks or genogram sheets which will distract from more critical issues and pressures on the family. Moreover, crisis-oriented families typically need much more trust and time to share their past.

We look at the past to see themes which recur in the family—losses, placements, etc.—and to better understand current family patterns. Current strengths and problems are seen within the context of the family's past and future. This process emphasizes our intention of working with family members as they move through time and also shows them that we respect their uniqueness and traditions.

Since trauma tends to freeze psychological development, the family's time line helps to clarify the level of individuals' emotional and social development. The practitioner needs to be aware of the developmental age symbolized by clients' behaviors, e.g., the whining of the preschooler, the rebellion of the adolescent. Parents who act in many ways like adolescents often reflect unresolved tragedies that happened during their adolescence. Adults who dress and act like little children may be functioning emotionally at the age during childhood when traumas occurred and the child lost the safety, security, and nurturance needed for development.

We need also to be sensitive to the level at which we speak to each person. Am I speaking as I would to an adult, to an eight-year-old, or to a four-year-old? This reflects our sense of the client's cognitive or emotional age.

Past and Current Helpers

To avoid repeating past therapeutic failures, we want to learn as much as possible from past and current providers of service because this tells us how the family is likely to respond to us. We treat other professionals (past and current) with respect and establish a framework for coordination of services in a positive working relationship. This assessment must include an understanding of the interactions of professionals (physicians, clergymen, police officers, school authorities, counselors, lawyers, family workers, etc.) with the family. We need to learn how the family has been helped in the past. Who has been a helper? Who has not been a helper? What has helped? What has not helped? Who is currently providing services? How are we expected to help? From this we can learn a great deal about the family, its resistance to change, and the roles that outside professionals (especially previous family workers) have played.

Previous helpers should never be discounted—even if families say that past work with another therapist, probation worker, etc., was of no value or that the other professional was malicious. We can assume that family members would not be coming to us (a new agency) if they had not already discounted previous helpers and did not have a longstanding history of resisting change. Accordingly, one must avoid becoming the next "powerful" professional the family members defeat by demonstrating the intensity of their rage, reenacting their experience of betrayal, and eventually becoming embroiled in crisis once again. Instead, it is useful to tell families, "We're no different . . . but the time might be different." We can also repeat that, "It seems that you've had some bad experience. . . . I hope that doesn't happen with us, but if it does, I hope you can talk with me about it." This is the first step in helping people learn that they they can take control.

Many families insist that they are helping themselves by themselves. We don't argue with this. We need to remember that many families referred for chronic and severe problems function emotionally at a level typical of two- to four-year-olds. Rather than getting into a power struggle, it is useful to think how one would work with that age group. The practitioner can lean back and say, "You have done a great deal. I can see you have done so much especially with all the pressures on you." To offer direct recommendations or require the family to change at this stage of work would almost certainly lead to the family fighting the practitioner and proving that the recommendations were faulty. In fact, from a developmental perspective (after Erikson, 1986), telling the parent what to do would be a mistake; our objective is to help the parent to develop greater independence, autonomy, and competence rather than to experience massive shame.

In looking at interactions with past or current helpers, we examine the family's use of boundaries, i.e., who is allowed into and out of the family. Some families share their innermost secrets with multiple helpers, friends, and neighbors. Other families have incredibly rigid boundaries, with doors locked and shades drawn. Such families allow no one into the family's sanctum and may allow individuals to leave only if they become "crazy," "sick," or delinquent. Lyman Wynne and his colleagues (1958) have talked about families with a rubber fence—they let you in and then shoot you out.

In some families key members, e.g., the father, are simply absent. While recognizing the absence of family members and the important role they play in the family, we do not demand that an absent member participate in family sessions, since that would be a challenge to the family and start an unwinnable battle for control. Instead, absent members are seen as respecting the family's needs and the door is left open for them to join when they feel it is safe enough for the family and for themselves to do so (after Selvini Palazzoli et al., 1978). The key here is not to ignore, not to deny, and not to wage battles with missing members.

Past Placements

The strength of attachments and the multiplicity and severity of past losses are important indicators of the family's ability to face current stresses. We ask about previous placements in the family's history. Who was placed? When were they placed? How long were the placements? Where were they placed? What was the effect on the family? Who was most upset at the placement? Who was least upset? How did the family cope? Were connections maintained? Who cared for the child (grandparents, babysitters, relatives, neighbors, foster care agencies)? The history of placements through the parents' generation reveals the tendency for cycles of loss and rejection to be replayed. By exploring past placements, we validate the family's experiences of loss.

The history of placements also provides clues as to where possible future resources might be found. For children in placement, we want to understand who they have been attached to in their early years and from whom they have experienced the greatest sense of loss or rejection. We are especially concerned about separations for children under the age of five, when positive attachments are critical. Who was there for the child at different ages?

With whom could connections be rebuilt? Abandonment and loss are the greatest sources of terror for most crisis-oriented families—much more so than the ongoing trauma and abuse they may experience. Accordingly, we want to know as much as possible about how past placements outside the home have worked, with special attention to the duration, times of placement, and attachments to helpers.

The assessment process examines the meaning and impact of placements on children and parents. For example, if a parent is expected to return following a two-year prison sentence, the family may simply be putting all issues "on hold" until that parent returns.

A mother was convicted of a violent crime and sentenced to five-to-ten years in prison. Her five children, ranging in age from three to ten, were placed in a children's residential treatment center and later in group and foster homes. All attempts to link the sibling group with another family failed because the oldest daughter and the maternal grandparents continued to give the children the message that their mother loved them and would return from prison soon to rebuild the family. The fantasy of the mother's love and caring kept the children in a "limbo" status. They grew up unattached, resentful, and clinging to the myth of the wonderful mother who would rescue them.

This family needed help dealing with the reality of the mother's limited ability to care for her children. The children should have been taken to visit their mother consistently in keeping with their goal of reuniting. Ideally, work would have focused on whether this could be a reality.

For the child entering placement, time has stopped. Until he or she can move through the grief process, return home and/or form reattachments, the child's emotional development is blocked. Resolution of family conflicts may also be put on hold until the expected length of placement has been completed.

If a family is working on preventing further placements or on getting a child home from placement, we focus work by asking: "What is going to be different? What has changed in your home? What do you think needs to change for Johnny to return home?"

Assessing the family's history of placement gives us clues as to what needs to be done to work on helping the family reunite or to prevent placement. The county social services department can use legal leverage to promote change. State mandates, e.g., New York State's Child Welfare Reform Act, require that social services staff make "diligent efforts" to help families reunite. At the same time, parents must work to bring the child home within one year or make a decision to "surrender" the child for adoption. The assessment team must find out what time frame the family, placement agency, and county authorities have for the length of placement of any family member.

Family-Worker Dynamics

The first home visit gives us a chance to assess the interaction between family members and the worker. How reactive or passive is the family? Do family members permit people to come in and take over or do they quickly show us they are enraged and will defy pressures to engage in counseling? Who sets the limits in the family? Who is the peacemaker? Who is the moderator? Who controls the interview? Who speaks for whom? And who does no speaking at all? Who acts out covert emotional themes (e.g., sexually provocative behavior, defiance, violence) during the meeting? Does this "acting-out" demonstrate a need for help or signal that the family is frightened, angry, and wants us to leave?

We ask family members to identify important members, present or not present, and whether they will be a resource to them in the present or in the future. We may be told that there is no one else involved in the family. However, a little probing brings to light absent members, peripheral helpers, and "significant others." For example, a mother may have a series of live-in boyfriends who are initially seen as rescuers and may end up as abusers, confirming once again the family rule that one cannot trust, and yet must remain dependent on, potentially dangerous men. These often absent and serial adults play critical roles in the family.

From the information we have gathered about how outside professionals interact with the family, we can develop a hypothesis about how we might fit into the family. What roles have past family workers played? Are we likely to be seen as rescuers, persecutors, or parent figures?

The worker may feel pulled—to protect, to rescue, to blame, to fear, to work hard, etc. Such reactions and feelings, e.g., feeling scared or angry, wanting to transfer the family to another worker, are all clues to the dynamics between family members and practitioners. Will the family worker be drawn in as an enabler for future growth or as a stabilizing force to maintain current roles, however dysfunctional? Does the worker feel a strong need to save a child, protect a mother from an abusive boyfriend, confront a parent, or leave at the earliest opportunity? Self-awareness and use of supervision and consultation can help the worker understand these feelings and use them as tools for assessment and intervention.

ASSESSMENT IS NOT A ONE-WAY STREET

The family worker seeks to understand how crises fit with the rules, beliefs, patterns of interaction, and emotional process. We feel the family's pain and seek to understand the dilemmas (after Papp, 1983) that keep the family locked into their dance of despair. The family worker begins to connect the family's presenting "crises" and problems with their pain.

It is not enough, however, for a family worker to analyze the family, make a report, and file it with his or her colleagues. The process of engaging a family in making changes means sharing with the family the strengths, problems, feelings, and dilemmas perceived and experienced by the therapist. This is also necessary so that the family worker does not take these feelings home and act them out upon spouses, children, etc.

Family members also assess workers. They notice if we are frightened, if we try to judge or control them, if we are detached, if we have any hope, if we like them, or if we feel only disdain and hopelessness. Will we push them too fast without respecting their needs?

A worker visiting a family referred for abuse asked, "Why did the mother do it?" The father responded, "She didn't do it." The mother left the room.

Family members want to know if workers can be trusted. We stay in touch with our own feelings in response to the family as well as to hear and see the family's verbal and nonverbal behavior. If we feel scared, this tells us of fear in the family: perhaps a terror that something horrible might happen. When this happens, we ask family members if they are afraid of something terrible happening. What do they think will happen? How and when will it happen? Who will be included? We ask other family members if they feel the same or different. If we feel detached and uncaring, this also may reflect the family's position. We ask if everyone has given up hope. Does anyone think things can change? Assessment means using ourselves to hear the family's messages.

We look for the dominant emotions evidenced in the family: fears, pain, and primary defenses (e.g., rage, avoidance, withdrawal). The driving forces that underlie repeated crises are often revealed by metaphors and sensed (but often not expressed) dangers of family change. The worker can use his or her "gut" to feel the emotional process in the family and can work to understand the dilemmas which leave family members feeling stuck and hopeless.

At the end of a home visit, we take time to share what we have experienced, validating the dilemmas and pain sensed in the session and conveying our perception of some reason for hope that things can get better, e.g., a parent's determination to get her children back, a mother's ability to get so many service providers involved, a woman's skill at caring for pets, or even the family's permitting this session to be held.

The initial assessment process concludes with an offer to work with the family members; at the same time we respect their option to work or not work with us. "We would like to work with you. Would you like to work with us?" We also want to end the session with a message of restraint to the family. "We will work very carefully. Please tell us when we are moving too fast." We restrain ourselves by recognizing that assessment is ongoing and never limited to our initial sessions.

The nuclear family is universal and has four functions: sexual, economic, reproductive and educational . . . no society has succeeded in finding an adequate substitute for the nuclear family to which it might transfer these functions.

—G. P. Murdock, *Social Structure*, 1965

CHAPTER 3

Engaging Families with Chronic and Severe Problems

M OST FAMILIES ARE TRAPPED between the need for change and the need to protect their current patterns, roles, and organization (Bell, 1963). Families can protect their ongoing patterns with a child institutionalized as unmanageable, delinquent, or psychotic. Similarly, families can maintain a fragile balance with an adult incarcerated as a criminal or institutionalized as an alcoholic or as mentally ill.

Resistance, from this perspective, serves to protect the family from dangers which may be feared much more than the decisions of judges or the warnings of social service workers. In chaotic families, disintegration, abandonment, exposure of sexual abuse, etc., are major concerns. Loyalty to the family (Boszormenyi-Nagy & Spark, 1984) and maintaining the family's precarious balance become more important than the personal development or well-being of individuals. For each individual in the family, change may risk loss of their identity in the family, feelings of failure, accusations of betrayal, collapse of the family through separation and divorce, and isolation from other family members resulting in unbearable loneliness. Resistance can be seen as a positive statement of dedication to the family. In the pages that follow, we show how we use a family's resistance to change as a means of identifying underlying dynamics, engaging families, and developing effective strategies for initial interventions.

WORKING HYPOTHESES

Ongoing crises are a powerful form of resistance which in effect enable families to avoid facing critical issues. Care for oneself, care for one's children, and self-development become secondary to protecting fragile relationships and escaping overwhelming pain. The family in perpetual crisis appears at one level to be desperate for change, and yet, at a deeper level, to be comfortable with a repetitive series of crises. Crises stabilize a family and distract from the need to move on to a new stage of integration in terms of the relative power, independence/dependence, and responsibilities of each family member.

The challenge for practitioners is to utilize resistance to change in order to understand the family's interactions with the family worker and develop strategies for building positive relationships with families. Resistance is not "bad"; instead, it offers us a chance to gain insight and leverage in working with "hard-to-reach" families. The following working hypotheses have provided a foundation for this effort:

1. *The family worker must begin where the family is.* Services must be relevant to the needs and wishes of clients (Maluccio, 1979). This basic principle is often overlooked because of the dangers and risks perceived and accepted by professionals working with these families: continued physical and/or sexual abuse and neglect of children, risk of injury, violence to family members and the community, threats to helpers, self-destructive behavior, and eviction or abandonment of a family member. Community agencies and practitioners often feel a greater urgency for change than the families themselves. This pressure can easily lead an otherwise sensitive practitioner to expend great energy probing into a family's background in a desperate search for causal factors or old wounds. Family concerns may be very different, centering on such issues as dealing with the shame of being in therapy, the dread of an upcoming court hearing for a neglect petition or custody settlement, or getting child protective services "off (their) backs." Ignoring these issues can leave a family feeling unheard and resentful.
2. *Resistance often reflects unresolved issues with extended family*

which are acted out with community agencies, family workers, etc.
Conflicts which cannot be managed within a family are often played
out with police, teachers, or family workers. Practitioners need to
know the context for a family's behavior in order to understand its
meaning (Bateson, 1979); for many families referred to child welfare
and social services programs, this context is extremely harsh, built
upon generations of abuse, losses, abandonment, and chronic
problems.

3. *A family's level of resistance to change corresponds to the pain
   inherent in confronting the family's dilemma.* A family that has
   worked with multiple agencies over many years without progress
   can be assumed to be stuck with extremely difficult problems that
   allow for little flexibility and movement. Therapeutic responses
   must address the actual dilemma in order to be seen by family
   members as recognizing the stress inherent in their situation. For
   example, a family may be preoccupied with fear that the mother will
   resume drinking, become violent again, and return to prison. A
   practitioner's efforts to look at the children's behavioral problems
   or confront safety issues for the children may be resisted until
   mom's drinking is addressed. With the very essence of the family in
   jeopardy, little energy can be expended on other issues.

4. *The type of resistance utilized fits the emotional stage of individuals
   in the family and serves to maintain the family system at its current
   stage of development.* Families go through stages of development
   just as individuals do (McGoldrick & Carter, 1982), and family
   problems may serve to protect a family from difficult transitions
   (Watzlawick, Weakland, & Fisch, 1974). Explorations of family
   histories often reveal that the grandparents, parents, and children
   have experienced massive losses, abandonment, or abuse; in fact,
   the repetition of abuse from generation to generation has been
   reported in many studies (see Frommer, 1979; Oliver, 1977; Spinetta
   & Rigler, 1972). The emotional development of family members
   often appears to have been stymied, with current acting-out behavior typical of an earlier stage of emotional development. From this
   perspective, a parent's frequent moves correspond to a child's running away, and the physical fighting of a parent is similar to the
   tantrums of a child.

5. *Resistance serves as a test of the usefulness of the family worker-
   family relationship.* From this perspective, resistance provides a
   valuable screening technique for families to determine if it is safe to
   build a relationship with a particular family worker and if risky and
   painful changes are possible. Can the family worker handle their
   pain, their secrets, their misery, and the awful things they think
   they've done, e.g., incest or abuse/neglect of an infant? Can

family members talk with this person about their primary fears: panic over feared abandonment, fears of being alone, a yearning for one's mother despite years of abuse, etc.? Can the family worker help them and at the same time understand how frightening change can be? Can they trust this person after working with so many professionals who have left after short periods of time? Will the family worker reject them, as so many have apparently done before? In the context of generations of abandonment and rejection, the development of a positive relationship with a family worker is a major accomplishment.

BASIC PRINCIPLES FOR ENGAGING FAMILIES

Work with resistant families involves careful navigation through seemingly endless roadblocks. Time and again the family worker's persistence and sensitivity to a family's dilemma are tested. We have found the following strategies useful in skirting some of the major obstacles in work with troubled families:

1. *Coordination with referral sources and other service providers.* Involvement of all systems, e.g., schools, other family workers, the probation department, child protective services, etc., is essential. Unless services are coordinated, the professionals involved will tend to reflect conflicts within the family, blocking any change. Service providers need to meet together and develop an integrated plan based on a shared understanding of the family's problems, strengths, and goals. Whenever possible, the family worker should be introduced to the family by the referral source. Roles should be clearly delineated. Intake and quarterly review conferences are critical times for coordination of various service providers' efforts. Conferences also provide opportunities for the family worker to see how the family interacts with all of the agencies and professionals involved.

2. *Outreach.* For extremely closed and chronic systems, including those presenting with incest and child abuse/neglect, as well as those referred by the court, home visits provide a means of communicating a family worker's concern and allow for person-to-person contacts.

3. *Maintaining respect* and validating all members of the system. Family systems approaches (see Fisch, Weakland, & Segal, 1982; Morawetz & Walker, 1984; Papp, 1983; Pittman, 1984) have described problems as creative solutions to underlying dilemmas. From this perspective it is possible to respect a family's efforts, to respect the efforts of other professionals, and to identify the positive aspects of

an individual's behavior. Without this respect, family members tend to be defiant and engaging the family in a working relationship becomes impossible. Genuine respect is not a pretense. For instance, we don't want to commend family members for coming to a session when they were court-ordered. Instead, we empathize with the fact that they came to the intake session against their will.

It is essential to identify dilemmas as involving all members of the system, including absent members, with empathy for their needs and contributions to the family. This includes validation of past treatment efforts and family helpers by checking on the family's perception of the value of these services and asking for past assessments by other professionals. Another important area for inquiry involves negative and positive networks and connections with friends, relatives, and religious organizations, etc. Typically, families referred are isolated. Supportive networks with friends, relatives, other professionals, and neighbors are needed to facilitate and maintain change.

4. *Avoiding symmetrical power struggles* (Ausloos, 1985). The family's *avoidance* of such painful issues as loss and grief may increase as pressure for change is experienced from professionals. It is important to not take over for parents and to promote their making choices. A family's options can be stressed at the time of referral, e.g., to work with another clinic or go back to court to try to change an order for counseling if the family wishes. All too often, family workers find themselves escalating pressure on a family to reveal important information or to change as a family's resistance increases. A deadlock then develops as the relationship turns adversarial. In the end, the family will reassert the importance of protecting its own integrity over compliance with outside demands.

Sensitivity to the family's need for stability is crucial (Weitzman, 1985). Restraining changes and urging the family to carefully consider the advantages and disadvantages of change are useful techniques (Fisch et al., 1982). This helps to differentiate the family worker from child protective services workers, probation officers, and the police. Family members need to feel that the family worker respects their efforts and both the enormity and difficulty of moving beyond their "problems."

5. *Triadic questioning to expand perspectives*. The process of asking triadic questions developed by the Milan associates (see Selvini Palazzoli et al., 1980; Tomm, 1987, 1988) and described in Chapter 2 is effective in expanding a family's perspectives and options. Questions and redefinitions which add a time perspective, connecting current problems to the past and future, as well as to continuing

relationships with extended family, can enlarge a family's views while introducing new information.

6. *Maintaining presence while addressing painful dilemmas.* Family workers must demonstrate genuine concern, persistence and belief in their work. This involves a full use of oneself as a family worker: humor, warmth, "I" messages, and feelings as indicators of the family system and flexibility. In addition, to maintain objectivity and potency, the family worker needs support from supervisors, consultants, and colleagues. Use of teams (see Bergman, 1985; Breit, Im, & Wilner, 1983; Papp, 1983) and working within a training-research model provide the context needed for staff to work with resistance and painful dilemmas and to test and refine approaches.

PRACTICE STRATEGIES FOR ENGAGING FAMILIES

Specific strategies to engage and promote change with crisis-oriented families must be based on hypotheses about how the process of resistance protects families from their primary fears and tests the family-family worker relationship. Table 3.1 outlines a process for identifying typical patterns of resistance encountered in family work. A family worker begins to utilize resistance by identifying his/her own reactions and feelings when faced with a stern-looking father who sits stiffly with arms crossed or when greeted at the family's home by large barking dogs, strange odors, and a blaring TV. The family worker's internal "gut" feelings provide clues to pressures and unstated messages in work with families. These reactions can be used as indicators of the family's feelings and fears. We can then formulate a hypothesis which addresses how the behaviors that form a pattern of resistance make sense in terms of the family's dilemma. This hypothesis provides the foundation for creative interventions to engage the family and to begin the process of change, i.e., "to get a family past its snag point" (Pittman, 1984).

Following Clues to Basic Patterns

By tracing patterns of resistance encountered and identifying the therapist's and family's feelings, a family worker can develop a hypothesis about the function of resistance in therapist-family interaction. This hypothesis can then be used to help the family worker understand the family's experience and to engage family members in terms of their primary issues and pain.

For families referred for neglect, and where parents appear worn-out or overwhelmed, the primary issue is often the predominant need of the parent to be fed and cared for—to receive what she never received while growing up. Such parents are confronted with the primary need to avoid abandonment

Table 3.1

WORKING WITH RESISTANCE: A FRAMEWORK FOR ASSESSMENT
AND TREATMENT PLANNING

I. IDENTIFICATION OF PRIMARY RESISTANCE PATTERNS	EXAMPLES
1. Denial	"No problem."
2. Blaming	"It's all _____'s fault."
3. Labeling	"He's been diagnosed as _____."
4. Fragility	"Don't push too hard."
5. The Driven Parent	"If I don't do everything, nobody will."
6. Induction	"We like you. You're part of our family. So don't . . ."
7. Avoidance	"He couldn't be here." (absent member or family)
8. Discounting	"It hasn't helped . . . you're no good."
9. Helplessness	"What's the use?"
10. Environmental Hurdles/Dangers	"Cockroaches, lice, . . . 'the pits'"
11. Family Worker's Resistance	"I can't, shouldn't, or must . . ." (lessons from our own families)
12. Crises	"We're in terrible trouble."

II. IDENTIFICATION OF FEELINGS
    1. *Therapist's reaction/feelings in response to resistance*
    2. *Family feelings/beliefs: what family fears most*
III. DEVELOPMENT OF STRATEGIES TO ENGAGE FAMILY AND PROMOTE CHANGE
    1. *Hypothesis: function of resistance in therapist-family interaction*
    2. *Specific strategies*

and the terror of finding themselves totally alone. If the parent has developed enough competence to be seen as autonomous from her own parent, she may risk losing the only support (however inadequate) she has known. Or, the parent may feel a need to remain incompetent in order to give a grandparent or some other significant party a role in the family. From a developmental perspective, in most cases of neglect we need to feed the parent first.

When families are referred for abuse, we can look at violence as energy within the family. The parents' desperate need to blame and protect themselves is also a cry for help. Here we need to deal first with the family members' fears, the terrors in the family. This often involves fears of past traumas being repeated or of someone going crazy. We need to look at the pressures on the parents and help them to find enough relief so that they can look at what has happened and what is happening—what they risk losing if things continue as they are.

If a parent is physically limited or retarded, we assess how much the parent can actually do and how long additional resources to the family will be needed. Are the parents able to manage children now? Will they be able to handle them as they grow up? The family needs to be helped to deal with the painful issue that it will become more and more difficult (or impossible) for the parent to care for, supervise, and protect the children as they enter adolescence.

For the family with a scapegoated child who continually draws his/her parents' wrath, we focus on how that child has become an active participant in choosing this role. A change in this role would mean a loss to the child and other family members.

These and other hypotheses help us to identify primary issues and decide where we will begin and what stance we will take. We do not need to share our initial hypotheses with the family but we do need to have them clearly in mind to guide our work and to maintain our focus while experiencing the family's multiple crises.

Within the framework outlined in Table 3.1, it is possible to develop specific strategies for dealing with various forms of resistance. This is illustrated in the case of the P. family described below.

THE CRAZY ODOR: WORKING WITH MULTIPLE PATTERNS OF RESISTANCE

The P. family was referred by a child protective services worker who stated that the P.'s oldest daughter, Elizabeth, had not attended school for one-and-a-half years. Elizabeth (age 14) had been hospitalized approximately one year prior to this referral. At the time of the referral the family had exhausted the staff of three agencies. In one instance, Elizabeth had smashed a lamp at a mental health clinic, telling one and all that no one should see the family.

Elizabeth's mother, father, and five additional siblings lived in a three-bedroom, run-down house. The family owned two dogs (one rather large) and five cats. The home was rather smelly and dark.

Elizabeth was at imminent risk of placement in either a residential treatment facility or hospital, and the family was being taken to court by the department of social services on educational neglect. It was apparent that the family members would not seek help on their own.

The family worker's first role was as coordinator between the child protective worker, the school, and the court. Everyone needed to be involved in holding back the process of placement in order to permit the family worker to intervene and work with the family as a resource for change. Since the family was such a closed system, it was necessary to contact the parents by letter and set up a home visit. They mistrusted professionals and had sealed themselves off from the community. To begin engaging the family, a strategic "don't trust" message was incorporated in a letter (see below). The letter had the paradoxical effect of permitting staff to make an initial home visit.

August 15, 1985

Dear Mrs. P.:

I would like to begin by asking you *not* to trust me. I know you have had many caseworkers before me, and because I am just another caseworker and a stranger to you, there is *no* reason why you should trust me.

Please allow me to introduce myself as both your and your daughter's new caseworker. I realize, Mrs. P., that it has been a while since you have been involved with a caseworker from this agency and that it can be pretty hard having to talk with a stranger. What I really need, Mrs. P., is your help in planning for your daughter's future, so that we can work together in making permanent plans for her.

Again, Mrs. P., I know it can be scary having to talk with someone you do not know, especially when you do not have the option of choosing that person yourself, but I would like very much to have the opportunity to meet you. Would you be so kind as to contact me at 555-2222, so that we may arrange a convenient time either here in the office or at your home, whichever you prefer. Thanks so much for your anticipated cooperation.

I am looking forward to meeting you.

Very truly yours.

This letter led to a call from Mrs. P. and arrangements were made for a home visit.

On the first visit, the family worker had to deal with the following:

1. *Environmental resistance*: Terrible smells permeated the home; dogs barked and snapped.
2. *Denial of the problem:* "She's not crazy." "They called her schizophrenic, but she's my right hand." "We can't be without her help."
3. *Little trust in helpers:* The shades were drawn, the windows and doors were locked.
4. *The driven parent:* "We have tried everything for her and our other kids, but no one seems to be able to help."
5. *Helplessness:* "And we don't think anything will change. Look at my husband and myself—we have been sleeping in the living room for over seven years."
6. *Blaming:* Everyone in the family stated that it was the outside world that was to blame. "If it weren't for the school," or "if it weren't for child protective services and the neighbors," they would be all right.
7. *Fragility:* The family seemed frightened, constantly on guard, and fearful that Elizabeth would do something dangerous. (She had once tried to stab her father.)
8. *Induction:* The parents attempted to get the family worker to agree with their views about the outside world and to become a part of the family. Moreover, any disagreement led to the feeling that the family

worker would be betraying the family and could be evicted summarily from the home.

9. *Crisis:* The family members feared Elizabeth's forcible removal from the home and the breaking apart of their closed system.

All these resistances masked the family's greatest fears — the death of a family member and the dissolution of the family, never to reunite again. No one would voice this fear; however, the family worker, feeling frightened and on guard, anticipated an unpredictable and scary crisis.

To engage the family it was necessary to deal with the many presenting resistances used to fend off the outside world. The family was again instructed in the initial visit "not to trust us." The family worker put herself in a "one-down" position, stating that she was no better than previous helpers and perhaps worse. The family worker would try to work with them, but only if they wanted some help, not because they were referred or ordered to have help. The "don't trust me" message and the placing of the family worker in a "one-down" position gave the family little opportunity to discount the family worker and at the same time told the truth: The family worker was new to the family, knew little of the family, and really shouldn't have been trusted at that time.

Denial, labeling, and the environmental obstacles of this very dramatic family were approached through dramatic statements and gestures. The family worker coughed and said that the smell was making her choke. She began to use the word "crazy" as a descriptive adjective in order to redefine Elizabeth's (and the family's) label as "crazy" and diffuse its potency. Whenever possible, the family worker used the word "crazy" in a humorous nonconfrontive manner: "Those crazy drivers." "That crazy smell." "It's pretty crazy to sleep sitting in a chair for seven years." At the same time, her continued visits helped the family to recognize that the outside world could come into the home without threat.

Since the family worker became anxious with each intervention, the family's fragility had to be addressed. The family worker recognized her own concerns around someone's getting hurt, and transferred these feelings to the family by talking generally about everyone's fearing that someone could get hurt — especially by the outside world. The family was told that all work would proceed very slowly and very carefully, in order to deal with the fear that the family worker as an outside world representative might also hurt them. This restraining message also helped the family to feel some control over the pace of family work, which was especially important for a family that was so fearful of losing control and that had often been out of control. Family members were also given the opportunity to set their own goals, with little pressure to change. A goal as simple as, "the parents will make a decision on what goals they wanted to work on," was accepted. In this family significant decisions had not been made for over 14 years. The messages given by the family worker, especially that of restraining change and setting simple goals, worked paradoxically to help the family react a little faster.

The fragility and possible induction of the family worker were addressed by informing the family that the family worker would be bringing the team consultant to the home. It was explained that this consultant was for the family worker's assistance to enhance her work with such a mind-boggling family. The family worker also addressed her own fear of Elizabeth's unpredictable behavior, such as throwing books and other objects down the stairs or running unexpectedly into the room, by openly stating how startled and scared she was. The family worker's fears were reflected back to the parents and siblings, opening up discussion around their fears.

Crisis was addressed by exploring the parents' view of their current risky situations. All the details of the current crisis, as well as the initial crisis that got the family involved with the psychiatric, social services, and legal community, were explored. Having mapped family patterns and each member's "acting-out behavior," the family worker could predict future crises and thus help the parents begin to anticipate and change patterns of behavior.

Using these interventions, this very resistant, isolated family was able to work with the family worker on a weekly basis. The drawn shades were opened. The "crazy smell" drifted out the opened windows, and many of the animals were given away. The parents, given permission to work slowly on developing a single goal, were able to agree on going out together once a week and looking for a new home which would provide everyone with adequate sleeping space.

As the parents' behavior became less "crazy," they were able to perceive that Elizabeth was not the only problem. Elizabeth began to understand that she no longer had to sacrifice herself to keep the family safe from the outside world. Despite strenuous effort on her part to maintain her role, she eventually ceded power to her parents and began to explore training programs in an adult education center.

With the help of the family worker, the family slowly began to negotiate successfully with the outside world. Further work could then begin, as longstanding problems and family cutoffs surfaced.

Traditional techniques of family therapy are of dubious value to
the severely dysfunctional family.

—Jack Weitzman, 1985

CHAPTER 4

Getting Past the Door: Practice Strategies for Working with Resistance

In Chapter 3 (see Table 3.1) we listed typical resistance patterns of families in perpetual crisis. In this chapter, we outline interventions useful for building a working relationship with these families. Most crisis-oriented families, of course, use more than one type of resistance. Our intent is not to fit families into rigid categories, but rather to use a family's primary pattern of resistance to help us to utilize what we feel and what we see (the emotional and behavioral transactions in family work) as clues—clues which can help us to engage a family.

DENIAL: "IT NEVER HAPPENED!"

Families referred for assessment and counseling often expect to be blamed and so assume a defensive position befitting an adversarial relationship. Given the problems of abuse/neglect, sexual abuse, incest, alcoholism, etc., the last thing parents want is for a "helping professional" to ask them a series of questions about sensitive issues in their lives. The experience of being referred or court-ordered for counseling will evoke feelings of shame and resentment. The claim of "no problems" serves as a simple block to questions and a shield against probing into painful situations, e.g., problems with grandparents, past abuse, conflicts with live-in friends or lovers.

The family worker seeking to engage involuntary families who have not admitted to abuse/neglect must avoid becoming locked into a battle—an adversarial relationship—with families. It is important to recognize that denial reflects a struggle for self-esteem. The family worker's task is to take a respectful position and recognize situations as *serious* without assigning blame. If a mother describes an injury to her child as "an accident," we avoid a judgmental stance and redefine problems or accidents/injuries as events happening when people are under stress.

The family worker can gently probe with such questions as: "What was going on? What were the pressures? What else was happening at home, at work, with relatives, etc.?" These questions help to expand the family's perspective and to support the redefinition of problems occurring when there is great stress.

In a repetition of the "don't trust" message, the parents can be reminded that they did not seek counseling or a family evaluation and that they should be aware of the legal mandates which require a social worker, psychologist, teacher, physician, etc., to report abuse or neglect to state authorities.

We tell families that initial sessions are meant to determine whether they would like to work with us and we with them. Even court-ordered families have choices and can ask their child protective worker to refer them to another agency. Moreover, we as practitioners are not court-ordered to work with them. We have the choice of working only with clients who want to work with us.

Such forthright, honest, and respectful messages free the family worker from a covert battle with a "client" who feels forced to comply but inwardly resents and distrusts the family worker. Taking this position also frees the family worker from becoming locked into a role as a monitor, rescuer, or persecutor of the family.

Many families referred for outreach services may identify the referral source (e.g., child protective services, schools) as their only problem, despite the many problems that have brought child protective or other community workers into their lives. The family worker can accept the client's definition of the referral source as a genuine problem and make an initial contract with clients to get child protective services out of their lives. With this goal, the family worker and family can examine what would have to happen to end monitoring and visits by child protective services, etc. This approach, of course, requires a coordinated and sometimes rehearsed effort with the referral source. The roles of the family worker, child protective services, or probation staff need to be carefully delineated and shared with the family.

Progress can be facilitated if the family worker can join with the family in grappling with what it will take to meet clear and concise objectives. For example, if the child protective service worker states clear demands for ensuring the safety of children in the family, the family worker can take a meta position which validates the needs of the parents *and* the children. The family worker can join with the parents and children in recognizing their needs and pain, while the child protective worker provides monitoring and consequences. The combination works well to stimulate change (Reid et al., 1988). Once a client is engaged in a working relationship, it may be possible to focus on recurrent problems and the risks the family is taking by leaving them unresolved, e.g., a youth ending up in jail or placed in residential treatment, a family member being hurt.

In many cases we need to ask ourselves what is not being said. Families locked into denial may appear on the surface to be very motivated but leave the worker feeling that something is missing.

Mr. and Mrs. F. bitterly blamed the county department of social services, the family court judge, and their attorneys for keeping their 12-year-old daughter in placement for three years following the daughter's report that she was sexually abused by an older sibling. Mr. and Mrs. F. complained about how they had been victimized by the county and expressed a strong desire to get their daughter back. Both parents appeared outwardly sincere in their wish to reunite their family; however, they never expressed concern about what had happened to their daughter.

The workers in this case were concerned about the parents' denial of the sexual abuse and about the likelihood that it would recur if the daughter returned home. With all the children present, we said, "When children speak about sexual abuse, we believe them." For cases of sexual abuse, we need to validate what happened to the victim and operate under the assumption that the abuse will continue until the parents believe and protect their children.

BLAMING: "IT'S NOT ME!" "IT'S NOT MY FAULT!"

Mrs. M. rigidly sat facing me with her arms crossed and a stern and angry look in her eyes. Her 13-year-old son sat to her left with his head

down. Mrs. M. blamed her son for all their troubles: He threw rocks at girls,
was accused of molesting a neighborhood girl, and, most upsetting of all to
Mrs. M., tried to sexually molest his younger half-sister. Mrs. M. denied any
other problems (past or present) and refused to bring her daughter to this
consultation session or to invite her live-in man-friend, with whom she had
had an on-again-off-again relationship for many years.

In talking with Mrs. M. and her son, the consultant sensed the mother's
tension, anger, fear, and fragility. The mother's nonverbal behavior con-
veyed: "Don't push me!" The mother's tight grip and frozen posture sug-
gested how much effort she had to make to hold herself together, while the
boy's reported behavior suggested that he needed to act out intense con-
flicts around sex and violence.

When someone blames and denies, we make it clear to the family that,
"We are not here to judge." The family worker needs to make contact with
each family member and to recognize and validate the stresses on each
person. Soliciting everyone's perception of the problem and clarifying different views help to enlarge the family's perspective of the problem, which in
turn can open up new alternatives. "Sometimes things that everybody knows
are only dimly understood or even misunderstood." As we continue to work,
we help individuals clarify their own thinking and communicate better with
each other.

If one member of the family is being blamed, the others can be com-
mended on the fact that they are aware of the problem. At the same time we
offer an empathic response to the blamed person: "It must be hard for you
to hear all of this." If blaming is being carried to an extreme and is dominat-
ing a session, the family worker needs to restrain the blamer and take charge
with a nonjudgmental stance: "Hold on. We have a lot of time to address
this in our work with you. . .but only a limited amount of time now to
explore a great deal." We introduce the idea that each member of the family
may perceive the problem differently. For example, "He perceives you as
abusive. You may not be but it is important to know how each person feels."
Or, we might say in another case, "Your perception of your son is that he is
very bad and possibly crazy." We would then ask the son, "Do you agree
with your mother's perception of you?"

Our intent is to empower the family and at the same time to validate the
dilemmas experienced by each member, including the person blamed. The
family worker can accept the seriousness of the family's concerns (e.g., a son
acting just "like his father" who went to prison) without blaming either the
family or individual family members. We ask a blamed family member, "Do
you want to stop being blamed?" This process leads to setting a goal for
change and an opportunity for the family worker to restrain each family
member from changing too fast. Subsequent sessions can be used to expand

the context of the problems described and to link problem behaviors to other dynamics and concerns.

In later sessions, a co-family worker, consultant, supervisor, or unnamed "expert" authority can redefine the role of the blamed individual within the family context. For instance, the blamed individual's behaviors can be described as a family contribution, a sacrifice, or naive meddling (Selvini Palazzoli in Simon, 1987). Sometimes change is possible if this "contribution" can be presented in a way that is unacceptable to the family. For instance, a son's failure to do his schoolwork could be reframed as a way of distracting the parents from the father's business failures and of telling the parents that he will keep himself uneducated and a "failure," this would ensure that he can remain at home to protect his father from his mother's anger (after Papp, 1983).

With Mrs. M., described above, the consultant and family worker took a slow and gentle approach — commending Mrs. M. for her concern, validating her perceptions, bringing out themes from the past, reinforcing the seriousness of the charges and the mother's fears, and stressing the need for the mother's help. They operated on the hypothesis that Mrs. M.'s denial and blaming were essential defenses to protect against something much more painful — most likely a reexperience of early traumas, e.g., sex abuse, rejection, abandonment. Accordingly, the consultant affirmed that it was "okay not to share" in order to give Mrs. M. more control. The consultant redefined problems as things that happen when people are under great pressure and helped mother and son to look at what had been going on. What were the pressures?

With the worker's supportive and nonjudgmental approach over several sessions, Mrs. M. learned to trust enough to share how she had to leave her home when she was her son's age, how she had a "nervous breakdown" when rejected by the boy's father eight years earlier, and how she had been repeatedly beaten in a violent relationship with another man. Soon after we began working with Mrs. M. and her son, they had a fight during which she wanted to stab him. She called the agency. The family worker responded to this crisis by asking if she could put her knife away and separate herself from her son while they talked on the phone. Mrs. M. said that her son had provoked her. The worker redefined this as the boy testing to see if she would break down again. The worker helped Mrs. M. to share some of her fears of falling apart again. Mrs. M. was asked if she could keep things together until the worker came out to the home the following day. This defused the crisis.

As Mrs. M. developed trust in her family worker and trust in herself, her son perceived that she had enough strength so that he could express some of his conflicts directly to her rather than through aggressive behaviors. Mrs. M. was better able to take charge of herself and her family without having to resort to physical punishment or threats of placement, as she had before.

LABELING: "HE IS SICK."

Defining a family member as "disturbed," "psychotic," "sick," or "bad" is a form of blaming that can stabilize a family but leave it powerless to change. If a child is assumed to be mentally ill (i.e., a medical disorder), then that child can be helped only by skilled physicians specializing in treatment of the child's disease. Family members are relieved of responsibility and at the same time placed in the position of being ineffectual bystanders to the treatment process.

As with the "blaming" family, we accept where the family "is at," confirming the family's concerns and taking a respectful position regarding past assessments. We explore the value of past treatment programs and determine what everyone has done to make things better. Careful coordination with other service providers is essential to avoid becoming locked into a covert (or overt) conflict with other professionals.

Many families will request further evaluations, e.g., a psychiatric or psychological evaluation, when a child has been labeled as deviant. Commending their concern, the family worker assists them in obtaining the psychiatric or psychological assessment. These evaluations can be used to help the family to see how symptoms fit with (or serve) multigenerational family issues.

FRAGILITY: "I CAN'T TAKE IT ANYMORE!"

"I've been known to throw things," said one heavyset woman as she glanced at a nearby toy truck lying on the conference room floor—the heavy metal kind, of course. Some clients can be quite direct in saying: "Don't push me or I will . . . (explode, collapse, place the children, leave)." In other families fragility will be a covert issue leading to a paralysis of the family worker-family relationship. With an awareness of his/her own fears, the family worker can identify a relationship built on fragility. The family worker must sense clues (e.g., stomach tension, needing to be especially gentle, a feeling of working hard to not disturb the family, or a subconscious expectation of an explosion occurring at any second) that the worker is getting caught in a fragile relationship and is becoming too fearful to deal with sensitive issues or to confront the family. The family worker can use these feelings to understand the family's fears and inability to act or make changes because of an omnipresent anticipation of disaster.

With families showing fragility, one must avoid a power struggle over control and responsibility for some unnamed calamity or recurring trauma. All helping professionals fear clients' hurting themselves, committing suicide, or hurting others. The unpredictability of crisis-oriented family members triggers our own fears around losing control or death. The family worker can reflect the fears of the family from an "I" position, e.g., "I'm worried about giving you another heart attack," while giving clients responsibility for controlling the pace of family work, e.g., "Tell me if this is going to be too painful. . . . Tell me if we are going too fast."

In enormously fragile families, individuals are often isolated and cutoff from extended family members. The fear of violence or breakdowns blocks dreaded transitions, e.g., a young adult leaving the family. Building supports and rebuilding relationships with relatives may give family members the strength and courage to directly confront one member's assumed fragility. The challenge for the family worker is to build a working relationship with the family that will allow for exploration of how the family is stuck, support for dealing with current dilemmas, and later confrontation about where the family is headed, e.g., a child ending up in jail or a treatment center, a parent hospitalized.

Mrs. V. began an intake consultation session in her home by saying that she was "chemically imbalanced." She had had a series of psychiatric hospitalizations, shock therapy, and trials with many psychotropic medications—all to little avail. Two years before this session she had tried to kill herself, and the family appeared paralyzed by the fear that she would try again—and succeed.

Mrs. V.'s husband also appeared extremely depressed and isolated and reported a history of longstanding rejection by his parents. The oldest daughter was involved in many outside activities and appeared to be doing fairly well. However, the middle child, an 11-year-old son, was identified as depressed, doing poorly in school, and having no friends.

Mrs. V. wanted counseling for her son because of his school problems and increasing conflicts at home around his habit of passively taking hours to do simple chores. Mrs. V. would typically become enraged at her son, and her rage would mobilize Mr. V.'s anger as well. In this way the son energized his mother, united his parents, and brought their suppressed rage upon himself. His passive behavior seemed in many ways to represent his mother's extreme depression. Mrs. V. was also obsessed that her son would sexually abuse her daughters and feared she would physically abuse him.

With two words—"chemically imbalanced"— Mrs. V. established a contract for family work based on her biological fragility and an unspoken injunction: "FAMILY WORKER BEWARE!" To avoid becoming paralyzed, the consultant shared his fears of upsetting Mrs. V. and said several times, "Tell me if this is going too fast, if this is too hard to talk about." The consultant accepted Mrs. V.'s self-diagnosis of "chemical imbalance" and set an initial contract in which Mrs. V.'s work on her "medical" problems would continue to be managed by the two doctors (a psychiatrist and a psychologist) who had been working with her for the past several years. A coordinating session was held with Mrs. V.'s personal psychologist, as were meetings with school officials regarding her son's academic problems.

With this approach the family worker was able to begin a working relationship, despite Mrs. V.'s "chemical imbalance." Later the worker could explore: (1) how Mrs. V.'s fragility fit into her family system from a multigenerational perspective; (2) how her son's behavior symbolized trauma and stress experienced in the family; and (3) what Mrs. V.'s fears were about change and collapse of the family if secrets were exposed.

THE DRIVEN PARENT: "I'VE GOT TO DO IT ALL; NO ONE ELSE CAN . . . "

Most of us are in this business because we want to "help families." Driven parents make our work almost impossible because they cannot allow someone else to "help" them. No matter what we do we always seem to fail. Feelings of failure and impotence create much anxiety and frustration in family workers. If we are not aware of this process, we become so angry at our clients that we discount them and avoid them. The driven parent cannot allow people to help: all who attempt must be discounted and the parent ends up feeling discounted. By understanding that the "driven parent" must be validated, the family worker can avoid getting into battles for control.

"Driven parents," who have a very fragile sense of self-esteem, often grew up trying (but failing) to prove their worth to their parents. They are very afraid of change because it would mean facing their own painful issues. Driven parents operate at a tremendous pace in all areas of their lives. To slow down is impossible—unthinkable—because of the unspoken risks involved.

The first step for family workers is to be in touch with how angry we often get with parents who have to do everything. We need to respect the parents' efforts and give them the message that, "Parents know their own children." We can validate the parent's concerns and at the same time ask family members, "Who else should be concerned?" Then we can persuade other family members to help driven parents to recognize that they need to take care of themselves. This is a crucial step; if family members help, everyone's role must change. Meanwhile, we look at what this change would mean for everyone.

Some "driven parents" may balance underfunctioning (often alcoholic, chemically dependent, or handicapped) spouses. The family is often in complete denial that alcoholism or other substance abuse is a problem. Overfunctioning parents may neglect their own needs in order to devote themselves to needy members and to stabilize the family. As stress mounts, they will often feel as though they are being driven "up the wall."

In such families, one parent is overresponsible, the other underresponsible in caring for their children and themselves (Bepko & Krestan, 1985). This pattern stabilizes the family and prevents feared changes, e.g., separation, divorce, or a child's leaving. Overfunctioning individuals have just *got* to be there; there is no other perceived alternative. Life repeatedly confirms their paramount belief that there is no one they can truly count on and that everyone will disappoint them in the end.

With overfunctioning parents, it is important to begin by listening to their concerns, commending their massive efforts, and confirming/validating the pressures they are experiencing.

Mrs. R. was referred to the Parsons' Prevention Program by counselors at her son's school, who complained that Mrs. R. constantly badgered teachers and staff about her son's needs. Mrs. R. thought that her son had been inappropriately placed in a classroom for "emotionally disturbed" children, when he had, in her opinion, a learning problem. In a family assessment, Mrs. R. described John, her nine-year-old son, as "ruling the roost." John refused to go to bed and wouldn't eat with the family. He refused to go on his school bus unless Mrs. R. rode with him.

In school John was seen as a behavior problem. He refused to do schoolwork, was oppositional to teachers, and occasionally had loud tantrums. As John's behavior became more serious in school, Mrs. R. took on more and more of an adversarial relationship with school officials.

Mr. R. was physically present in the home but had little or no relationship with family members, including his wife. Mrs. R. had gradually taken on total responsibility for her son and the other children.

Mrs. R. was also caught up in a longstanding battle to prove her worth with her mother, who demanded daily reports on John's behavior and always told her to work harder and do better but never to value or take care of herself. The well-established roles of Mr. and Mrs. R., John, and John's maternal grandmother depended upon Mrs. R.'s continuing to be the "driven parent" and upon John's continuing to have trouble.

We began to work with Mrs. R. by validating how important it was to work with the school and to negotiate an appropriate educational program for her son within a school system that had become very angry with her. We then wondered if Mrs. R. wanted to work on what she could get for herself and what her husband could provide for her. We sidestepped the marital issues and instead asked Mrs. R. what help she could get from her husband for John. If Mr. R. was involved too quickly, Mrs. R. would lose her role as John's caretaker and what little power she had. The change would have meant that Mr. and Mrs. R. would have had to face issues in their marriage, perhaps before they were ready. In addition, it would have interfered with the maternal grandmother's supervision of her daughter's care of John.

Over time the family worker was able to help Mrs. R. develop a better relationship with school staff. John was reevaluated and diagnosed as hav-

ing dyslexia in addition to an "oppositional disorder." Mrs. R. had been right all along—John was inappropriately placed. As a persistent parent, she was initially labeled as "interfering." Previous workers discounted her knowledge and engaged Mrs. R. in battles of control.

The family worker and Mrs. R. were able to get John into a more appropriate educational program. With this settled, further work could begin on other family problems.

The family worker needs to recognize that overfunctioning serves to avoid pain just as underfunctioning does. Often the overfunctioning parent is tremendously afraid of failing and losing what may seem to be a fragile grasp on security and stability in the family. Yet, the pattern of overfunctioning/underfunctioning typically leads to escalating problems which in turn require even greater efforts—until finally the system collapses. Such cycles may end with the overfunctioning individual hospitalized, or more often, the children placed.

INDUCTION: "YOU'RE A PART OF
OUR FAMILY . . . BE MY FRIEND . . .
DON'T ROCK THE BOAT."

As we walked up to the isolated, half-finished house on a tree covered hillside, we were greeted by three large barking dogs rushing toward us. Mrs. C. and her granddaughter welcomed us into their house and guided us through the kitchen. We could see and smell the savory aroma of Italian sausage and spaghetti sauce simmering on the stove. Mrs. C. invited us to sit on soft couches and offered us coffee, tea, or juice; she wanted to feed us, to make us feel at home.

The C. family had been referred because of the seven-year-old granddaughter's overactive, distractible behavior, and poor academic work in school. Annie had been living with her grandmother since eight months of age. As an infant she had been severely neglected and starved by her mother, Mrs. C.'s daughter. When Annie turned five, Mrs. C. went back to work. She privately arranged a placement for Annie in a neighbor's home with weekends at the grandmother's home. This placement ended due to allegations that another child was sexually abused by someone in the neighbor's home. Mrs. C. then took on the total responsibility of supervising Annie. At the time of our visit the C.'s also complained about their marriage, with Mrs. C. describing an incident in which she had become so upset with her husband that she walked away from the house and did not return for hours.

Sitting on the soft couch and sipping our beverages, we found it extremely difficult to address important issues with the C. family: Would the grandmother leave the home? Would the grandmother and grandfather

separate? Was the girl sexually abused in her foster placement? Critical
questions involved the current role of the child's mother and the repeated
history of placements in the grandmother's family.

From what little history we had, we knew that the C. family had experienced at least two generations of physical and emotional neglect and multiple placements of children. Mrs. C. praised a family worker who worked
with her daughter many years earlier when her daughter was in placement.
Mrs. C. remembered this worker as warm, comforting, and friendly. With the
pleasant aroma of delicious foods and the warm welcome, it was very difficult
to see past the positives and very easy to ignore the hostility of the dogs and
the impermanence of the granddaughter. The intake assessment session ended much like the condition of the grandparent's house: unfinished.

The worker is inducted to fill a missing role in the family—"the good
mother," "the strong father." Once we step into this familial role, we no
longer see problems. To avoid becoming incorporated into the family's emotional process, a family worker first needs to recognize his or her own need
to be loved and fear of losing clients—the practitioner's own fears of abandonment. It may seem preferable to be loved than to bring up sensitive
issues; yet this almost certainly leads to the family worker's becoming frustrated and eventually leaving the family. It is better to confront honestly
than to abandon. With recognition of one's own needs, the family worker
can avoid being trapped into a circumscribed role.

It is critical for family workers doing outreach work to step back and
view their work with a consultant and/or supervisor. When that is not
possible, family workers can use peer consultation.

Taking the time for a brief meeting of staff before the intake conference
with the family and other helpers is useful. Often this can be worked into a
break between the assessment and conference portions of the intake. However, this is difficult to do on a home visit. During a home visit where the
family worker, consultant, and supervisor are uncertain or feel in conflict
about how to begin work, we tell family members that we will share our
initial impressions with them but have to come back another time to give
them more carefully thought-out opinions.

To avoid induction, one must use distance and maintain a clear perspective. Returning to the office and talking about the family assessment with a
supervisor or consultant helps to identify the induction process that occurred, the dynamics of this process, and how to work with the family.

Review conferences held with the family, workers, supervisors, consultants, and collaterals are needed minimally every three months to assess the
value and progress of family work and to develop future strategies. Viewing
work from a team perspective, the family worker can bring in messages from
the consultant, supervisor, etc., and then take his/her position pro or con.
For instance, the family worker may say that a consultant believes that the

family needs to have things remain as they are (i.e., no change), while the family worker sees positive strengths with which the family can achieve its goals. Another useful approach is to have experts disagree in front of the family (or for the family worker to take a position of "on the one hand, on the other . . . ") and then to ask the family to decide who (or which position) is preferable (after Papp, 1983).

All these approaches are designed to enable the family worker to step back and avoid becoming locked into a stabilizing but limited role in the family. The family worker must be flexible and yet strong enough to help the family address critical and painful issues.

AVOIDANCE: "HE COULDN'T BE HERE"

Many family workers and clinics insist on seeing certain family members or even the whole family. This is often impossible with families characterized by chronic and severe problems. Instead, much, if not most, of our work involves merely engaging the family in a process of change — building up a minimal level of trust with individuals who have little reason to trust in professionals.

Engaging family members requires respect and persistence. If a family is motivated to work but a family member is unavoidably absent, it is possible to reschedule a session after meeting for a respectful amount of time. "It's too important not to have _____ present. Let's set up another time when it is possible for _____ to come." With many crisis-oriented families, it may take several months to engage a missing member. In such cases, the family worker can note overtly who is missing and express a need for his/her help. When there is resistance, pushing harder will not help, but taking a meta position that _____ will know when it is safe enough in the family for him/her to attend may make a difference (after Selvini Palazzoli et al., 1978).

Avoidance of therapy by the family or some of its members reflects a fear of annihilation or castration. The family worker can note the absence of a critical member and how important that person is for future work. The fact that someone is missing is itself a problem that the family may take for granted but one that we can work with them to solve. Moreover, avoidance must be recognized as a universal human characteristic shared by clients and workers. Families who appear to reject us, families who are frightening, and families who appear unpleasant often experience cancellations or even "no shows" from the family worker. The family's avoidance of the family worker, as well as the worker's avoidance of the family, reflects the overwhelming need to avoid dealing with painful issues. In many such cases, the family worker's feelings (e.g., rejection, anger, animosity, repugnance) reflect the family situation and need to be addressed as clues to the family's dilemma.

If this is not done, the family worker may end up acting out the family's avoidance.

DISCOUNTING: "IT HASN'T HELPED . . . YOU'RE NO GOOD"

The family worker can expect at least some level of discounting, which in many ways reflects clients' need and desire to bolster self-esteem, to prove that they are "something," to ward off feelings of dependency, and to avoid intrusion into their lives. Moreover, from a realistic point of view, why should family members trust a worker assigned or referred to them and why should they want to work with *another* "professional"?

Family workers need to be sensitive to feeling put down and to use perceptions of being discounted to identify this process. We give choices to the family, "You may need to go and see another practitioner or at least review options for counseling so that you can make the best decision." Even court ordered families can request another agency, clinic, or family worker.

We avoid taking a one-up position, and instead ask for the family's help. With families that have worked with many family workers, we say, quite honestly, that there is no reason for them to expect success in the current counseling after years of therapies with multiple social workers, psychologists, psychiatrists, etc. A "don't trust" message is also very useful. Then, to empower the family we ask, "What would *you* do at this point? I don't know if I have the answers." This approach helps to avoid idealization of the worker. Idealization leads to disillusion, which eventually leads clients to move onto the next worker.

HELPLESSNESS: "WHAT'S THE USE?"

Many families referred for abuse and neglect appear overwhelmed, exhausted, and extremely depressed. The family worker may sense "deadness" in families where both the children's and the adults' needs have been chronically unmet. These family members expect people to tell them what to do and have, in effect, adopted a lifestyle of being helpless. The family worker must avoid getting trapped into either the role of accepting the helplessness of family members or the role of cajoling/nagging/demanding them to change.

At the beginning of work with such families, one may simply listen and reflect overwhelmed feelings (e.g., "It must be very tiring. It must look like a long road ahead"). The family worker can go with the family's depression while continuing sessions. For some families that appear stuck in the past, it is useful to take a strong stand and to redefine the helplessness as protective of a certain hierarchy or family interaction. Helplessness may even be described as an important function that may need to continue despite the

consequences. The family may even need to get used to certain situations/
disabilities (after Watzlawick, Weakland, & Fisch, 1974).

By taking a stance contrary to the paramount efforts in and out of the
family to get the helpless person to move, the family's cycle can be altered. A
consultant or supervisor can stress that the whole family and outside helpers
need to get used to the helplessness of an individual because this helplessness protects the family and is a sacrifice of the "helpless" family member.
This stance redefines the helpless person's position and may make him/her
angry or others angry enough to change the family patterns of interaction.
We ask families what happens when people tell them what to do. Most of
those referred for chronic problems say that they don't follow recommendations or that the advice never worked. Many families will proudly boast that
they have done the opposite of professional advice. It is also helpful to ask if
family members like having people giving them advice/demands and, if they
do not, whether they want to change this. If family members want to
change, an intervention used is to have them select two people to whom they
want to say "no" — and to have them choose the practitioner as one of these
people.

Many helpless families almost invite the practitioner to tell them what to
do and thus to become identified as another adversary of the family. In such
cases we tell family members that we want them to point out when we slip up
and tell them what to do: "Stop me if I try to tell you what to do."

ENVIRONMENTAL HURDLES: COCKROACHES, LICE . . . "THE PITS"

Extremely scared and closed families need to keep the world out and
nothing works better than bugs, lice, or offensive odors. The family worker
entering such a home is likely to be repelled and frightened of becoming
infected or bitten. We quickly become angry at the situation and want to
escape. More often than not, however, family workers do not address the
environment, instead dealing with it through avoidance — the case is referred
to another practitioner or agency — or through rigid demands (e.g., scheduling requirements) that encourage the family to drop out of services.

Environmental hurdles and dangers serve to protect the family from
much greater risks. A therapeutic approach to such families needs to address
these risks despite the difficulty in doing so. Thus, if there is a growling dog,
the family worker may say, "Is it safe for me to come in? Will he bite?" If
family workers are uncomfortable, they must tell the clients that they feel
uncomfortable for fear of being bitten, etc., and ask the family members
what it is like for them. When safety is involved, strong straightforward "I"
messages are called for. If there are guns in the house, the family needs to be
told that they need to be locked away because they are dangerous, and

sessions cannot continue with guns lying around. "I am not comfortable and cannot work with you when your shotgun is out and not locked up."

Lice and mites, in particular, keep everyone out, including family workers. We don't know any client who is not as uncomfortable as we are with lice, cockroaches, etc. We ask, "Is it uncomfortable for you?" Often, we find our clients are used to being uncomfortable and so they see no hope for change. This becomes a vicious cycle. The hopelessness to change one's environment keeps professional helpers out. Poverty is demoralizing and leads over time to depression. Family workers must recognize that joining the search for better housing may be the best way to help the family.

We ask some families to come into our offices for sessions until they have cleaned up their home and made it safe. We then address how lice, mites, etc., keep family members isolated from friends and enemies alike: "The bugs keep the world out, and you may not really want me (and others) working with you either."

Environmental dangers need to be looked at in terms of the context of the situation.

For instance, a family with a child in placement was reluctant to bring the child home permanently, while agency staff were becoming increasingly angry when the youth came back from home visits with reinfections of mites. The mites served as a test of whether the agency would take over the child and relieve the family of responsibility. Group care staff were reluctant to send the youth home for fear of his returning with mites to his cottage and infecting other children and staff. The consultant in this case told the family that, instead of terminating home visits, the agency would discharge the child to the family if the mite problem continued. Home visits needed to occur if treatment were to proceed towards the parent's stated goal of the child's returning home, and the family needed a safe environment to carry this out. After this message the family cleaned up the house and the mite infections ended.

Environmental dangers keep family workers out and maintain stability in the family. The best strategy in working with such situations is to be dramatic (e.g., cough at obnoxious smells), to talk about such problems as dark or dangerous stairway landings, and to demonstrate a desire to work with the family while modeling the need for safety for oneself.

MULTIPLE CRISES AS A WAY OF LIFE: "WE'RE IN TERRIBLE TROUBLE"

Sometimes we are most impressed simply by the number of crises a family presents. The D. family described in Chapter 1 was referred by a school psychologist because of the children's inability to concentrate on schoolwork and the eight-year-old son's statements in school that he wanted to join his deceased grandparent. The children's mother presented a long chronology of crises, continuing unabated into the intake consultation session, during which an eviction notice for failure to pay rent was delivered. Evictions had been a recurrent pattern for the family, and the family had been previously investigated by child protective services for sleeping in their car for a week.

At the time of the intake session, the family was only minimally engaged. The mother and her son appeared extremely depressed and all four children were at risk of placement, particularly for not having a home. The family worker and consultant felt great anxiety about further violence in the family, a desire to do something (e.g., pay the rent), and yet a sense of hopelessness—nothing would change and the family would be evicted again. Several crises appeared to be swirling out of control.

Utilizing the framework outlined in Table 3.1, the consultant and family worker used their own emotional reactions—feeling overwhelmed—to help identify the primary feelings of the family: our own anger because Mrs. D. forgot her appointment with us, lack of trust that Mrs. D. would really work with us, and hopelessness that we could facilitate change. The family's current crises were repeated patterns of the mother's childhood experience. She had been physically abused by her father and sexually abused by an uncle; she fought physically with her mother and observed violent battles between her parents. Repeatedly, incidents of physical conflict with men led to a climax in which she would say, "Just try!" In many instances this was followed by physical fights with boyfriends or husbands, injuries, rejection of the spouse or boyfriend, and the family's need to move because of loss of their financial support. These incidents repeated a theme of violence leading to eviction—just as the mother had had to leave her own parents as a teenager with nowhere to go after being abused and rejected.

Crises helped the family avoid facing the pain implicit in the mother's longstanding conflicts with her parents. Repeated violent incidents with men and evictions kept the family locked into a negative and dependent relationship with the maternal grandmother and in effect symbolized the mother's inability to move on developmentally from her position as an abused (and abusing) adolescent and to ever have a home of her own.

Presenting the worker and consultant with both current and chronic crises tested the worker's willingness to work with the intensity of the family's conflicts. The message, "Don't change me," posed a test to the worker. This message was also similar to Mrs. D.'s message to her boyfriends—"Just try" to change or control her. In these first few sessions Mrs. D. was asking if the family worker would be willing to help and whether the family worker, like most authority figures, would become locked into a position of trying to control and change her.

Crises help families like the D.'s to avoid painful issues. The urgency of addressing multiple problems prevents the family from facing issues and in effect prevents the family and its members from making developmental transitions. Battles are being fought at all times, but nothing seems to change. The war is never won. And, as problems escalate in severity, new recruits from outside the family (family workers, probation officers, child protective services, school officials, etc.) are often brought in to help fight threatening problems.

When a family worker is presented with a crisis-oriented family, it is important to stay with the family through a series of typical crises. Family workers need to find out what crisis got the family referred for services, even if that particular incident is no longer seen as a current issue. A crisis-oriented family will most likely be preoccupied with another critical event and may need some coaxing to recall what precipitated the initial referral. For the D.'s, this meant going back to the family's needing to sleep in a car and the school's fears about the son committing suicide. Information on previous crises and, in particular, the family's first major crisis (e.g., the first time the D. family had to sleep in the car) can be very helpful in determining repetitive patterns and themes. Collecting details on what happened, what was done, family reactions, community reactions, etc., can reveal the family's typical cycle of behaviors.

By presenting the family worker with a series of crises, the family members are, in effect, testing whether the family worker will help them, whether the family worker can deal with the intensity of their problems, or whether the family worker will be scared away and reject the family. It is therefore essential that the family worker provide information and concrete help in dealing with immediate problems, e.g., driving a client to the county welfare office to apply for benefits or helping a parent look for another apartment. When we help clients obtain needed services, they recognize us as their helpers. Our cars can become one of our best therapeutic tools.

After gaining acceptance by the family, the family worker can begin to predict future crises based on the family's past experiences, which have been shared with or experienced by the family worker.

The family worker works with the recognition that multiple crises reflect intense emptiness and that the family members' problems are symbolic messages of their deeper fears. By recognizing the exhaustion and/or excitement in the family without demanding change, the family worker is communicating an ability and interest to go with the family—even if that means facing much more difficult issues than the current list of problems.

To begin to engage the D. family described above, the family worker needed to share her overwhelmed feelings, slow down on dealing with the family's long history of crises and events, and instead work with the family on the current needs. "I'm feeling overwhelmed with what you've shared. You must be overwhelmed as well." "Sometimes we have to recognize that we can't solve everything all at once but we can work on one thing at a time." "I don't know anyone who can do productive work without a roof over their heads." "We need to deal with keeping a roof over your heads."

Since lack of trust was such a major issue, the family was asked not to trust the worker and consultant: "You must not trust us. We too might tell you what to do. If I do, please tell me." This helped the worker to address current crises and to understand and experience with the family repeated patterns of stress without rejecting the family, becoming locked into an adversarial relationship, or telling Mrs. D. what to do.

After staying with the family members and helping them go through a series of incidents, the worker was in a position to help the family members predict future crises based on recurring patterns. They could be presented with their options for making choices within the larger context of these repetitive patterns. For example, keeping a "roof over their heads" was a message to the grandparents that their daughter (Mrs. D.) was responsible and making decisions as a parent in her children's best interests. Coordination with the school was similarly based on the family's need to have a roof over their heads, since the children could not concentrate in school if at any minute the family could be evicted. And more importantly, if the family had to move, the children would have to leave the school.

FAMILY WORKER'S RESISTANCE: "I CAN'T, SHOULDN'T, OR MUST . . . "

Working with families with chronic and severe problems requires family workers to use their own feelings and to address their own needs in order to be comfortable. Only by so doing can the practitioner be in a position to help the family to address critical issues.

Donna was an extremely agitated woman who talked incessantly and appeared to engulf her three-year-old son and nine-year-old daughter in all areas of their lives. She appeared to be obsessed about conflicts with the father of her two children and locked into ongoing conflict with his new wife and him. When questions were asked of Donna, she would turn to her daughter and ask her daughter what to do. During sessions her complaints were interrupted only by her need to manage her three-year-old son, who demanded food and threw temper tantrums.

Donna described a history of multiple losses. She never knew her biological father. As an infant she was placed privately by her biological mother into a foster home, where she stayed until age three. At that point her biological mother returned and took Donna from her foster mother, whom she never saw again. She lived with her biological mother and stepfather until age 10, when she was placed in a residential center for children. At age 13, she managed to get herself evicted from the residential center by burning a bed and by engaging in other defiant behaviors. She returned to live with her mother for two years and then moved out on her own, traveling around the country with different men. Donna had learned in her life that she couldn't trust anyone and had to continually fear abandonment.

The family worker appeared ill at ease talking to Donna. She dealt with her own anxiety by trying to write down every detail about Donna's traumatic past, which Donna related with great relish and energy. The consultant enjoyed listening to Donna's animated and obviously bright discourse but struggled with how to help the family worker work with Donna and her family.

Donna was a woman who appeared to engulf her children and any adults who came close to her. Separation was intolerable for her and appeared to reflect her own traumatic losses at age three when she was taken away from her foster mother and later at age 10 when she was placed. Ominously, her own two children were at or approaching the ages when she had experienced massive abandonment.

The consultant sensed that, while one session with Donna was very stimulating, working with her on an ongoing basis would be extremely difficult because the worker would have to always fear upsetting Donna. If the worker got close to Donna's problems, Donna would most likely find eventual termination (separation) intolerable. With this in mind, the consultant recommended that the worker address the issue of abandonment from the beginning. The consultant suggested that the family worker tell Donna, "Many people have left you and someday I will have to leave you also. I can and want to work with you on the most important thing right now—helping you and your children so that you won't have to leave them, so your children won't have to experience what happened to you when you were young." To increase real anxiety with Donna, the consultant recommended emphasizing, "This is crucial in this next year because your children will be at the same ages when you experienced traumatic separations and we know that history often repeats itself." The consultant also recommended that the worker begin with messages, "You should not trust that I won't leave you or that any helper wouldn't leave you." The worker could begin to engage Donna by talking about the worker's own experiences of loss and abandonment. By dealing with issues of abandonment from the onset, the worker freed herself from fears of being engulfed by Donna's manic and agitated behavior.

Most family workers have never experienced chronic abuse, neglect, sex abuse, or the intense abandonment of crisis-oriented families. We have, however, experienced losses and acquisitions which we can use to help us get in touch with these emotions. An exercise we use with staff is to ask them to remember losses in their family and what happened. We also ask staff to visualize themselves being placed at different ages (preschool, latency, and adolescence) and imagine themselves in a foster home, in a room in a residential treatment center apart from their families, in a detention center, etc. How would they feel? What would happen to their family and what would they do? It's helpful to put ourselves in our clients' places. This helps us to better identify our own feelings of anger or fear and to better understand the families we work with.

We need to avoid narcissistic beliefs and externally imposed mandates which impede our work (e.g., expectations to heal all clients, to understand all situations, and to love everything about our clients). It is valuable for family workers to understand their own families, so they can distinguish issues in their client families from their own family issues. Therapist's Own Family work (Bowen, 1978; Guerin, 1976) is very useful in helping family workers be sensitive to their own issues, their own pain, and how these lead them to distance or pursue a client. The family worker who is able to address painful issues in his/her own family will be better able to work with the extreme pain and despair in chronic crisis-oriented families. Given the intense emotional climate of families in perpetual crisis, practitioners must be capable of feeling their own emotions and keeping themselves free enough to both understand their position in family-practitioner interactions and intervene in the turmoil around them.

Therapy is an act of aggression in which the therapist attacks, however gently and indirectly, the patient's most cherished pathology.

—Frank Pittman, 1984, p. 7

CHAPTER 5

Home-based Family Work: Moving Beyond the One-way Mirror

CRISIS-ORIENTED FAMILIES are masters at engaging family workers in a pattern of interactions entitled, "I will let you victimize me and become my persecutor. Then I will lose you." Practitioners and families often repeat a pattern of interaction in which the helping professional is seductively drawn into the role of yet another perpetrator of abuse upon the family. The well-intentioned but unknowing practitioner is tested to see if he/she will repeat what everyone else has done with the family before: move in too close and push the "client" into intense pain. This reactivates the client's feeling of inner terror from earlier trauma and the inevitable need to avoid the practitioner. The lesson for the family is clear: Never trust!

The family worker's seduction from a role as "rescuer" and "helper" to yet another "abuser" is a complex process which often goes unrecognized by the practitioner until it is too late. Another crisis will take place (e.g., removal of a child by child protective services for abuse, arrest of a youth for stealing a car) and the practitioner will have to "close" the case. In the end, the practitioner is kicked out of the client's life and the client reaffirms the need to avoid working on sensitive issues.

With more secure and competent clients who have experienced severe losses or traumas, the therapeutic process moves forward directly from assessment to helping family members within a supportive relationship to reclaim their traumatic past as part of their history and identity. Such clients can be helped to understand what has happened to them, to grieve, and to let go of both the trauma and past distortions of memory which once were necessary for survival (after Rieker & Carmen, 1986). This work includes helping individuals to discover and rebuild connections with people they have loved and to understand what made that love so hard to bear (Vaillant, 1986). Psychotherapy optimally includes recovering people the client has loved (but lost) and building new connections with an understanding of what led to earlier emotional distress.

We need to follow a much slower course with families in perpetual crisis and to restrain change while moving ever so slowly to join the family. Otherwise the risk will be too great that families will slip into intolerable feelings of terror and rage.

The need to move slowly was dramatically illustrated in a case involving a new family worker and a mother, Julie R., referred following a chronic history of neglect of her son, now four years old. Both Julie and her son had been physically abused by several of Julie's boyfriends. Julie had a long history as a victim of incest and multiple experiences of rape. As an adult, she appeared to allow anyone and everyone into her life.

The family worker constructed a genogram with Julie and helped her to examine her past in order to confront and overcome the horrendous traumas she had experienced. This was done in one intense session in which the family worker believed that he was engaged in "real" therapy and touching the core pain of this client. Julie experienced great pain during this session and began crying. Following this session, Julie was not at home at the regularly scheduled time for the next session, nor did she appear for any session for the next month. At the end of the month, the family worker was informed that there had been a "crisis" in the family and that the county child protective services unit had to place the four-year-old boy into foster care because he had been left alone by Julie for an inappropriate amount of time.

In this case, the family worker was enticed into probing into the pain and trauma of a chronic victim of rape. By pushing verbally into areas of extreme pain (a form of emotional rape), he replayed Julie's recurrent pattern of "victimize me and then I will lose you."

Crisis-oriented families test us by asking through their behavior: "Are you going to do to me what everyone else has done?" We are seduced into replaying patterns of abuse that reflect the parents' experiences. By moving too fast in our drive to heal and cure (the definition of therapy), we fail the parents' test of whether they can trust us to understand their extreme dilemmas and why they cannot change. Then they feel that they must escape and avoid us. These parents give up any hope of change rather than getting too close, touching their pain, and connecting with all of the tragic losses they have experienced.

In Julie's case, the family worker was helped to see how he had become seduced into the role of repeating a pattern. Fortunately, there was another opportunity to work with this parent.

Another family worker in the same program was able to engage Julie by talking about what had happened and stressing that she needed to give her control of how fast and how intensely they worked on painful issues. The family worker and Julie agreed on working to help her to avoid further victimization. After setting this goal, the family worker asked Julie to remind her every time she began to "victimize" her by going too fast into sensitive areas.

With the son now in foster care, Julie was confronting a major crisis in her life, which evoked tremendous pain. The family worker was able to engage Julie to work on getting her son home while at the same time not being a victim. She joined with Julie based on her genuine concern and her understanding that family workers had victimized her and pushed her too quickly into terrible pain. As a relationship with Julie developed she began to elicit a beginning sense of trust based on the understanding that no one can touch so much pain so quickly and survive.

In work with Julie, as with so many crisis-oriented individuals, we must recognize that it is not the past traumas, e.g., rapes, violence, that are the cause of current discomfort. We as family workers are often shocked and at the same time intrigued by the horrors experienced by our clients. We must realize, however, that these past traumas, no matter how gruesome or horrendous, are often not the primary concerns of our "clients." The challenge for the worker is to eventually understand the patterns of crisis in the family and help family members avoid repeating past traumas.

GOING WITH THE CRISIS

We work to help families with their crises while learning to be aware of how crises work for them. We probe gently for what families fear most and what must be protected; at the same time, we validate the crisis and recognize everyone who is involved, including other professionals, friends, and neighbors. Our task is to involve everyone in understanding the family crises, to get everyone to recognize who is participating in and affected by the crises, and most importantly, to identify the stresses on the family before each crisis.

What is the family's pattern of response? What is comfortable for the family as a whole? Can we identify cycles of interactions among parents, grandparents, and children? Asking such questions, the worker begins to recognize the painful experiences that exist in the families' unique histories, which have taught them to prefer having crisis after crisis over facing conflicts. We help the family to see that crises are addicting. Crises are exciting and provide temporary relief from problems. Crises keep everybody from feeling anything. Experienced, well-trained staff are needed because of the intensity, timing, and sensitivity required for this work.

Well-trained master's level staff can use concrete services as a way to engage and help a family. This can involve taking family members for medical examinations, helping them find a new apartment, helping a parent apply for financial assistance or for job training.

WORKING WITH MULTIPLE PROBLEMS

Rather than focusing on a single problem, we look at the crisis pattern, including all details of the crisis, what led up to the crisis, every individual's responses (before and after), and the meaning of recurrent crises in the family.

The J. family was referred to help prevent replacement of Amy, age eight, and Susan, age ten. Both girls were uncontrollable at home and in school. Mrs. J. and her daughters had been repeatedly hospitalized for both imagined and real illnesses while her second husband, to whom she had been married for one year, complained about the impending loss of all their possessions because of the family's tremendous medical bills. Marital tension was punctuated by frequent incidents in which Mrs. J. had to be rushed to the emergency room. Sexual intimacy between Mr. and Mrs. J. was impossible because of the wife's continued need for medical treatment for her physical problems. Sexual abuse of the children by Mrs. J.'s first husband had been the cause of a previous placement for over two years.

With the J. family, we needed to look at the family's initial crisis that led to placement. The family's *many* crises served to help the spouses avoid painful issues around their lack of intimacy and Mr. J.'s constant fear of total abandonment if Mrs. J. should die and leave him responsible for her children. Symbolically, a woman who repeatedly goes to the emergency room is saying that the family is in "emergency." In effect, the family was asking for a quick and urgent intervention before someone repeated the initial crisis of sexual abuse. The husband and children were worried about losing everything—the mother's life, all their belongings, etc. They were all frightened by their own behavior, loss of control, the hidden potential for sexual abuse, the lack of supervision of the children, and the mother's inability to take control and supervise.

Our work began by recognizing the multiple and chronic crises that had led up to the present referral. We then stressed how these crises could and most likely would be repeated in the future. Given the history of sexual abuse of the two children by their biological father (and sexual abuse of the mother as a child), we alluded to recurrent crises as "something serious going on in the family that cannot be directly dealt with." Were family members worried about sexual abuse occurring again? What needed to happen for sexual abuse to *not* occur? What needed to happen for the children to be safe and to remain at home? After addressing these concerns, the parents began to verbalize problems in their marriage. The family worker could then provide initial marital counseling and help the parents address such concrete issues as obtaining health insurance that would cover mother's and other family members' medical bills.

In family sessions, the new stepfather needed to hear what had happened to the children so that he could be more sensitive to their fears about what fathers can do. Mrs. J. needed to give the children a message that she wouldn't die. To help Mrs. J., the family worker needed to validate her medical needs and work to engage her trust.

Our approach operates on the premise that we will not tell family members what to do but will instead give them support in developing autonomy. From a developmental perspective, the growth process means that the parents need to take control. Adults in crisis-oriented families are often functioning emotionally in Erikson's stage of "autonomy versus shame" (Erikson, 1986). Our task is to help them to make choices and to take risks that will enable change and growth.

PREDICTING THE CRISIS

After working with family members as they experience several crises, we can slowly begin to predict upcoming crises based on the patterns we have learned to expect from the family. We explore the meaning of crises for each family member. What would happen if they accomplished their goals? What are the parents' greatest fears? What would stop them from accomplishing their goals, e.g., the anticipated loss of helpers, the end of a needed role for the maternal grandmother? We help the family to predict the next crisis, e.g., loss of a job, loss of an apartment, redefining it as predictable and based upon avoidance of the family's pain. Thus, family members who have had a crisis every time a child has threatened to grow up and leave home will be advised that, with their next son approaching the age of 16, they can probably expect a violent episode similar to what happened when each of the older children turned 16. With a family in which, over three to four generations, girls had been raped or became pregnant at the age of 14, we warned that their 13½-year-old daughter might become pregnant. Our intent is to help families to recognize the meaning of crisis and to deal with the painful past and present which they have long avoided. Very, very slowly crises are understood as a way of life and as an addiction. Like all addictions, crises mask pain.

We are careful to predict crises at all major life transition points, including when children come home from placement, when the parents stop working and go on a vacation, when holidays approach, or when a relative visits. We predict crises especially when things are going well. Families may interpret "things going well" as a signal that our work is ending and that we will soon abandon them. This or any other action that elicits feelings of abandonment will provoke another crisis. For example, if the parents fear that no one will be home for Thanksgiving or that a child will get a job and move out of the house, feelings of emptiness and loss, as well as the predictability of a crisis as a response to this pain, must be dealt with.

Crises are likely when a family worker is actually terminating with the family or transferring the case to another family worker. Crises at this point not only keep family members from dealing with the loss of someone they have begun to trust, but also bring others in by demonstrating to the world that they are not ready to move on without a family worker, child protective services worker, etc. The message to the family worker is: "You really haven't helped." Thus, the family's gains and progress will suddenly seem to disappear.

One Primary Family Worker

The family members, especially the parents, need to develop enough trust so that they will allow us to touch their pain. Given that these parents are often emotionally very much like young children whose dependency needs have not been met, we help them to begin to trust that we will not abandon them in the next crisis. This contrasts with the extreme pain most of these individuals have experienced through rejection and abandonment by their own parents.

Our approach involves family members' growing very gradually by facing their pain within a supportive relationship with one primary family worker who continues to work with them over time. This approach differs from most home-based counseling programs. Prevention-of-placement programs in the United States typically have focused on the presenting crisis, with time-limited counseling, typically lasting two to five months, and involvement of a team of professionals (Norman, 1985). Our approach emphasizes the need to offer ongoing family work in order to build the level of trust necessary both to help crisis-oriented families through the presenting crisis and to provide them with opportunities to work on recurrent toxic issues.

One primary family worker can be "real" from an emotional sense in a way that a team of professionals visiting the home can never be. The family worker operating alone demonstrates both a vulnerability and a sense of courage and determination to work with what most professionals would consider to be chaotic, disorganized, incompetent, and sometimes violent families — the exact opposite of the YAVIS clients (Young, Attractive, Verbal, Intelligent, Successful) that respond best to psychotherapies. To "get in the door" of crisis-oriented families, the outreach family worker must be genuine, honest, and respectful of the family's integrity. The primary family worker can offer the support and guidance needed for families operating at an early developmental level, demonstrating persistence in contrast to their history of abandonment and enabling family members to make choices rather than leaving choices up to community authorities and professionals (including the family worker).

This involves collaborative work with child protective services, foster care workers, staff at residential treatment centers, probation workers, and other mental health family workers. County authorities need to take strong positions based on their mandates to protect children in cases of child abuse or neglect. Similarly, probation workers need to take strong positions on the need for family supervision and the end of dangerous behavior in cases under their jurisdiction. When county authorities take their statutory roles, the family worker is freed to work on joining with families to address their concerns and dilemmas.

Mandates by county authorities are used as leverage for change. This creates anxiety and an impetus for change in the family. For instance, parents may need to make certain changes in order to get their children home from foster care or to prevent placement. This could include removal from the family of a sexually abusing boyfriend, treatment of chronic alcoholism, providing beds, providing sufficient food, installing doors on the bedrooms to provide minimal privacy, or even satisfying the basic need of establishing a home.

THE ROLE OF THE THERAPIST

If family workers do not have a clear focus on their role, they will soon find themselves acting out the family's dilemma. The family worker's first task is to engage the family in a working relationship, as outlined in Chapters 3 and 4. Typically, families will test the family worker with a series of crises to find out: How much is the worker willing to help? Will the family worker get impatient and leave? Will the family worker bring in more professionals, showing the parents again how hopeless and helpless they are—as well as the hopelessness and helplessness of the family worker? In these beginning stages, we show the family that we will be there and persist in coming. Recognizing that these families are testing whether we will abandon them or fall into typical roles of investigator, prosecutor, or simply stabilizer, we help them to secure concrete services, both as a way of nurturing them and as a way of learning the patterns of family crises. If clients have to go to court, we go with them. If clients are being evicted, we help them look for housing. Such interventions foster a trusting dependence on the worker, which is needed for the client to grow. Clients show us in their crises where they are stuck developmentally; this is where we need to join them and help them move on.

Working with crisis-oriented families means dealing with the intense feelings and needs generated by their dilemmas. It is a mistake to leave our feelings unaddressed and take home intense feelings that we were afraid to express during sessions. Instead, we try to recognize our feelings (in our guts and in our heads), and identify them as worries, fears, anger, etc., that the family is experiencing. In this way we stay comfortable enough to continue to work with the family. By addressing feelings of fear, anger, sorrow, etc., we show the family that feelings can be talked about and that we are willing to deal with them. "There is nothing so scary it can't be talked about." We need to remember that the family members' biggest test is whether we can like them or whether we will add to their shame and abandon them.

Workers also fear being abandoned by the family and feeling the "shame" of failing to be a helper. As we learn more about the family, we can ask, "Who would not like to be here for the next session?" We can predict that the family might not want to have another session and/or won't be there for the next session since painful feelings have been shared. We caution the family to stop us and not let us move too fast into sensitive areas. By addressing issues of abandonment, the worker can avoid being paralyzed by fear.

Family workers will experience a strong pull to do everything for the client or feel overwhelmed by the family's needs and back away by setting rigid limits and withholding support. It is helpful to remember that some crisis-oriented families have few limits and tend to become involved in many activities (even taking in homeless persons), while other families remain withdrawn and isolated. Visualizing the crisis-oriented family with either nonexistent or rigidly closed doors can help the practitioner understand what needs to happen and what must be avoided. We need to be especially careful not to move too quickly and take on the responsibility for averting disaster with a family that is perennially on the brink of calamity.

WHY OUTREACH?

Many crisis-oriented families have gone from agency to agency attending one or two sessions, ventilating, sometimes sharing a great deal, and then never returning. In many cases families have shared something, become fearful, and immediately abandoned the family worker. Some families in perpetual crisis become known to every agency in the community. Outreach is often seen as a last resort for attempting to engage families who have been referred to many clinics and agencies but have never become engaged in counseling, despite court orders and efforts by experienced family therapists.

Outreach provides a means for the family worker to come back again and again and thus to demonstrate persistence. For families who have been cut off from relatives and the community, outreach brings people into the family. This opens the family system and brings in new information and the possibility of new relationships. Holding conferences in the home (for instance, with school staff and referring workers) can allow for contacts and the beginning of constructive relationships which the family would otherwise not risk.

Working in the family's home also helps establish boundaries. The family is left in control in a concrete fashion, e.g., where we sit and who will be present. Issues of privacy and confidentiality are brought up, as the family needs to choose what will be private and what will be public, e.g., to decide whether they wish neighbors involved. Decisions on who should be present (e.g., should the children be involved in a session) are structural moves. For instance, seeing "Mommy" first and then having a family session stresses that Mommy needs to be in charge and to take care of herself. This can also be a lesson for children in learning how to wait and for Mommy in setting limits in her own home. Moreover, by going to the family's turf, we are always taking a one-down position which emphasizes the parents' control and ability to make choices. This, again, is a key developmental task with parents who are often functioning socially and emotionally at a level typical of young children.

Outreach contrasts sharply with bringing a family into an office. In an office setting, the practitioner controls the environment and is immediately perceived as being in a position of power over the family.* Most families in perpetual crisis, involved in an ongoing battle to maintain distance and avoid getting too close to their pain, continually rebel and fight to stop people from controlling them. If they feel they are getting too close or

---

*For those practitioners who see families in their offices, we urge them to use at least one home visit. Seeing the family in the home enhances and enlarges our understanding and feeling of the family's reality. Primary issues, e.g., lack of physical safety, are striking in the home but may be hidden in office visits. Moreover, practitioners whose clients do not show up for their next appointment are frequently never seen again. A home visit offers an opportunity to pursue. "Try it, you'll like it!"

sharing too much with an engaging and empathic family worker, they will stop coming to the office.

Overpowering family workers frighten crisis-oriented families. One strategy to engage families is for the family worker to stress his/her powerlessness, while at the same time serving as a catalyst for the family to make choices and change in a way that feels safe.

The L. family (stepfather, mother, and three children) was referred by child protective services. Mr. L. discounted any suggestions that were made by previous workers and the psychiatric consultant. No matter how the family worker intervened with the family, Mr. L. needed to believe it was his idea and his decision. The family worker helped Mr. L. identify the problem and tried to help Mrs. L. and the children make suggestions. The family worker then took a one-down, helpless position, stating that she had no answers but that she would like the family to explore solutions. Mr. L. came up with creative solutions which enhanced his self-esteem. These solutions eventually led to the family's discharge from child protective services.

By modeling powerlessness and giving choices to the family, we can help family members to take control of their lives and their interactions with others. This is a tremendously difficult process, as crisis-oriented families are constantly demanding that other people take control of them. By going to the family's home we concretely demonstrate that the family is in control and not us. The one-down position of the family worker may be necessary only until the family is engaged in family work or with families experiencing tremendous shame and low self-esteem. Once engaged, the family worker can make powerful interventions and consider alternative settings for family work or group activities at the office or at school playrooms, etc.

The one-down position of the worker can be complemented strategically by using a consultant and holding treatment review conferences. At these conferences, messages can be given by referral sources, e.g., child protective workers, on their roles as monitors of the family, time limits confronting the family, and consequences if change does not occur. At the same time, consultants and supervisors can give strong messages bringing out the dilemmas facing the family if change occurs (after Papp, 1983). Strategic messages can be given by supervisors or consultants about the immense difficulties family members would face if they were to change and the probability and predictability that they will continue to have crises or repeat past behaviors rather than achieve their goals. While consultants are predicting failure and crises, the family worker can continue to support family members by recognizing their strengths, their positive efforts, and their ability to do what is needed to accomplish their goals.

Conferences are critical times for coordinating work and recognizing the role of each practitioner with the family. All practitioners must work towards the same family goals. Many cases end in failure when multiple helping professionals are working toward conflicting goals, e.g., for and against placement of an adolescent. In addition, with families fearing abandonment, we need to deal with the grief and loss of a service provider leaving the system — even if the termination of services reflects improvement by the family. For instance, the closing of a child protective case can lead some family members to panic for fear of loss of control and renewed abuse. Conferences provide a time to address these fears and losses and to identify their remaining support system (individuals and organizations).

Conferences also often bring out the powerlessness of the community to help crisis-oriented families who have given up responsibility for caring for themselves. The conference helps agencies refocus on attainable goals and workers regain energy.

Mrs. W. was visited by a child protective services worker weekly. She had a family worker provided by a child welfare agency who provided counseling for her and her children. Mrs. W. also was given parent training by childcare workers. She had a worker who met with her weekly in a crime victim program and she participated in a mothers group at her church. In addition to these counselors, she had a public assistance worker and a probation worker.

At the first treatment review conference, everyone was struck by how busy this mother was in being a client with so many professionals and how she was not doing what she needed to do to get her two oldest children out of placement. Mrs. W. had become accustomed to and felt very comfortable with seeing everyone involved. She really cared a great deal about each of these workers. They had provided connections and given purpose to her life; they had become her "family."

By gathering together, the workers were hearing and seeing for the first time what an overwhelming group they were. This meeting helped everyone to recognize the problem of too many services. Yet, abrupt dismissal of some helpers would have been a terrible blow to Mrs. W. Instead, services were slowly consolidated so that Mrs. W. could begin to take charge.

WORKING WITH ONLY ONE SPOUSE

We may ask that the whole family come to a session, but respect the family's wisdom in deciding who actually appears. We work with those who are present, while recognizing the importance of those who are absent (see Chapter 4).

In working with a marital couple, we begin with the assumption that prolonged work (e.g., more than five sessions) with only one spouse on marital issues would be tantamount to helping that person to end the marriage (Gurman & Kniskern, 1978). We advise marital couples in which only one member comes to the session that, if we continue to work beyond five sessions on marital issues, this could contribute to the end of the marriage.

If the absent spouse conveys a message that our meeting together with the couple could be explosive, we stress again that *we need them both* to work on marital issues, reassuring them that we are aware of the risk to the marriage involved in either addressing issues together or having one spouse not come in for sessions. To lessen tension we emphasize that this office (or session in the family's home) needs to be a safe time/place to share feelings and that, as their workers, we will stop them if they become too intense. The couple is asked to agree ahead of time that they will end the session if it becomes too painful or provocative.

Sessions are designed to give couples an opportunity to learn new ways to listen and share their feelings and ideas. Each spouse helps to set the pace of work on sensitive issues and is given the option to leave at any time if things get too intense. Asking family members to do homework, such as writing down feelings, is helpful to defuse anger. We are aware that couples continue to deal with issues after sessions and couples are told that they can call the worker if issues become too toxic. This process provides a framework in which each individual can begin to make choices about working to stay together or to separate.

WORKING WITH NEGLECT

Some parents appear to be quite calm while others move in a frenzy around them. Such parents may be referred for neglect and may be seen as not providing needed medical care for themselves, not getting their children to school, or in general not seeming to care. Many are extremely depressed, have had little experience being nurtured themselves, and have experienced abandonment at an early age or prolonged and repeated separations from their own parents as young children.

Many of these parents were also "parentified"—given the responsibility of caring for younger siblings at an early age: so early that they missed the critical stage of childhood in which the child learns to play and master the environment.

The A. family was referred because the children came to school dirty and unfed and their home was filthy and vermin-infested. Mrs. A. was extremely obese and rarely moved outside of her apartment. Mr. A. had a history of alcoholism but was a steady worker. The A.'s five children had been in foster care for one year and during this time Mrs. A. became pregnant with her sixth child. Following return of the children from placement, patterns of neglect, lack of food, poor hygiene, and poor school attendance resumed. The mother's weight steadily increased until she weighed approximately 300 lbs.

The family was provided with after-school activities for the oldest boys, monitoring by child protective services, family therapy on a weekly basis, group involvement for the parents and children, parenting groups for Mr. and Mrs. A., and assistance with obtaining food. Yet the three oldest boys continued to act out in the community, running in the streets and in general showing disruptive behavior at home and in school. In response, Mrs. A. threatened to file a PINS (Persons In Need of Supervision) petition in family court on her sons and to have them placed in institutions. In spite of the intensive help given to this family, the situation remained the same, with Mrs. A. getting heavier and heavier and the children acting out more intensely the conflicts in the family.

With parents referred for neglect, it is important to have a strong child protective service presence to create some anxiety that can lead to change. The family worker can then nurture and support the needy parent. Parents are seen separately at first, as many such parents cannot even tolerate the jealousy of seeing their children nurtured while they are momentarily ignored. It is important to engage parents around their own unmet needs and what they would like for themselves. It is only after they feel nurtured that they can nurture their children. Family sessions thus follow parent sessions.

Setting a time to meet with "Mommy" or "Daddy" helps to establish the parent in a special position in the family hierarchy. When the children are present, we look to the parent for decisions on what and when to give to the children. This models that the parent is in charge and responsible for nurturance to the children.

Meeting with the parents weekly and holding weekly family sessions starts to set new family rituals. Often these may be the only times that a parent looks at his or her own needs or that a family gets together. Family work becomes a ritual which stresses the importance of family and of taking care of oneself.

For parents who have never been nurtured themselves, the use of play during family sessions helps both parent and child. It is helpful to leave play materials in the home so that they can continue to play after the session.

In cases where there is no change, we have used the following strategy. After building a supportive relationship with passive and neglectful parents, we gently tell them that they will have to get used to their situation—living with vermin, disease, child protective services monitoring, children in placement (after Fisch, Weakland, & Segal, 1982). It is useful to be dramatic and point out in graphic detail what that could mean in one year, five years, ten years. Using this approach, the family worker avoids beseeching the parents to change or rescuing them from their problems. Instead the family worker joins with the family in recognizing the tremendous obstacles to change (e.g., what it would mean to relatives, what the family might lose, etc.) and the almost inevitability of staying the same. Hope is brought out through recognition that family members do have resources to face the difficulties they would encounter if they were to change.

WORKING WITH TIME AND CONTEXT

Several techniques are useful in enabling clients to broaden their perspectives and gain control over their lives. Construction of a genogram (McGoldrick & Gerson, 1985) with the family may help to reveal positive or negative attachments, cutoffs from other family members, generational patterns of crises, neglect, abuse, acquisition, and abandonment. This not only expands the family's perspective but also promotes a realistic understanding of past connections that may have been very toxic.

Over and over, we are confronted with the child who has been neglected and abused and yet says, "I love my Mommy and want to go home." Many of our clients have memories that combine love and pain divorced from the feelings of rejection, engulfment, or abandonment experienced in their past. The past is often idealized and seen alternately as all-good or all-bad. For instance, a mother of five children living in a lice-infested home isolated from the world told us, "My parents were wonderful." Later in the same session she revealed that both she and her children had been sexually and physically abused by these "wonderful" people.

As we work on the genogram (see Figure 5.1), we involve the entire family in looking at the past and slowly coming to grips with reality and pain. The genogram belongs to the family members and we leave it with them.

Many individuals, however, are not ready to work on past or present relationships. For such families, the genogram can be used almost like parallel play. If parents cannot relate to one another, we let them take turns talking about their families, and by so doing slowly learn to listen to one another. The process of gently learning about the past within a supportive relationship can facilitate their dealing with their choices about the present. When parents reach the point of saying, "This is what my parents did . . . and I don't want to do it," we can build on their positive desire to make things better.

Idealization can be addressed by taking individuals to visit a family member in jail, writing relatives in another city, or encouraging a parent to correspond with relatives to find out needed information. When significant relatives are deceased, visits to the grave site can assist in finally putting them to rest. Not only does this help the parent to grieve his/her loss, but the child sees the reality of death and learns to mourn. This process helps families to begin to look at the deceased person realistically. With crisis-

Figure 5.1

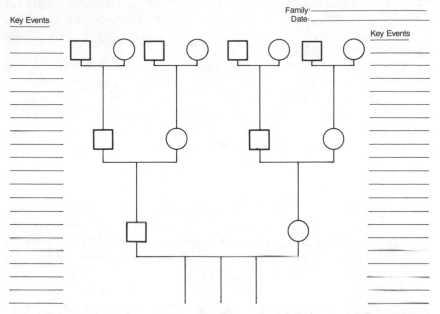

oriented families, the work of connecting or mourning must be concrete, e.g., getting a gravestone for a deceased grandparent.

We use the basic genogram (McGoldrick & Gerson, 1985) and list key events on the side in the client's own words (see Figure 5.1). For example: "Their grandfather was a 'dirty old man' who was never home. Grandmother thought land was the most important thing in life. They came to this country and bought a farm in 1932. My family lives very far away; I don't know them. I haven't seen them since I was 16." This process reveals pieces of the family's script.

Constructing an ecogram (Hartman, 1978) with the family, visually illustrating positive and negative resources in the community, expands our understanding of the family's network and potential supports.

All Work, No Play Makes . . .

One important need that is often overlooked is the family's taking time for pleasure and enjoyment. We model nurturance by bringing cookies for sessions if the parent can provide tea or milk. For many of our families, the dinner hour means sitting in front of the TV with one or two members at the table. We invite families to have dinner at the agency and use the dinner hour to sit down together—to talk and to listen.

Many of our families live below the poverty level and move from one place to another, often losing rather than acquiring furniture with each move. If we model family dinners, we must also help the family to acquire the chairs and table to do this at home. As the family builds strength, its members are better able to participate in community activities or agency programs that allow families to have a good time and at the same time to meet and learn from other parents and children.

Once a family is engaged, we no longer have to work as hard. Learning about what a family has done, blow-by-blow accounts of events, or "taking tea time" (Bergman, 1986) can then be dealt with in a lighter vein: "You know this has happened before. How can this be avoided next time?" Or, "You had all this happen and you didn't call me. What am I — chopped liver? . . . Next time call me!" (K. Pratt, personal communication, 1985).

BUILDING CONNECTIONS

Crisis-oriented families typically have few or no resources to call upon or, at the other extreme, too many resources that overlap. Some "friends" are seen as "stabbing you in the back," while changes within the extended family are considered impossible. The risk of placement and replacement of children is directly correlated with the lack of supportive relationships with people whom the parents can actually rely on (Reid et al., 1988). The relationship with the worker is vital because over time the worker acts as a transitional object as the parent begins to feel secure enough to make choices about which extended family members, neighbors, friends, or community organizations can be resources. Some family members can never be a resource.

For isolated families with limited resources, we offer a program which brings families together to build skills and have fun. The program offers parent support and therapy groups and varied activity groups that meet the needs of clients, e.g., a cooking, nutrition, and shopping group, a parent-child play activity group. Clients can initiate time-limited groups on issues of concern, e.g., sexuality, developmental tasks of children.

The program offers basic supports, e.g., a thrift shop and assistance with securing employment, housing, and educational programs. This program is only offered to families who have an ongoing family worker. As clients network with one another, they build skills that help them connect with others in the community. As clients build relationships in the community, they often wish to bring their new friends back to the program. This is a positive sign of growth and an indication that the family is building a supportive network. Over time, family members can become volunteers to the program, changing their role from client to a services provider.

"LEARNING TO HOLD IT"

Once a family has been engaged and trusts that the family worker will be consistent and genuine, the next step is to help the family to learn how to manage crises. Since crises are a way for family members to make sure they are not abandoned, the worker needs to ask if they can hold things together until their next meeting. Although families often need this experience more than once, most can hold on and learn how to tolerate frustration and master impulses. As sessions continue, family members will begin to bring the crises into sessions rather than acting them out in the family or in the community. We thank them for bringing a crisis or painful issues into the session, since that's where we can best help.

ENGAGING FAMILIES OF COURT-MANDATED YOUTHS
IN AN ALTERNATIVE TO INSTITUTIONAL PLACEMENT*

Some families will need at least short-term placement of an acting-out youth in order to give the family a chance to regain control and avoid immediate risks to family members or the community. We have found that the families referred for prevention-of-placement services with the highest likelihood of placement are those with the least resources (people they can count on) and with youth who are demonstrating numerous problems (Reid et al., 1988). Parents in such families often rely upon the judicial system to manage their children.

The CRY for Help Program was developed in conjunction with the Albany County Department of Social Services and the Albany County Probation Department. This program provides a 30 day "emergency" placement in a foster home which helps to provide relief and respite to the family while at the same time providing family court judges with an effective alternative to institutional placement in cases where youth cannot remain at home. The goal of this short-term placement is to engage the family and youth, with the intention of returning the youth home within 30 days. In addition, it provides a comprehensive assessment of the family and coordination of needed services. When return is not possible within 30 days, the youth can be considered for continued placement in the foster home in which he/she has resided rather than in an institutional facility. In every instance efforts are made to return the youth within six months.

This program of short-term placements is focused on our ability to engage family members in counseling and to help them cope with current stresses. The program promotes engagement and assessment of a youth within the family, rather than in an institutionalized setting with the family often distant from the assessment and treatment process. The parents are approached as a necessary resource for change rather than the cause of problems and unable to help their son or daughter.

Inherent in most family court hearings is the attribution of blame. Parents often stress in court that the child is the problem but end up feeling blamed by judges and probation officers sympathetic to the plight of their child. Family workers work to empower the family and to defuse labels and

*Portions of this section are revised from Kagan, Reid, Roberts, & Silverman-Pollow (1987).

accusations that the youth alone or the parents alone are the cause of the problem.

Family workers facilitate engagement by conducting home visits in almost all cases prior to a formal family consultation with a consulting psychiatrist and an intake conference involving collaterals and referral sources. After a youth has been referred to the program, the worker meets with the family, preferably in the family's home, thus emphasizing the importance of the family's being together in its own home. The worker tries to detoxify their feelings of failure. When the parents describe their child as "horrible" or "terrible," the worker recognizes their efforts and need for respite, suggesting in most cases that they have exhausted themselves by working so hard. When a youth sits silently, supressing great anger, or accuses the parents of abuse or of not understanding, the worker recognizes his or her pain and validates that there are many family issues involving the parents and youth that need to be dealt with. A short-term respite with the child in a foster home can then be offered.

Placement of the youth in a foster home rather than an institution promotes anxiety and competition between the biological family and the foster family. For parents in crisis-oriented families, an institution is a place for children who have been bad and deserve punishment. With foster care placement, the biological family is essentially confronted with another parent or parents managing their child. This competition initially increases the parents' discomfort and prevents their giving up responsibility, as often happens when a child is placed in an institution managed by multiple staff. The anxiety inherent in this situation activates the parents to consider return of their child.

All children placed by family court are "limbo" children. Someone is saying, "We want you placed; we want you out of the family."

Mrs. C. filed a PINS on her daughter, saying that she was not attending school, was staying out to all hours, and was a member of a street gang. At the same time, the county child protective services department received a hotline report that Mrs. C. was leaving her three younger children alone in the house and was suspected of using drugs. Both agencies referred the family for a 30-day assessment, asking that Charlene, age 13, be placed.

The family worker's first impression was that Mrs. C. was extremely depressed and lacking in energy and that Charlene was very angry at her mother, especially for not taking care of her younger siblings. It was soon learned that Mrs. C. had had a serious head injury and was using drugs indiscriminately as a way of dealing with the pain. As the assessment progressed, we realized that Charlene could not go home until her mother received appropriate care, which would in turn relieve Charlene of worry. Charlene was able to see that her involvement in a street gang kept her from being home to watch and worry about her mother and her siblings.

THERE IS NO CURE

For parents who have experienced intense and repeated abandonment at early ages, there really can be no "cure." Emptiness and further abandonment are too painful to risk. Thus, we do not expect any final closure with a family. Our objective is not to say "goodbye" but rather to get family members to the stage where, the next time they need help, they will call us rather than act out a crisis that brings in help from outside authorities. Family members who call for help in the future are given priority for provision of services.

We also recognize that the family's changing may be very difficult for extended family members to tolerate. Intense pressure will be placed on the parents to resume old roles as dependent and irresponsible individuals. Again, we predict these countermoves by family members and look at what pressures will be brought on them from all possible sources to fall back into old patterns.

The intensity and suddenness of such forces can often catch the family worker off guard. The key here is to remember the context and to help family members see how pressures serve to keep them in an older and less functional role.

Mrs. N. had been repeatedly hotlined for neglecting her children and living with an abusive boyfriend. With counseling, she made a good deal of progress in managing her children, providing a safe home, and setting boundaries. Unfortunately, she then became involved in an auto crash in which she suffered internal injuries and as a result was awarded a large monetary settlement by an insurance company. Suddenly, hotline calls resumed, alleging that she was psychotic and threatening her children. Mrs. N.'s mother and sister called Mrs. N.'s physician and asked that she be institutionalized. At the same time, the maternal grandmother and sister sent letters to Mrs. N.'s lawyer asking for a share of the monetary settlement as compensation for their efforts in caring for Mrs. N. after her injuries. They wanted to take over Mrs. N.'s legal rights and act on her behalf. These efforts put a great deal of pressure on Mrs. N. to return to earlier behaviors or act in a psychotic way so that she would end up living again with her mother. Without knowing the context for the hotline calls, community authorities initially began to see the mother as needing institutionalization and to plan placement of the children with the maternal grandmother.

In this case, pressures from the extended family were augmented by the enticement of sharing in a large monetary settlement. In other cases, messages may be much more subtle. For example, a maternal grandmother brought cakes and pies to a mother who had been able to control her weight through dieting—a step towards controlling other factors in her life. We need to recognize such messages in terms of the larger family's fears of abandonment and pressures on the parents not to betray relatives by changing. By predicting these actions we can help the parents to choose what they will do.

As we approach the end of family sessions, we recognize the family's fear of abandonment and predict crises. In fact, we may challenge or even bet family members that they can't go through life without another crisis; it would be too difficult. They can choose to repeat what has happened before or move on to a different stage with the support of new resources and connections. However, they cannot do this if they avoid dealing with the pain of separation. Despite long, hard work, many individuals cannot say how they feel; the worker, however, can. The worker's expression of his or her own feelings of loss at discharge or transition is a vital part of family work.

There is no experience to which the young child can be subjected more prone to elicit intense, violent, and persistent hatred of the mother-figure than that of separation.

—John Bowlby, 1973

By the time I was in my third home, I came to know that any moment I could be sent off again.

—A foster child cited by Tom Seligson, 1988

You sometimes feel like a cereal box going from shelf to shelf.

—A foster child cited by Trudy Festinger, 1983

When I'm eighteen, I'm leaving the country. There won't be a family for me to come home to anyway.

—An 11-year-old child after three years in a residential treatment center and multiple previous foster placements—cited by Claire Berman, 1987

CHAPTER 6

When a Family Experiences
Placement

THE PHILOSOPHY OF PERMANENCY is based on the principle that "children are best raised in families and that family ties can be an important support throughout life. . . . Permanency Planning is . . . the effort to secure for each child a caring, legally recognized, continuous family in which to grow up. . . . The permanency philosophy seeks first to preserve and support the child's biological family as the most natural environment and, when this is not possible, to secure an adoptive family. If neither of these alternatives is beneficial or possible for an individual child, then services should be directed to insure the greatest possible continuity of relationship with nurturing parents or caretakers" (Cole, 1985, p. 4)

Placement occurs most often with the abused and neglected youngster, the youngster who is negatively, but strongly, bonded to his/her parents, or the youngster who is not bonded at all. Youngsters coming into care from the child protective system, the probation system, and the mental health system have permanency as their underlying dilemma regardless of where the child is placed — in a psychiatric hospital, a residential treatment facility, a group home, a foster boarding home, etc.

Despite the excellent work of many facilities, youngsters who enter placement often remain in placement for long periods of time. Many move from one placement to another or from home to placement to home. For those youngsters a permanent plan is either tentative or nonexistent.

If removal from the home occurs, we examine where the child should be placed to best meet his/her needs and the needs of the family. How will this placement affect progress toward permanency for the child? We must address how each move by the child from placement to placement represents an additional loss and acquisition, and in most cases, additional bonds or attachments to an environment that cannot be a long-term resource.

The philosophy of permanency provides a framework for developing options for children who are in out-of-home placement or at risk of placement. Preservation of family life and of the child within his or her biological family is the very first option. The family creates the strongest bond, whether negative or positive. This family bonding is not only to parents, but also to siblings, extended family members and, often most overlooked, to the family's community. Initial service interventions to families in crisis should focus on prevention of placement and on reinforcement of the family bond. When this fails, placement in the least restrictive level of care is needed.

In this chapter we describe the process of permanency work when parents and children have been separated through placement. This approach is based on the premise that "You can't give up anything until you've had it" (Schlosberg, 1987). Permanency work must be based on the struggle for attachment and can only take place when everyone involved works to help a family enhance attachments or to face painful realities when reunion is not possible.

Bonding is essential for children to have a consistent, predictable place to grow. Only when the parent and child have been involved in every facet of the effort to enhance attachments can a parent be helped to accomplish the tremendously difficult task of reattachment or surrender. One cannot regain or give up a fantasy, only what is real.

THE NEED TO BELONG

Maslow (1962) wrote that belonging is a more basic need than self-esteem or self-actualization, and it is our belief that until belonging occurs, self-esteem and self-development cannot be achieved. Attachment, consistency, and nurturing in the child's early years are critical (Bowlby, 1960; Goldstein, Freud, & Solnit, 1973; Mahler, Pine, & Bergman, 1975). Spitz's (1945) well-known research on the need for infant attachments documented the lack of development and deaths of infants deprived of ongoing nurturance and love, while Steinhauer (1974) described how children experiencing prolonged and repeated losses without reattachment will develop into antisocial personalities. Family disintegration, marital fighting, and rejection of family members stand in the way of belonging for children referred to child welfare agencies.

Placement of children is accomplished by six major routes:

1. voluntary placement through departments of social services;
2. placement by family courts and child protective services for the protection of the child;
3. placement by family courts and the juvenile justice system for delinquent or "ungovernable" behavior;
4. placement by school systems for disruptive behavior and learning disabilities;
5. psychiatric hospitalization for behaviors diagnosed as psychiatric illnesses; and
6. placements privately arranged by parents.

Placement of children through these primary routes can provide relief to a family by reducing immediate stress; moreover, the community (state, county, school district, or health insurance) will often cover the costs involved.

Trying to help families with children in placement often feels as useful as throwing a life preserver to a drowning swimmer who refuses to take it. Many parents do everything in their power to maintain some distance between themselves and anyone who tries to help them. Typically they have already experienced multiple separations and have learned to cut off the normal grief process in order to protect themselves from feeling the pain of losses. They often provoke others to reject them and confirm that everybody hates them. At the same time, they maintain the hope, however unrealistic, of reuniting with their children.

Dorothy was referred for outreach services to help her reunite with her five-year-old son, Bart, who had been placed at age three after being sexually abused by Dorothy's boyfriends. She was also referred for guidance in caring for her three other children, who appeared unfed, unsocialized, and neglected. Dorothy came from a family with a long history of alcoholism; in addition, her parents had surrendered three of her siblings. She showed little affect and appeared hostile and withdrawn. Dorothy wanted no services and had resisted every offer of help from her child protective worker.

Dorothy also refused to recognize that Bart had been sexually abused. Bart, fathered by a different man from the father of her other three children, was often blamed for her problems. The bond between Bart and his mother appeared extremely fragile; yet Dorothy stated that she wanted him back. Bart appeared attached to his older brother and had remained distant from his foster mother.

Even though Bart had been in placement for two years, Dorothy had made little progress toward getting him home. She gradually decreased visits with Bart, continued drinking, and appeared preoccupied with new men in her life. Bart felt unwanted and unliked by his foster mother, who found Bart to be unmanageable, detached, and unresponsive to any reward or punishment.

Often early losses come back to haunt families when a child becomes an adolescent.

Bill S. was placed at age three for one year after repeated reports of abuse and neglect by his mother and abandonment by his father. Bill returned home to his mother and was placed again at age five. His mother, an alcoholic, surrendered him while he was in foster care but never said "good-bye" or gave him a message to grow up in an adoptive family. Between the ages of five and ten, Bill moved through five foster homes; he was then placed in a residential treatment program. From there Bill moved into a treatment foster family and then an adoptive family but "disrupted" and was returned to the treatment foster family. This placement also "disrupted" and Bill moved to a second treatment foster family, then back to the first treatment foster family, and then again to the second treatment foster family who adopted him. At age 16, Bill renewed contact with his biological mother who was still an alcoholic. He rebelled against his adoptive parents and asked his biological mother to take him back. He could not give up the bond he never had.

Bill's caseworker needed to help him connect with his mother and recognize and accept the reality that he could not live with her. Five-year-olds are concrete thinkers and cannot believe a verbal statement from social workers that their mothers cannot take care of them. Bill could never be loyal to a foster/adoptive parent when he was still emotionally loyal to his biological mother.

If belonging is the primary need, abandonment is the primary terror of children. The toddler with the scraped knee and no one to turn to, the four-year-old locked alone in a dark closet crying out to no one, and the six-year-old on his way to his tenth foster family all share the terrible emptiness of abandonment and the feelings that they are "bad," worthless, and unloved. Such children have idealized the lost parent — "Mommy wouldn't do this if I weren't so bad." All have conflicts of loyalty when placed in a warm, nurturing foster home.

Even the threat of placement can elicit feelings of abandonment in children, who experience placement as a message of being unloved and worthless. Children, who have had multiple placements are likely to distrust their parents and all adults out of fear of further rejection. They hide their feelings behind a mask of indifference or belligerence (Moss & Moss, 1984). Children like Bart become inured to pain and have no expectation of attachment. Year by year, the slender threads of attachment break; the hope for bonding weakens and eventually dies.

Despite behavioral gains made during placement, children may still face enormous pressures and conflicts when they return home if no work has taken place with the parents. Even if a child returns home, replacement in a foster home or group care facility becomes highly probable. In fact, higher rates of disruption leading to replacement have been reported (Seltzer & Bloksberg, 1987) for children returning to their biological families than for children who are adopted. The recidivism rate of children returning from foster care systems to their families has been reported to be as high as 43.6 percent for youths aged 13 to 15 and 22.6 percent for children aged 10 to 12 (Block & Libowitz, 1983). Other studies have found that between 17 and 32 percent of children returned to their biological families end up back in foster care (Claburn, Magura, & Chizeck, 1977; Fanshel & Shinn, 1978; Fein, Maluccio, Hamilton, & Ward, 1983; Sherman, Neuman, & Shyne, 1973).

THE FUNCTION OF PLACEMENT

Placement reduces anxiety and takes away the family's immediate pain. For families in perpetual crisis, placement of a child not only relieves the current crisis but slows down time. The family becomes fixated, with crises becoming a repetitive, structural feature of the family. The child's connections to the family remain but at a distance; crises recur whenever this "temporary" status quo of the family is threatened.

Bob, age 14, and his brother Bill, age 16, were referred because of disruptive behavior in school, fighting at home, and running away from home. Their mother expressed hopelessness and exhaustion; she had taken on a full-time job since the incarceration of her husband for assault and had little or no energy to deal with her sons. When the boys' father was about to be released from jail, both boys accelerated their fighting at home and ran away repeatedly. Their mother filed a Persons In Need of Supervision petition and asked for their placement. In effect, Bob and Bill focused attention on themselves and their acting-out. This avoided the real pain and fear in the family—what would happen when their dad returned home. Placement helped them avoid being caught up once again in recurrent fighting, violence between the parents, and their father's alcholism.

Placement also helped their parents to focus on the boys rather than their relationship and longstanding conflicts.

With a child or children in placement and the family feeling more comfortable, crises will recur at predictable moments to avoid change. These crises typically prevent the parents from getting their child back. Children will typically act out unresolved conflicts in their homes and conflicts arising from a growing attachment to foster parents. For instance, a sexually abused girl masturbated blatantly, upsetting the sensitivities of her foster parents, just as she was beginning to feel at home in foster care. A sexually abused boy became involved in a sexual relationship with another child in his foster home just as his parents began asking for longer visits. Such acting out will continue as long as problems in the family (i.e., sexual abuse in these cases) remain unresolved and/or the child feels tremendous conflicts of loyalty.

Joe ran away repeatedly from his father's home and continued to run away after placement in a foster home. Services were provided with the goal of returning Joe to his father as soon as Joe's behavior improved. Joe's father was both alcoholic and actively suicidal—behaviors which had been only tangentially addressed. Joe needed someone to say that he could not go home until his father was no longer alcoholic or suicidal. He continued to run away until the family workers involved recognized and addressed the father's need for help. Joe's running away served as a signal that the treatment plan needed to include help for his father.

PLACEMENT AS A CATALYST FOR CHANGE

We propose a model of placement that works to create enough pain to stimulate parents to make a decision on whether or not their child can come home and to take the steps necessary to carry this out. Not every child can go home, but every child deserves a "permanent" alternative offering ongoing nurturance and guidance.

Children are often placed because their parents are "acting out" conflicts, abuse, and neglect experienced in their families of origin or severe trauma experienced in the current family. Community resources are activated to provide help for the family through placement. When a child can no longer remain at home because of abuse or neglect, the first choice for placement is a foster home. Placement in an institutional or group care system gives parents the message that their child is so "bad" or so "sick" that he/she cannot be managed in a home setting. When a child is placed in a foster home, the parents have to confront feelings about another mother and father accomplishing what they could not do.

PERMANENCY WORK: CRITICAL STEPS

The first step once placement occurs is to have everyone involved (i.e., the family, group care staff, foster parents, and community authorities) meet to develop a permanency plan (see Appendix B). Parents and children need to hear a permanency message: "The children cannot keep going back and forth into placement." Children need to be permanent (see Finkelstein, 1980; Maluccio et al, 1986). Whatever the recommendations of court, probation, social services, etc., a permanency plan needs to be developed.

The permanency plan needs to outline what has to change for a child to go home and stay home. All present need to hear what will be happening as a result of placement. It is at this first meeting that everyone involved hears the details of what caused the need for placement, what may happen in court, and what needs to happen as a result of placement. Whether placements occur on a voluntary or involuntary basis, it is very important to include conditions which spell out what the parents must do before the child is returned home. Children, parents, group care staff, or foster parents need to hear what kind of visits will occur. If supervised visits are necessary, the reasons must be established.

WORKING WITH FAMILIES OF CHILDREN
IN PLACEMENT

The second step in this approach is to engage the biological family around the crisis of placement and the need for permanency work. What pressures were the parents and children experiencing at the time of placement? If the goal is for the child to return to the family's home, it is important to identify the crisis that got the child into placement and what would have to happen to prevent replacement. This brings out what needs to happen to ensure that the parents can manage the child and provide a safe and nurturing environment. The needs of the family must be discussed and priorities listed for what must happen before the child can return.

When a child is placed, we establish who the legal parents are and make every effort to engage them. The parents' rights must be recognized. Parents who want to fight a placement need assistance in understanding what they legally can and cannot do. At the same time, they need to hear that, despite their battles with the court or agencies, their children need a permanent family.

The foster parent who can serve as a model for parenting has a crucial role in this approach. The foster parent must:

1. respect the importance of the child's family despite the reasons for placement;
2. understand the child's position in the family, the context of the

child's behaviors, and the child's feeling of divided loyalty between his/her biological family and foster parents;
3. be heard and recognized by the biological family and caseplanners as having a role in the treatment process;
4. work towards the parents' and child's goal, e.g., supporting visits and communication between child and family.

Foster parents need to recognize that, if the child can attach to them, the child must have been given a great deal from his/her original parents. They must understand their own vulnerabilities and have support from friends, relatives, and professionals, so that at times of crisis they can understand and deal with their own feelings and problems rather than evicting the child.

It is essential that foster parents be involved in treatment planning and participate with the family and child in reviewing the plan. Their input on how the children are doing before, after, and between visits is extraordinarily helpful. When they share strategies for managing a child's behaviors, this models effective behavior for a parent during visits. Often they can join with parents in grappling with the difficulty of caring for the child.

Foster parents can easily become overidentified with the child (or the parents when a child is especially difficult) and begin to covertly sabotage progress toward reunification. A child caught in a loyalty conflict between foster and biological parents will often act out in a way that is most upsetting to the foster family. The child may in effect say through his/her behavior: "A pox on both your houses." This leads to a crisis and the threat of eviction. The family worker needs to help everyone involved understand the child's dilemma and how the acting-out fits with the child's caring about both the parents and foster parents. Regular meetings with foster and biological parents are used to promote communication and understanding of the children's behaviors and the family's goals.

Most parents say they want their children back and most children say they want to live with their parents despite experiences of abuse or neglect. We recognize this and make every effort to validate the parents' and child's wishes. However, so often these wishes are not reality and there is much ambivalence about return of the child. We ask parents, "What would happen if your child was returned tomorrow?" Parents often respond (1) "nothing will happen; he'll be fine" (denial), or (2) "there will be trouble again" (recognition that the crisis can recur). The role of the family worker is to work with every member of the family to identify how a child could be placed again and how repeated crises have led to placement. Then parents and children can focus on preventing such crises.

At a meeting with a mother, her three children (currently in placement), the foster care worker, the foster parent, and the family worker, what needed to happen for the children to come home was discussed.

FAMILY WORKER   Could we review how the children came into placement? And everyone, mom, and you kids, please feel free to add what you remember happened.

FOSTER CARE WORKER   Well, according to the child protective report, the children were found alone in the apartment with no food in the house. They had been drinking from half-filled bottles of stale beer. The child protective worker had no way of reaching you (the children's mother) and waited for you throughout the night. You did not return until the next morning. The report also said that the children were dirty and had bruises.

MOM   I left them with a baby sitter. I want my kids home right away and that won't happen again. I'm not going to leave them with anybody.

FAMILY WORKER   That would be hard for any mother to do—to stay home with three kids without ever going out. Sooner or later, it would get pretty lonely and overwhelming. It looks like you don't like your kids being in placement or going back and forth from home to placement. (The children's mother nodded her head.) I also notice that everybody (foster care, child protective workers, the judge, even the children) is telling you what to do or not listening to you. Do you want the decision to be yours about what happens to the children? (She nods.) Then it's important for you to pick goals that will get the children home as soon as possible. But, if you see that it is not working, do you want it to be your decision about where the children live and not the judge's?

MOM   I don't want other people to make any decisions for me. I want to do it—but I still want them home.

FAMILY WORKER   Okay. Then let's put that down as the first goal—that you'll make decisions for your kids and that you want them home as early as possible. Now let's look at what we can work on so that when the kids come home, they can stay home. I've been noticing at this meeting that the kids are quite a handful—they're all over the place!

MOM   Well, I could use help getting the kids to mind me so I don't have to hit them.

FAMILY WORKER   Okay. Would you like to set a goal that you will work with me on understanding what each one of the kids needs and how to set limits and consequences so that they will listen to you? I also know that if you leave the kids alone again or with a baby sitter you can't trust, that they'll be right back in placement again . . .

At the end of this meeting, the children's mother also agreed to set two goals for herself: (1) to go for an alcohol assessment and treatment and (2) that she would work individually with the family worker on how to safely plan taking time off from her children.

Professionals often become ambivalent in cases where little change is seen as the visits continue. The worker, carrying the pain and fear about what could happen, may fear expressing concerns about the child, the foster parents, or the biological parents. Painful as it may be, professionals must admit their concerns and then address them in meetings with the family and children present.

The child and family must experience the reality of working to return home and the pain if that goal cannot come to pass. Avoiding pain is a natural tendency. A child cannot detach from his/her family and attach to a new family without pain. In fact, we worry most about the child who feels no pain.

WORKING WITH THE LEGAL SYSTEM

The third step in this approach is to use the legal system to maintain pressure upon the parents and child. The child's social services worker asks: "What legally will happen if the family fails to act? What can happen in court if the parents fail to make the necessary changes to get their child home?" When failure is discussed, such possibilities as adoption, finding another family, locating a missing father, and making connections to relatives or significant others are addressed openly. Children need to know that they will not fall into a void if their parents fail. They need to hear, "If Mommy cannot take you back and the family you are living with cannot keep you, everyone will be looking for a family just for you." The law (e.g., Public Law 96-272 or state statutes) is explained and time constraints (typically one year of diligent efforts) outlined to all involved.

When we focus on these questions, the child's and family's anxieties increase, but at the same time the primary issue of abandonment is addressed. The child hears that he or she will not be left adrift in a state of "limbo" (after Finkelstein, 1980). The child will not continue to bounce like a rubber ball between the family and multiple placements—not knowing where he or she will be getting breakfast tomorrow, sleeping next week, or celebrating Thanksgiving next year. Identifying goals and a time limit creates anxiety in a homeostatic system, brings reality to the myth of reunion, offers direction for work, and includes consequences for success and growth—or failure and growth. Ongoing consultation with legal staff is essential throughout this process. Thorough reports to judges enable them to make the most appropriate decisions to meet the child's needs.

USING TIME AND CONSEQUENCES

The fourth step of this process involves using time to motivate change: to encourage the parents to make the decision about their child's returning home or being adopted rather than leaving this decision to the court. The plan must include what has to change within a defined time period. Help must be offered to the parents and the children so that they truly believe that everything possible has been done. When this occurs, everyone can feel more comfortable with making final decisions.

Often children will act out to help their parents avoid making a decision. However, children cannot be allowed to make decisions by their acting-out behaviors, as this would simply reinforce their roles in maintaining the status quo in the family.

The B. children were evicted from several foster homes and two of the children had been moved to residential care resulting in a total of five moves for the children. All four children were angry and thought that their parents were not getting enough help to get them home. They ran away from their placements to search for apartments and to check to see that their parents and social worker were looking for an apartment. Mr. and Mrs. B. had moved five times during the time their children had been in placement. The children and parents continued to battle all those they perceived to be in authority and no progress was made on returning home.

The B. children needed to see concretely that they could not get an apartment for their family, i.e., they could not buy beds, make a rent deposit, etc. The children needed to know that everything possible was being done to help their parents get an apartment and that only the parents with their social worker's help could accomplish this task.

Crisis-oriented families are used to having others make decisions for them, while they essentially remain unchanged. Making decisions is difficult and brings up basic conflicts. It's much easier to focus on a child's changing before he/she is allowed to return home. The child thus retains control of when and if he/she goes home. If the child senses that things have not changed, he or she is likely to repeat enough of the behaviors that originally resulted in placement to ensure that he/she remains in placement.

In this model, we stress to parents the problems of having the child or a judge tell them what to do and encourage them to make their own choice, stressing how much better it can be for the parents, rather than someone else, to make the decision. We predict that the child will try to reassert control by acting out, in essence attempting to make a decision for the parents — again taking away the parents' authority to choose what is best for the family. We point out that it is likely the parents will have crises that will prevent the child's returning home, again leaving decisions up to the judge. We work from the premise that parents have rights and are in the best position to make choices in the interests of their child and their family.

The family worker must look at the entire system with a time-oriented perspective on the child's developing from the past to the future with the possibility of moving into an adoptive home or returning to the family. The child needs to see his or her parents make a decision rather than an outside authority or the child. In order to be free enough to grieve and reattach to another family, children need to see that their parents really cannot raise them. If return of the child is not possible, the worker's task is to help work with parents through their grief and loss. Many parents cannot permit this because the pain is too great; however, the agency can still offer assistance.

Mr. J. was a chronic alcoholic who had sexually abused his daughter but had a loving, nurturing relationship with his older son, Doug, age 12, who was in placement. His wife was retarded, "impulse-ridden," and had such difficulty saying "no" that she often brought strange men into the home. Work with the J. family began with such basics as getting them to put a lock on their door and to set boundaries for privacy and safety.

The parents voluntarily surrendered their daughter for adoption. The social worker involved in the case did not believe the parents had the capacity to raise Doug. Doug, however, was a parentified child and refused to consider any other home, despite a long history of abuse, neglect, and multiple placements. It was very important for the family worker, the foster care worker, the foster parents, and the law guardians all to show Doug that they were doing everything possible to help the family achieve their goal of reuniting with Doug. Doug needed to see if his parents could do the simplest tasks, such as getting a lock for the door and keeping strange men out of the home. Only after Doug saw his parents receive help and yet still fail to accomplish these tasks could he accept that his parents could not raise him. He then began to consider living in another family.

Understanding that children must be involved in the process of diligently working to reunite with their family enables the worker to continue permanency work in cases where failure is likely.

Gloria F. had a longstanding history of relationships with abusive men and her youngest children (ages five, seven, and eight) had been sexually abused and were placed due to Gloria's denial of the abuse. For the children to return home, it was necessary for the boyfriend who had sexually abused the children to be out of the home and for Gloria to have enough support so that she would not need to associate with abusive men. The children were in terrible pain—afraid to disclose the sexual abuse for fear of angering and possibly losing their mother. Yet, in order to go home, they needed to feel safe enough to tell their mother if they felt threatened by any further sexual abuse. They also needed to hear from their mother that she would keep abusive men out of the house, act to protect her children if they were threatened, and carry out a plan of visitation. We supported the children in sharing feelings directly with their mother. When this was not possible, we asked the children's permission to speak for them.

Dilemmas such as this one in Gloria's family create enormous pain for *the worker. The usual response is to want to protect the children — to shield them from past, present, and future pain. This, however, would prevent change and block the children from ever being with their mother or with any other family (foster or adoptive). Despite the high probability of Gloria's failing to get her children home, the worker needed to join with Gloria and the children in working towards their goals. The children needed to see if their mother could succeed in safely bringing them home. Until this happened, the children could not be safe and could not trust.*

Crisis-oriented families must experience the efforts to reunite and strengthen the family as intense and sincere. At the same time the child needs to know that the parent(s) may or may not do what is needed to bring the child home. It is the parents' choice, not the child's, and not ours (as family or childcare workers). This is tremendously painful work. If a parent decides to surrender a child, he or she should be given help to deal with their loss, shame, guilt, and pain. If a parent does what is necessary to bring a child home, help must be ongoing, since the most vulnerable time for a family is after return of the child.

ASSESSMENT OF ATTACHMENT

A careful assessment of whether or not there is a bond between parent and child is crucial and forms the basis for the treatment plan and contract. A child cannot be asked to give up something that he or she never had. Nor can a parent be asked to give up an attachment to a child which never existed. In many cases, parents of children in placement were also separated from their parents as young children or adolescents. Many such children and parents never developed an attachment.

Most parents who are not bonded to their children will fight to have their children returned despite long histories of chronic violence and multiple placements. In some cases, parents appear to have less attachment to the child than to the never-ending "fight" with authorities to get their children back. We may address lack of attachment by talking about "the chemistry is not there or was not right" (see Chapter 9). This helps to reduce the pain of making a decision to surrender.

We ask children in placement for their first three choices of where they would like to live if they cannot go home. The people identified are actual or potential connections for the children and can be developed as resources and supports for a child, whether or not he/she returns home. If the parents decide they cannot raise their child, we use the child's list of where he/she would like to live to begin the search for another home.

A psychological assessment of the child can help to determine who the child feels most attached to and where the child's behaviors fit into the family. With older children, projective questions may reveal the quality of their attachments and how they view any possible separation or rejection. We use such standard questions as: "The three people I like the most are _____"; "If a magician came into the room and told you you could have three wishes, what would you wish for?"; "If the magician sent you to a desert island (elaborated), would you want to take anyone with you? . . . Whom would you take?"; "If you were given $1,000 and a one-week vacation, what would you do? . . . Whom would you spend your vacation with?"

Sentence completion questions concerning parents, e.g., "I wish my mother (father, grandmother, foster mother, etc.) _____," "If I could, I'd tell my father (mother, etc.) _____," "I wish my mother (father, etc.) knew _____," can also generate valuable information. The Thematic Apperception Test (TAT) (Murray & Bellak, 1973) and Roberts Apperception Test (Roberts, 1982), ask a child to make up stories about pictures of typical family scenes and can uncover dynamics. It is also useful to ask a number of "pretend" questions about what the child would say and do if mother, father, brother, foster parent, etc., knocked on the door of the room. Would the child let this person in? What would the child like to do with him/her? What would the child say if the parent came in? How would he/she feel (happy, scared, angry, sad)? Nonverbal children can be asked to mark on a series of thermometers (after Walk, 1956) from 0–100 degrees how happy, scared, sad, or angry they would feel if their biological mother, father, etc., came into the room.

Our assessment includes an evaluation of what the loss of a child has meant and would mean in the future for everyone involved—siblings, relatives, grandparents, aunts and uncles, etc. What has it been like in the family with the child in placement? What do they imagine it will be like when the child comes home? Was placement a relief? Was it difficult? Who was most upset? We look for the parents' empathy and understanding of the child's needs and the amount of actual work they have done to maintain connections with their child. How often have they phoned? How often have they visited? How often have they communicated through letters? Are they aware of how their child is doing in school? Are they aware of the child's likes and dislikes? Are they aware of the child's strengths and problems? Are they aware of what the child needs and wants?

We pay special attention to attachments to missing parents. Too often diligent efforts are carried out with the parent who has been the primary caretaker, forgetting that children have an image of a missing mother or father who will someday come to rescue them and care for them. For example, Billy, a seven-year-old child in placement, believed his father would come to save him on a white horse. His one memory of his father was of him riding on a horse.

The Family's Network

Different ethnic groups have different standards and norms for who will care for the child and whether the child can or will be surrendered. In some ethnic groups, surrender is not tolerable. In others, it is more acceptable. In some groups, a neighbor or relative will fill in as a matriarch to care for children who cannot live with their parents. Looking at the larger network for the family enables us to determine who will be available if the parents cannot raise the child, as well as what constitutes a cutoff in the family (e.g., moving out of the county or violating the family norm about teenage pregnancy) and what can be done to rebuild connections. Often this involves another crisis in the family or some form of self-punishment, confession, and recognition of the pain of others which resulted from one's behaviors.

Visitation

In fairy tales, parents and children are reunited and live happily ever after. In real life, when children return from foster care, the family may experience renewed problems and an escalating cycle of conflict, leading to further placement (Seltzer & Bloksberg, 1987). Simply returning a child to a crisis-oriented family does not work.

The focus of treatment during placement needs to be on helping the parents to reunite with their child. This is done through a graduated series of visits based on the special needs of each family. Weekly visits need to occur in the early stages, and extended visitations are important as work progresses.

We are aware that staff working with families in child welfare are often overburdened and overwhelmed. Still, we recommend frequent visitations for children and parents, so that they might maintain or build a bond and experience the reality of being together. For infants in hospitals we recommend that the parent sleep in with the child. For young mothers with infants, a placement for both mother and child is needed, preferably in a foster home. The younger the child, the less sense of time they have, so it is important to work as consistently and quickly as possible with preschoolers.

Graduated visits may begin with visits as short as a half-hour and progress to several hours' duration and or entire evenings. Later, day-long visits, overnights, weekends and extended visits can be utilized. A progressive series of visitation maintains parents' connections with *and* responsibility for their children. The positive and conflictual issues that arise out of both scheduling these sessions and what happens during visitations can be addressed in counseling. Frequent visits also make it easier to involve the parents in managing day-to-day problems. If parent skills training is needed, this can be provided. It is the combination of goal-setting, time limits, and intensification of visitation that creates the anxiety needed for changes.

CONTINUED SERVICES AFTER RETURN HOME

Support of the family in reuniting does not end with the return of the child. In many ways, the most intense and difficult aspects of permanency work occur after the child returns home. For this reason, from the day of placement we start preparing for discharge, asking, "What needs to be done so that you won't lose your children again?" Professionally trained outreach family workers can assist parents in strengthening positive connections, gaining resources, and maintaining gains made during placement. The family worker who worked with family members before and during placement is best able to help them predict and manage the crises that may occur after the child returns home. A continuum of care is provided by having a family worker who can remain with the family.

SURRENDER IS NOT THE END

When a parent decides to sign a legal "surrender" so that a child may be adopted, we consider the value for the child and other family members of maintaining a connection with each other. In all cases, the message that adoptive children and parents receive as to the reason why biological parents have surrendered or lost parental rights is crucial to a successful adoption. It is important to assess how able the child is to hear the facts. Children can understand their reality and adapt to knowledge within the limits of their developmental growth. As they mature, knowledge of events becomes enhanced with the child's increasing ability to comprehend. Children need to know why they are surrendered, no matter how awful the reasons were. It is especially important that secrets are not kept.

Sammy, age 9, was born as a result of rape and had long been the scapegoat in his biological family for all his mother's rage. He had been abused by his mother and sexually abused in an institutional placement by other youngsters. Sammy had never been told about his birth and always wondered why his biological mother hated and surrendered him.

Now, in his preadoptive home, he was getting in trouble and wondering why his preadoptive mother hated him and wanted him to leave. In counseling, Sammy and his preadoptive family explored what his birth had meant to his biological mother and why she "hated" him.

We help biological parents word an appropriate, realistic message to their child or children stating why they have decided to surrender the child and that they wish for the child to grow up in another family. The parents then convey these messages directly to the child, both verbally and in writing, in the family worker's presence. This allows the child and the family worker both to see the parent's verbal and nonverbal messages and to go back to the written message later. If a parent cannot give a verbal message directly to the child, then the parent must write his/her own letter. If the family worker writes the letter for the parent, the child may not believe that his/her parent really meant what was said. The child may simply blame the family worker for forcing the parent to write the letter or for putting words in his/her mouth.

Since messages from biological parents are very powerful, a child should never get a message that adoption is an interim step, e.g., that the child can come back to the parent at age 18 or after completing high school. If the parent asks a child to never forget him or her, the child may interpret this as a mandate to remain committed to caring for the parent and to finding a way to return to that parent—regardless of a legal surrender.

If the message cannot be a sincere wish for the child to have a family, no message is better than a mixed message. Working on a life book (see Jewett, 1978) with the adoptive parents and concretely exploring the past are essential steps, especially when a child gets a mixed message reflecting his/her parent's ambivalence.

THE CHALLENGE OF PERMANENCY WORK

The pain involved in permanency work is enormous. For this reason, professionals as well as parents avoid it. Our preoccupation with ongoing crises helps to avoid the pain involved in making such difficult decisions as whether or not the child can be raised by his or her parents. For parents who have lived from crisis to crisis, making a decision means acting like an adult. It means taking responsibility for considering the best interests of their child and recognizing their own strengths and limitations.

Permanency work means keeping everyone focused on what must be done and providing the family with every support possible (see Appendix B). This is both painful and extremely difficult; at the same time, pain can lead to change and growth. "No pain, no gain," the often-cited therapeutic maxim, is especially applicable to families with children in placement.

Blood is thicker than therapy.

—David Treadway, 1987

CHAPTER 7

Children in Group Care: Moving from Crisis to Context

I AM FOLLOWING JANE down the hall, escorting her back to her classroom, when she suddenly turns around, screams obscenities at me, and raises her leg to kick me in the groin. Jane is only 12 years old and not such a great kicker, so I escape—at least temporarily. But a bigger question looms: *How am I helping this girl? And, what am I doing here?*

The new boy in the cottage is A.W.O.L. for the third time in as many days. Last night, Sally, an attractive and seemingly mild-mannered 14-year-old ended up in the emergency room after ingesting 4 oz. of laundry deter-

Portions of this chapter were previously published in "When love is not enough: Creating a context for change," in C. Gorman & R. Small (Eds.), *Permanence and family support: Changing practice for group childcare*. Washington, DC: Child Welfare League of America, 1988, and in F. Alwon & R. Small (Eds.), *Challenging the limits of care*. Needham, MA: Trieschman Press, 1988.

gent inadvertently left in an unlocked cabinet by a temporary replacement for the last cleaning contractor, who abruptly terminated his contract yesterday. Then there is William, age 13, who loves to climb up on roofs of buildings and dare anyone to chase him. And my supervisor is distressed because three audits are scheduled for the next two months: the state department of social services, the state mental health department, and the Joint Commission on Accreditation of Healthcare Organizations. With my supervisor preoccupied with external reviews, Jane, Sally, and William seem to warrant little attention. *So what am I doing here?*

This chapter is dedicated to group care practitioners who have devoted their time and energy to what often appears to be a futile and unappreciated task: working with children and families with chronic and severe problems, problems so intense that the child's, family's, or community's very safety is at stake. In this chapter, we share conceptualizations and practice strategies which have proven valuable to us in our work with children and adolescents in group care.

How Do Children Get Into Group Care?

Children and adolescents referred to group care facilities in New York and many other states in the 1980s have typically been violent—to either themselves or others. Most have experienced physical abuse, sexual abuse, and/or basic neglect of their needs. Such children share the terror that comes from watching their father point a loaded gun at their mother, seeing their brother's head bashed into a wall, or hearing—but needing to ignore—the whimpers of their sister being assaulted by their uncle or their mother's boyfriend.

For the child who literally fears for his or her life or the child who has experienced the empty feelings that go along with neglect, little energy is left for the development of normal social and academic skills. Instead, each day becomes a reenactment of primary fears: abandonment, annihilation, or feeling smothered by a tremendous need to care for and protect a parent or siblings.

For some children/adolescents, foster care placement is not a viable option and placement into a group care facility is necessary. Many children are not able to tolerate the feelings generated by living in a foster family. The closeness of family life creates too great a reminder of what they have lost and too much need to act out and defend against feelings of abandonment. Such children have been abandoned and placed too many times to be able to tolerate another temporary placement into a family—however, loving and concerned the family might be. These are children who have experienced the emptiness of foster care drift—chronic placements, chronic losses, chronic separations, and chronic frustration of their basic needs to belong and feel safe in the family. A group care setting can provide the neutrality, safety, and support needed for such children to decrease their pain.

Placement into group care is also necessary for those children/adolescents who have multiple handicaps which cannot be managed in a foster home. Moreover, when abused and neglected children escalate acting-out behaviors to the point where they cannot be tolerated in a community or family setting, institutional placement may also be needed. For instance, the child who sets fires cannot in many states be placed into a foster home because of both the risk of harm and the lack of insurance for the foster family. In such cases, abuse and neglect have become unbearable to the child, and the child in turn has become unbearable to the community.

Group care can provide a neutral setting in which the child/adolescent *and* family can grapple with critical issues. The challenge remains the same as in foster care: to reconnect the child to a family. In most cases, this means helping the child's biological family make a decision on whether the child can return home or should be surrendered for adoption. Group care staff can recognize the family's pain and maintain a focus on the child's continuing needs for a family he/she can call "mine."

ACTING-OUT YOUTHS AND THEIR FAMILIES

Many "delinquent" and "emotionally disturbed" youth have provoked parents to say: "I can't handle you—you'll have to leave!" At the same time, they have often received such messages as, "You're responsible for my problems!" or "See what you have done to me!" Such youth are often given both responsibility for family problems *and* simultaneously a subtle but powerful demand to continue to fulfill vital family roles.

Increased acting-out behavior often results in requests from parents for placement and/or court-ordered institutionalization. The youth may improve in placement, but in many cases will bounce back and forth over the years between various forms of group care and his or her family. The youth often remains bound to the pressures and conflicts experienced in the family. The family may in effect say: "Go away for now . . . but come back." In such cases, the family's "elastic message" (Ausloos, 1978) functions like a rubberband, keeping the youth and his family together with little behavioral change, regardless of how far away a youth may run away from home or how far away he/she may be placed for treatment.

Children/adolescents in placement also function in many ways as ambassadors from their families (Ausloos, 1985). Changes in policy have to be cleared with the home government, or the ambassadors risk losing their positions, roles, and very identities. For this reason, behavioral changes seen in group care may be only temporary if children return home to ongoing conflicts and the need to play a role in protecting their families and themselves against unstated fears. From this perspective, Jane's kick or William's roof-climbing may be more honest reflections of their dilemmas than the youth who functions well in group care but regresses tremendously when placed back in his or her home and community.

Such youth have learned over the years to act the role of the "problem" child. Many of these youth have learned that when they are okay, their mother and father fight, threaten divorce, or one of their parents gets depressed. However, when they act "bad," the parents may unite to criticize them or a depressed parent may become energized again. From the youth's perspective, it is often preferable to get a lot of negative attention while maintaining an illusion of family unity rather than to sit by anxiously and experience their parents' conflict or pain (Ausloos, 1978).

Youths who provoke rejections from their families are involved in a system which gives them great power and attention at the cost of being "bad" or "sick" children. A youth, in effect, can keep his parents preoccupied in a way that maintains a delicate balance in the family and also protects his or her siblings from having to face their parents' depression or conflict (Ausloos, 1978). Moreover, the youth's "bad" behavior stimulates powerful external forces to intervene in the family, e.g., school counselors, the committee on special education, psychiatric clinics, neighborhood parents, family courts, probation departments, and residential treatment centers. Nevertheless, many acting-out and aggressive youth seem unable to respond to these interventions and improve. They seem stuck day after day in using aggressive and immature behaviors which maintain a fragile family equilibrium and which perpetuate a cycle of institutionalization, return to their homes, and reinstitutionalization.

Love is Not Enough

Practitioners in group care typically have a great desire to help children, to care, to be needed, and eventually to see progress. Children/adolescents in group care are desperate for love. We are drawn to take on the role of parenting these children. Often we become the "good parent" or the "bad parent" and end up acting very much like the child's actual parents. For instance, Jane's endless kicking provoked many staff to physically restrain her for her safety and the safety of staff. To Jane, being held down by two childcare workers reenacted the same overwhelmed feelings that occurred when she was abused in previous placements. Struggling with childcare staff also gave her a chance to release intense feelings of rage—feelings which she could not dare to express directly to her biological parents.

Caring is not enough for children/adolescents who are still attached to families where they have experienced chronic abuse or neglect. These children attempt to replace their families with staff in the institution and in effect reenact the conflicts they experienced in their homes. Group care staff will be drawn by the neediness of these children to help them and yet may soon find themselves the target of the children's rage and calling for help for themselves and more discipline for the children.

Children/adolescents placed in group care continue to be embroiled in family conflicts and most often have no conception of a solution to their problems. If group care is to help them, we as professionals in group care facilities need to help these children and their families confront painful dilemmas.

Jane was placed into a residential treatment center following a series of placements with relatives, her mother, and finally foster parents where suspected physical abuse, sexual abuse, and neglect had occurred. She perceived herself as "kicked out" and was caught in an endless cycle of aggressive behaviors which kept her distant from any adults who tried to get close to her and which made it appear impossible for her to return to her mother, a single parent. In several previous foster home and group care placements, she had accelerated her violent and sexually provocative behavior until she was "kicked out" once again. Meanwhile, her mother remained unwilling to work with social services staff.

What could group care staff do? Work with Jane had to focus on whether her mother would take her back. This would involve long-distance driving by both childcare and clinical staff (one psychologist and one social worker) to engage Jane's mother and holding sessions in the mother's home, which could both support the mother and help Jane to express her rage at being abandoned and rejected so many times. Jane's aggressive behaviors were focused on her central dilemma: getting "kicked and kicked out" of her mother's and relatives' homes with nowhere to go. With support from group care staff, Jane was able to express some of her anger directly to her mother rather than at teachers and childcare workers.

Jane's mother, a chronic alcoholic, needed support and help from clinical staff in order for her to make a decision on whether she could parent Jane based on the best interests of both herself and her child. To avoid blaming the mother and becoming locked in an adversarial relationship, childcare and clinical staff visited Jane's mother and came to understand her stresses and dilemmas. Childcare and clinical staff needed to approach Jane's mother not as a "drunken ogre" but as a parent who cared enough to make a painful decision.

Jane's mother made the terribly difficult decision of placing her daughter for adoption. This allowed both mother and daughter to begin to grieve the relationship they had never had and for Jane to move beyond her role as an angry and aggressive child. Group care staff could then help Jane focus her anger and depression on her loss. In time, she was able to move into a foster family and later into an adoptive home where she could get the parenting she needed.

The Meaning of Placement for the Child

Children/adolescents come to group care facilities with overt behavior problems but also with a history of relationships, losses, and struggles to meet their needs and be a part of their families. The group care practitioner must keep in mind at all times the meaning of placement for this child. Is this the first placement; if not, how many placements have occurred at what ages? When was the first placement and what led up to this placement? Why should the child be here *now*? How will this placement be different? What good will this do the child or the family? What are the costs to the child in being labeled and placed outside his/her home and community? What are the benefits for the child and family in changing critical behaviors? In short, the group care practitioner asks "So what if _____ is placed?" This leads to a critical examination of the value of a given placement, and more importantly, to what needs to happen to help a child and family.

Departments of social services and group care staff need to look at the tough questions, including whether or not a child can go home and by when. This leads to one of three directions: working on helping a child return home, working on helping a child and family find out within a limited and specified period of time whether the child can go home, or working on building new connections that can provide the parenting the child needs.

With childcare staff preoccupied with daily routines and activities, and with educators addressing the often tremendous learning problems of these children, the responsibility of keeping all casework focused on the primary issues of the child/family belongs to the caseplanner. The practitioner in this position must keep the entire team and referral sources focused on the meaning of different behaviors. If the child runs away, does this represent a response to a specific precipitating incident in the group home or a child's rebellion against being in the placement facility? The case planner can help staff to see that a child's anger and outbursts are his/her way of dealing with loss or pain. Therapeutic responses to behavior can be developed based on the predominant emotional needs of the child and family and what needs to change for the child to go home.

Working with children/adolescents in group care is extremely difficult because intense issues of abandonment, loss, grief, violence, and attachment must be addressed. Children in group care need to know that being in group care will help them and their families resolve critical dilemmas. If not, being in the program may appear pointless, and they may run away or continue to act out to such an extreme that they may be placed somewhere else. If this happens, the child, parents, and staff will experience this last placement as another in a long series of failures, confirming the inadequacy, helplessness, and despair of everyone involved.

A 16-year-old girl ran away repeatedly from her group care facility and placed herself in dangerous situations where she was sexually abused. In this case, staff were working to help the girl improve her behaviors (e.g., stop running away) so that she could return home to her father. This was her discharge goal. It was essential to explore what had happened in her father's family (physical and suspected sexual abuse) and help the family make a plan based on the girl's needs for safety and support and the parents' actual ability to protect her. Otherwise, working with staff simply did not make any sense for the girl.

Caring about this girl and developing behavioral plans to address her running away from the group care facility were not enough. Help for this girl meant working with her father on what had happened and what was likely to happen again (i.e., physical and sexual abuse). It also meant working with the girl's mother (who was divorced from the father) on making a decision on whether she could parent the girl. By working on these issues, staff were able to show the girl that they were addressing her real dilemmas, which included her needs, her parents' needs and abilities, dealing with past trauma, and developing a plan for the future.

DYSFUNCTIONAL ROLES THAT MAINTAIN PROBLEMS

The aggressive and self-destructive behaviors of acting-out children and adolescents are typically experienced as dangers by "helping adults" in governmental or private agencies, who then feel an obligation to impose stringent controls on the child/adolescent in order to protect the community, the family, the child, and often the agency itself from further injury or harm. Such children will often be given a diagnostic label and placed in a treatment center, with responsibility for the child transferred from the parents to an agency monitored by a governmental authority.

These are well-intentioned efforts to provide help and control for acting-out children. Nevertheless, these efforts frequently backfire by undermining families. Children, parents, and public and private agencies frequently become locked into dysfunctional relationships which serve to maintain children in powerful but dangerous roles.

Therapeutic programs must address the interactional dynamics that have led to a child's behavioral problems and placement. The responses of parents, public agency workers, private agency staff, and children often fit the classic triangle of: victim, rescuer, and persecutor (Karpman, 1968). The child may be initially identified as a *victim* with the public agency or private agency operating as a *rescuer*. Blame for problems is usually placed on the parents or secondarily on any of the individuals or agencies involved, for example, the police, school officials, or the child. At the same time, the "victim" is perceived as relatively helpless to resolve problems without the assistance of professionals.

When the child/adolescent is identified as the victim, parents are frequently blamed, and the youth is frequently seen as harmed or hampered by the environment of his or her parents' home, with relatively little control over his or her behaviors. This frequently leads to public agency workers or staff of childcare agencies telling parents to do things which are felt to be helpful to the child. Parents in turn often react with anger to these messages and to their mandated (e.g., court-ordered) involvement with public and private agency workers. Parents often become resentful of repetitive demands that they must do *more* when they, too, have suffered through years of physical abuse, neglect, and chronic instability in their relationships with their own parents, extended family, and spouses. Such parents often feel that their own needs are not being considered and that these personal problems and needs are overwhelming. They may even feel jealous of the attention and support they see their troublesome child receiving from group care staff. As a result, they may resist making any substantial changes despite the pleas or threats of professionals.

Interactions among children, parents, practitioners, and state authorities become fixed through repetitive crises and repeated efforts to determine (diagnose) a focused *cause* of current problems, that is, some person, thing, condition, or entity to *blame*. Fixed roles, in effect, help both families and professionals to avoid facing painful issues and consideration of each one's own participation in behavior patterns that lead to a child's repeated placements. We must go beyond a very natural urge to meet the isolated needs of a child and grapple with the dilemma experienced by the child in the context of his/her family and the child's need for ongoing guidance and attachment to parents the child can call his/her own.

CREATING A THERAPEUTIC CONTRACT

Guy Ausloos (1981) has written that children/adolescents in group care have left their homes through the window. The work of a therapeutic program is to help children return to their homes and leave through the door. Children can then bring with them a sense of their roots and strengths. Losses can be grieved, conflict-laden relationships changed, and attachments reformed, or if necessary, new attachments made.

The first challenge when a child/adolescent is referred to group care is to negotiate a truly therapeutic contract with the family based on an understanding of the reasons for placement—a plan for prospective work that addresses the dilemmas the family has experienced and provides some hope and opportunity for change. The contract must encompass a time-limited goal of where the child is going to live. A time limit maintains the anxiety needed to prompt both the family and the agency to address difficult issues. A clear time frame for group care also prevents the agency from simply stabilizing the family with the child growing up in group care.

The contract must include goals on what must change in the family for children like Jane to go home and not get "kicked out" again. The contract must also address the primary dilemmas for Jane and her family: Can she go home? If not, who will provide her with the love and discipline she needs now and into adulthood?

The therapeutic team must help the family examine what would get Jane placed again if she were to go home. The mother needs to be empowered by being placed in charge of Jane's going home. In that way, Jane is not caught in a triangle with the agency keeping her away from her home and the mother caught in an adversarial relationship with the agency.

If a child/adolescent is going into placement in group care, it is important that all parties involved, e.g., staff of the group care facility, social service workers, and family members, clearly identify the time frame for work, who will monitor progress, a schedule of family sessions and review conferences, and a schedule of family visits to the agency and of the child's visits to the home. This makes the plan real.

Just as in foster care placement (see Chapter 6), it is crucial to address the specifics of what must change for the child/adolescent to return home and then to use the context of group care to help the family to confront difficult issues. This will bring up problems and anxiety in the system which otherwise would be hidden until the child was close to returning home. If one of the criteria for discharge is that the child's mother secure a steady income and establish a home of her own with appropriate furnishings for an adolescent, this becomes one of the first objectives of permanency work. If return home is predicated on a youth's not becoming aggressive with his/her stepfather, the context and dynamics of how this conflict ties in with the family needs to be addressed.

A therapeutic contract recognizes that something happened in Jane's family for her to end up "kicked out" and that Jane's involvement is likely to continue in behaviors which repeat what has happened before (i.e., to be so out of control that county authorities had to place her in a residential treatment facility). The contract ensures that the family and Jane have established goals (e.g., Jane's return home). Group care staff need to clarify their roles and how they will help the family accomplish the family's goals within a specified time frame. The contract maintains the focus of all work on helping the family achieve its goals.

The second challenge when a child is referred to group care is to recognize the youth's burgeoning sexuality and age-appropriate striving for autonomy and independence. Tasks for adolescents in group care include:

1. To develop a sense of competence—the ability to succeed based on a realistic sense of their own capacities. Self-esteem follows from learning, work, and achievements.
2. To understand their bodies, their sexuality, how to keep themselves safe, and birth control.
3. To learn how to say "No" to yourself and others. Children of alcoholics (or substance abusers) and children who were sexually abused can benefit from group participation, i.e., children of alcoholics groups and incest survivor groups.
4. To plan for their future with the support of their family and group care staff—to realistically explore how they will support, house, and provide for themselves as they become young adults.
5. To understand what it means to be a parent and what it takes to raise children.

The therapeutic contract includes goals for the child/adolescent to master these tasks with the help of parents, group care staff, school staff, and departments of social services staff. Work on these goals begins in group care with the child/adolescent taking on age-appropriate responsibilities in the areas of personal health and hygiene, clothing, school, job, meals, use of living space and free time. Vocational training optimally begins by age 12 to ensure that each child/adolescent can succeed and survive in the community.

FAMILY WORK IN GROUP CARE

Group care can provide a child/adolescent like Jane with a safe place to learn appropriate ways to share feelings and to help her to share these feelings with her family rather than acting them out in the community. Group care staff can join with the family in learning to understand how Jane's getting herself "kicked out" fits in with family dilemmas and patterns. Others in the family may have been (or currently fear) being "kicked" or "kicked out." Group care staff need to understand the cycles of interaction between Jane and her family that have led to her placement and how this can easily be repeated within a group care facility.

Family work in group care involves a collaborative effort with public and private agency staff to utilize the power of a child's family to facilitate the growth and development of a severely disturbed and acting-out child (Finkelstein, 1981; Kagan, 1983; Keith, 1975; Keith-Lucas & Sanford, 1977; Littauer, 1980; Whittaker, 1981). Public agencies set time limits and use court hearings and possible termination of parents' rights as a consequence and a goal to help parents move through a terrifying decision process. It is important that the child hear about the reality and possible consequences of failed work. Group care staff can help the child understand that he/she cannot make a decision occur sooner. Group care staff can use the child's past behaviors to predict what the child will do to try to regain control over what he/she perceives as a terrifying situation. The message the child must get is that he/she can control only himself or herself and not the parents.

THE TEST

Families with children/adolescents in group care almost inevitably test the initial contract by not being able to take their child home for weekend visits, attend family sessions, or work with their child in the group care facility. "We can't make it this weekend, our car broke down. . . . We need to move this weekend. . . . She wasn't good enough this week. . . . " These statements reflect genuine concerns and real problems. They also present group care staff with a test of the basic contract. The parents may in effect be saying that they cannot help their child this evening, this weekend, or any time in the near future, or that other concerns must take priority. In such cases, they may be implicitly asking group care staff to take over their responsibilities for their child and to help them to avoid having to deal with painful issues, their child's behaviors, or making changes in the family. "Crises" afflicting the family confirm that the parent(s) are incapable of caring for their child and managing the stress the family is experiencing.

For the child/adolescent such messages repeat earlier themes of neglect and abandonment, which will also be experienced by staff. The challenge for group care staff is to experience the pain of *both* the child and family and emphasize to the parents that, "We need you in order to help your child" (Ausloos, 1981). Inconsistent visits, family sessions, etc., need to be approached in terms of the family's goals (e.g., to help a child return home or move on to another family).

The parents and child need to experience that the agency has made *every* effort to help them reunite and make things work. The agency can help families by arranging help with transportation, conducting sessions in the family's home, and providing an apartment for families in the group care facility. These are concrete messages by group care staff to the parents that we recognize their dilemmas and will do everything possible to help them achieve their goals. For families that repeatedly test the contract, it is essential to ask for a formal conference to reconsider the basic contract. Do the parents still want the child to return home? It may be necessary for the facility director or consultants to again state to parents: "We need you in order to help your child."

This is painful and difficult work; however, to neglect these issues leaves children feeling abandoned and betrayed, not only by their family but also by group care staff. Such children are likely to feel that no one really cares and often become involved in fights or disruptive behavior in the agency.

The child may end up physically restrained or placed in a more secure facility where he/she will be more manageable and where he/she will struggle with intense feelings of abandonment and rage.

GOING HOME: BUILDING SUPPORT NETWORKS

We begin working on discharge at the time of intake. By focusing on what must happen for the child/adolescent to return home, the "criteria for discharge," we continue to stress the importance of the family's involvement. We know, however, that our work will be incomplete if we focus solely on the interactions of the family unit. Families of children/youth in group care are typically families with massive cutoffs and a lack of resources (relatives, friends, organizations, financial backing, etc.) they can depend on when stress mounts. Accordingly, one of the key goals in work with families of youths in group care is to build, facilitate, and mobilize support networks which can help the family after the youth returns home.

Very often family members will become close to and fond of the family worker working with them. This supportive relationship can help empower them to make changes and to take charge of their lives and of their acting-out youth. The youth's behavior will improve. And then the family worker will move towards discharge. Suddenly the youth's behavior deteriorates and parents appear once again helpless, desperate, and unable to manage.

For the family worker, this could be considered a crushing blow to the effectiveness of all of his/her past interventions and work with the family. On the other hand, from a systemic point of view the family members are honestly reflecting the dilemma imposed upon them with the upcoming discharge. Discharge for many crisis-oriented families means a tremendous loss, a loss which also rekindles the pain of past abandonment and rejection. While the family worker is looking for a successful outcome and the challenge of working with a new case, the family will be struck by the loss of a positive relationship with the family worker.

Our task is to help families build connections with friends and relatives throughout a child's stay in group care and with supportive services following discharge. From the time of the initial assessment, we need to keep track of who is available to the family, who might be a resource for the family, and what unresolved conflicts threaten any change the family makes.

Construction of a family ecogram (Hartman, 1978) helps to bring out connections of individuals in the family. We pay special attention to relationships where contact has been cut off, as unresolved conflicts will likely resurface once the child returns home.

Ralph made great progress in a residential treatment program. His mother regained control of her family and Ralph was returned home. In

this family, Ralph's father had been described as having an unknown ad-
dress and not having been involved in the family for many years. The
mother insisted that contact with him was not possible. However, within a
year following discharge from group care, Ralph acted out in the communi-
ty, resulting in a letter being forwarded to his father by the family court
with his mother's indirect approval. This letter brought Ralph's father back
into contact with the family. The family then had to deal with issues of
Ralph's identification with his father and parental conflicts that had lain
dormant for many years.

These conflicts in Ralph's family needed to be addressed. The earlier
family therapy and group care experience enabled the mother and son to
reach a point where they could begin to address these issues; however, by the
time the father reconnected with Ralph the program was no longer involved.
They had to deal with these issues on their own or with the help of other
service providers.

In another case a similar, difficult lesson was learned.

An aggressive youth gradually made a great deal of progress in a residen-
tial program as his mother was able to become more assertive, secure
adequate housing, get a more stable job, and provide discipline for her
three children. The mother and children became very attached to the
family worker working with them. Discharge from the residential center
meant that family sessions could continue only another six months, ac-
cording to the policy of the funding agency. As predicted, the two boys in
the family began escalating fighting within three months of their return
home. The mother had been prepared for this but to the surprise of the
family worker she quickly stabilized the family by bringing in a new
boyfriend.

In effect, the mother replaced the family worker as a source of support
by returning to an earlier pattern of bringing in boyfriends who would
manage her sons for at least a short period of time. The lesson in this case
emphasized the importance of building supports for every family before
discharge and of recognizing the role the family worker plays in the family
(in this case, as a surrogate father figure).

If the family worker at the group care center will not be able to continue
to provide services to the family, the family must be linked up with other
family workers before discharge. This can be done in terms of future resources for the family members if they should desire. In other cases, services
can be arranged prior to discharge for ongoing therapy.

Discharges and transfers mean losses, and losses rekindle overwhelming
feelings of abandonment and shame. The critical issue in termination is

helping the family to deal with loss and building strong support networks. Ideally, the family worker can remain available for further sessions on an outpatient, as-needed basis. If this is not possible, the next best alternative is to connect the family before discharge from group care with family workers in the same agency or another family-centered agency who can continue to offer services to the family.

Too often our system, in focusing on the individual, endangers the group. When a child is protected, but its family is shattered, we are forced to question if indeed our process has succeeded. Or are we, in fact, living the cliche that 'the operation was a success, but the patient died'?

—Maya Angelou, 1985

Professional work of any permanent value cannot be done until we get beyond the management of crisis behaviors.

—Nadia Finkelstein, 1988

CHAPTER 8

Engaging Family Competence When a Youth is in Group Care

FROM ADMISSION TO GROUP care* through discharge, a youth's† recurrent crises will often lead to more restrictive forms of restraint and control. County and school officials, mental health officials, family members, and staff of the agency may seek continued placement, replacement in more restrictive institutions, or psychotropic medications in an effort to control the youth's behaviors. Readmissions to group care, referrals to locked psychiatric hospitals, prolonged treatment, high dosages of medication, and "PRN" shots confirm once again a child's powerful but self-defeating role as the "bad kid," a mother's or father's image as an inadequate parent, and an

---

*Group care includes residential treatment programs, group homes, or agency-owned boarding houses.
†"Youth" and "child" will be used to refer to both children and adolescents.

agency's sense of failure. Crises may continue while underlying dilemmas in the family, community, and agency remain hidden.

Group care programs need to facilitate family strengths in order to avoid long-term placements and foster growth and development of family members. When parents effectively take charge of their families, a youth can return home from placement, continue development, and eventually leave home as a responsible young adult. The success of this approach depends on maintaining the focus of work on building family strengths and connections within a defined time period. During this time, the practitioner can expect to be confronted with a series of almost predictable problems which can undermine the therapeutic process.

ROADBLOCKS AT THE AGENCY

Providing coverage for aggressive and self-destructive youth seven days a week, 24 hours a day, is an awesome task. Salaries for childcare workers have been dismally low, resulting in difficulties hiring competent staff, high rates of turnover, and often understaffed programs. A recent report by the Child Welfare League of America (1987b), showed that childcare workers earn less than garbage collectors. Demands on staff include: providing a nurturing environment while carrying out daily routines (e.g., waking adolescents up on Monday mornings [no easy task!], coordinating breakfast, lunch, and dinner, and providing appropriate and engaging activities for the children throughout the day), preventing and/or managing "untoward events" (i.e., violence and injuries), going to meetings and training sessions, documenting activities, writing progress evaluations, and completing case records. Coordinators of group care programs must also grapple with problems in the physical plant — often decaying or deteriorating structures in need of major renovation.

To some staff who are pressed simply to manage children in care, behavioral problems and emotional strife following home visits and family sessions will be incomprehensible and intolerable. Staff may call for limiting home visits and contact with parents if the child "acts out" following a visit. Denying permission for the child to have contact with the family provides illusory control for staff on a short-term basis; however, it leaves the child in an ongoing battle of control and the ever-present anxiety of not knowing what is happening at home and when (or if) he or she will return.

In family-centered group care, staff work to help a child in the context of his/her family. The agency must make a commitment to family work and carry this out in day-to-day practice. An effective program needs a clearly defined approach backed up by the allocation of staffing for family work and mandates from the executive director to be implemented by line staff. The focus of work then becomes helping a child and family change rather than just managing today's crises. Home visits and family sessions become the crux of efforts by group care staff to help children in placement rather than a source of interference with the daily routine. These same visits and family issues can be discussed in group sessions to help youths share their experiences and pain and to learn that they are not alone in having problems.

Crises can be predicted if everyone involved in working with a youth understands the youth's pattern of acting-out behavior and how it functions to avoid pain for the youth, the family, and the agency. These potential crises should be discussed in both family and group sessions. For example, in a group home in which five youth are going home for weekend visits and two are remaining with nowhere to go, the challenge for staff is to get the youths together and begin to predict what the visits will be like, how will they handle conflict, and how the two left behind will feel about not having a family to visit. Staff can stress that they will be having a family session early the next week to deal with what happened during the weekend home visit or, for the youths who could not go home, what needs to happen to help them have a substitute family for visits and a family they can live with after placement.

This approach helps youths learn to hold their feelings until the next family session. Feelings are validated. Staff help youths see that their dilemmas and pain are understood and support them in expressing their feelings and problems to other family members. At the same time, staff are helped to see that a youth's rage stems from his/her family dilemma and is not a personal attack on them. This in turn frees staff members to be more objective, more creative, and less reactive in dealing with the youth's behavior.

ROADBLOCKS FROM THE COMMUNITY

Even with the recognition that long-distance placements are harmful, county authorities often find themselves in the position of asking for placements hundreds of miles from the child's home. This may be simply because of a shortage of beds or because of the need for a specialized facility. Most often, long-distance placements are sought for youth who have repeatedly run away from local placements. Or, a community may simply want a youth removed to a distant location following a violent incident that has raised community fears, e.g., a physical altercation in which another youth was stabbed.

From the perspective of the group care facility, it may seem like the child is being "dumped" or that the agency is fulfilling a role no one else can fill. From the perspective of the county worker, however, the search for an appropriate placement outside the child's *original* community may reflect primarily desperation and hopelessness because of the inability or refusal of local agencies to take children/adolescents unconditionally. The result is the same: a youth placed at great distance in a strange community far from his or her family and unable to work with the parents on the changes needed for return home.

Other roadblocks include regulations from some funding sources (e.g., the New York State Office of Mental Health), which limit the number and length (in days) of home visits. Based on the premise that a child/youth is emotionally disturbed and needs professional treatment, some mental health systems have a fixed limit on home visits which precludes a child's coming home every weekend or for extended visits prior to returning home. These regulations reinforce the labeling of a child as dysfunctional and in need of individual treatment that only professionals can provide.

In child welfare agencies the *minimum* requirements for home visitations set by state departments of social services are often followed rather than the *optimal* number for breaking the cycle of perpetual crisis. This also minimizes the family's role, so that the burden of change falls on the group care facility. Caring staff feel compelled to fill in for absent parents and in turn come to experience the parents' frustration, pain, and despair until they too give up, distance themselves from the youth, or refer the youth to another agency.

Each agency must determine whom they can effectively serve and in what community. Agencies cannot serve a family if they have little or no knowledge of the family's community and cannot work with them in their community.

Distance can be an excuse for some families not to work with an agency and is in fact a tremendous barrier for poor families. Distance also supports family myths, e.g., "My mother is wonderful," "Johnny is getting better." Distance helps families avoid responsibilities while projecting blame on agencies for keeping family members apart.

Distance also exhausts workers who feel powerless to help the family. It feeds the belief that staff must focus on the milieu as the primary therapeutic approach, which in turn puts pressure on staff to manage and change the youth. The frustration inherent in this task in turn leads to staff feeling a great need to take care of each other as victims of poor funding and bad families.

Within a limited distance, agencies can negotiate the difficulty of getting children and families together. Some agencies provide minivans to bring parents to the agency for visits, family sessions, and activities. Agency-operated minivans can also be used to bring children home, as is done at Children's Village in Dobbs Ferry, New York. Other agencies, including our own, provide an apartment for extended visits.

When staff meet with families and learn to understand their needs and dilemmas, anger and resentment are reduced. Ogres turn out to be real people with long histories of being abused and neglected themselves. Such contacts also help everyone to feel more powerful, because the reality of a situation is often better than fears of what might be. Working with real people and real issues can lead to hope and creative interventions. Myths about families will be shattered and the focus of work will become clear and shared.

An 11-year-old boy was referred from a county to a group care facility 200 miles away because no other facility was available within a 200-mile radius. The group care facility took in the boy with an understanding that family work would be done by the referring county. No parents or family members came up for the intake and the boy seemed reasonably calm and was accepted into the program. The plan, however, left a split between the child and parents and made it impossible for the boy to take part in family sessions.

After a brief "honeymoon" period staff began to have difficulty managing the boy. The agency school was able to provide an educational program suitable for the boy's low developmental level—something that had been seen as impossible to provide at agencies closer to the boy's home—yet the boy spent most of his time acting out behaviorally, upsetting other children, and threatening staff, which in turn prevented learning. Through all of this, the boy frequently cried out "_____ city is closed." The agency found family work nearly impossible due to the distance and the unwillingness of the family to make the trip, and personnel from the referring county said that they could not provide services to the family because of the family's lack of motivation. One alternative was for the agency to discharge the boy back to the community—a position seen as abandoning the boy and unacceptable. Referral to another facility was suggested, but that, in effect, meant another loss for the boy.

The agency tried to recontract with the parents but was not able to send staff to work on engaging them. There seemed little hope of returning the boy to his family or enabling him to build lasting connections with a new family. From the boy's point of view, his past relationships were "closed" and the future unknown.

No matter what the funding source, children in placement are in "limbo" (after Finkelstein, 1980). Whether placed by school districts or departments of social services, mental health, or mental retardation, all children need to know that staff are maintaining links to their families or building bridges to another family who can be a resource to them as they grow up. Moreover, when children have accomplished the difficult task of separation from neglectful/abusive parents, they feel a tremendous need for attachments to a neighborhood, community, and friends. No agency can be a substitute on its own. Keeping youths distant from their "roots" leads to further alienation, lack of identity, and vulnerability to anyone who offers substitute parenting (e.g., pimps, cults, or gangs).

If agencies are to work effectively with children and youth in group care, they must recognize that they are only transitional objects with whom the child and family work out issues of abandonment, abuse, neglect, and trauma. Each child must have a place to call his/her home.

ROADBLOCKS IN THE DAILY ROUTINE—
ABUSE, NEGLECT, SEX ABUSE

Children who have been abused come into placement expecting all adults to do to them what their families have done. Childcare staff must understand the exact details of the abuse, what led up to it, and what followed.

Mandy, an 11-year-old girl, was placed into residential group care after her foster family of ten years refused to keep her. Mandy, who repeatedly got into physical fights with one particular male childcare supervisor, claimed that her foster father had sexually fondled her. Over and over, the same childcare supervisor was provoked to physically restrain Mandy—often ending up holding her down on the floor.

Mandy was getting agency staff to act out what had happened to her in the past. In Mandy's eyes, being held down and restrained by a male authority figure repeated her experience of being physically and sexually abused by her foster father. The childcare supervisor worried about hurting Mandy, asked for medication, and began to recommend replacement in a more restrictive institution. Rather than deal with all her pain around the losses of her biological mother, her foster family, and her siblings, Mandy provoked agency staff to reenact the abuse and abandonment she had experienced.

It is essential for childcare workers on all shifts to understand the child's and family's history and the crises that led to placement. This contrasts with the mandates from state agencies for detailed chronicling of incidents (i.e., crises and "events"—after Ausloos, 1986) and the pressure within group care programs for behavior management. Staff need to understand how a child's provocative behavior serves to maintain the only attachments and behaviors he/she has known. Understanding the function of the child's behavior helps staff to intervene before a reenactment of abuse, neglect, or abandonment occurs.

A family-centered approach to group care enables staff to see that a youth's behavior is not a personal attack but an acting-out of the child's and family's pain. Staff can then help a child and family work on impulse control—to think before they act and to begin to understand how provocative behaviors fit with past and present family relationships. Childcare staff need to be able to say, "Can you hold it until the family visit?" or, if there was no family visit, "I know it's painful that your father didn't come. We can talk about it rather than you getting all of us to do things to you that would repeat the painful things that happened in your family." Staff need to validate a child's pain and at the same time help the child to express it at an appropriate time. Simply distracting a child from the pain only reinforces the denial of the child's reality (Sacco, 1987).

Staff also need training to be alert to signs of physical and sexual abuse and neglect. Many children in abusive families are not able to share what has happened and what they fear might happen again. Instead, such children act out their fears and rage. It is up to us as professionals to understand the messages these children are sending.

Signs of physical abuse include provocative behavior which leads to physical altercations with adults or peers. Other signs of physical abuse include:

"• Overly passive or extremely aggressive
• Appears withdrawn, fears going home
• Reports injury to teachers or others
• Child's explanation of injury is inconsistent
• Wears long sleeves or other concealing clothing (often inappropriate for season)
• Low self-esteem
• Blames self for abuse, e.g.: 'I was bad and upset Mommy/Daddy'
• Does not feel safe in own body—acts as though he or she feels no pain or exaggerates small injuries" (Council of Family and Child Caring Agencies, 1987, pp. 1–2).

Signs of sexual abuse include excessive masturbation or masturbation at inappropriate times, encopresis and/or enuresis as well as running away. Other signs of sexual abuse include:

"• Poor relationships with children of own age
• Unwilling to participate in certain physical activities
• Unwilling to submit to physical examination
• Avoids being touched
• Withdraws into fantasy or unusual behavior
• Exhibits regressive behavior, even appearing to be mentally retarded
• Becomes truant
• Becomes delinquent
• Exhibits extreme interest in his or her sexual organs, in other children's or parents' (sexual organs)
• Older children may exhibit seductive or promiscuous behavior" (Council of Family and Child Caring Agencies, 1987, pp. 3–4).

Neglect is often indicated by:

"• Begging or stealing food
- Constant fatigue, listlessness, falls asleep
- Frequent absences from school or lateness
- Child reports no caretaker at home
- Uses alcohol or drugs
- Sucking, biting, rocking
- Antisocial, destructive
- Behavior extremes
- Compliant, passive, or overly shy
- Aggressive, demanding" (Council of Family and Child Caring Agencies, 1987, pp. 5–6).

The daily routine of waking up children, providing breakfast, getting them off to school, providing appropriate individualized educational programs, afternoon activities, dinner, evening activities, and managing bedtime is a course of study in itself (Henley & Plumer, 1978; Klein, 1975; Trieschman, Whittaker, & Brendtro, 1969; Uhlig et al., 1977). In family-centered group care, it is essential to view each aspect of the daily routine in the context of the child's needing to return to a family. Most children in group care are not from the middle class and need to learn how to live in their *own* families and neighborhoods. Children in placement need to learn to get up in the morning, to use an alarm clock, to help make breakfast, and to clean up. They need to be involved in making lunch and doing their laundry; this is part of the work of preparing them to return to family life.

Group care needs to model caring and supervision in families and to involve parents in providing a nurturing environment. Typically children will act out at times of the day which were difficult in their homes. If dinner meant a stormy and often violent interaction between mother and father, a child may reenact arguments and violence at the group's dinner in residence. Staff need to help the children to learn how to manage themselves around meals — how to sit, how to share, how to pass things, taking turns, being patient, and beginning to talk. Staff can also help the parents and children to learn how to accomplish the same tasks. Food represents nurturance and thus meals are key times for group care staff to involve parents and children and promote positive relationships.

Children's loyalties to their families may be demonstrated by doing everything in their power to get rejected by staff at critical times during the day. Group care practitioners need to keep in mind the symbolic meaning of the daily routine and how children bring the context of their families with them into group care. Without this awareness, group care practitioners will soon find themselves reenacting roles of other family members from each child's family. Abused and neglected children will almost certainly find staff members who have issues about losing control and torment them until they feel like abusing or rejecting the child. Staff must first become sensitive to what behaviors will "push their buttons." Whiny behavior can provoke one staff, while masturbation can upset another. Self-awareness of what triggers personal reactions can help staff to understand what each child has experienced in the past.

Birthdays and holidays (especially Thanksgiving, Christmas, and New Year's) take on a mythical meaning which must be understood in terms of the child's experiences. In our society holidays often are presented in the media as a time for joyous and almost perfect family unity. The child in placement watches families having joyful reunions on TV and then takes part in a party at the agency with music, good food, entertainment, and gifts. For many youths, these parties stand in marked contrast to what they would get at home and end up taking the place of going home.

Most crisis-oriented families are used to failure, and holidays are times to fail. Holidays are remembered as times when *everyone else* is having a good time. As holidays approach, staff need to be aware of their own worries about returning youth home and their own need to make each youth "happy." Because the youth is so needy, staff often become rescuers and strive to give the youth "that special something" that they sense the youth never received. Staff worry "Will they be able to go home? Will they be safe? Will they get hurt? Will they come back early or in a rage?" One way for staff to maintain a nurturing posture but avoid becoming a rescuer is to constantly ask themselves, "Am I ready to adopt this youth and be part of his or her life forever?" Staff need to focus on how to help *families* have a "happy" time. When there is no family, staff need to work on finding a family for the youth.

Staff can work with the family and youth to determine what will be the most difficult times during the holiday. In particular, we need to keep in mind the presence of other siblings who may or may not be placed and the special role of the youth in placement. Everyone will be looking for additional nurturance, and everyone needs to be prepared for the reality that this cannot happen throughout every moment of the holiday. Youth in placement and their families often are magical thinkers and need a lot of guidance predicting what will happen—the pain as well as the pleasure. By addressing the reality of holidays in advance, we begin to help the family to set more realistic expectations, to get assistance when needed, to plan, and to choose. This process helps family members to take more control of what they do (i.e., behavior management) and to receive support from group care staff as they begin to express worries and concerns that were typically acted out in the past.

Behavioral Problems as Metaphors

"Untoward events" and behavioral problems are symbolic of a child's or adolescent's emotional needs, current stresses, and lack of hope. When a child is involved in a dangerous act we ask, "Why now?" (Pittman, 1987) and "What function does the behavior serve for the child?" We look at the cycle of behaviors involving the family, community, and practitioners in a youth's "acting-out." For instance, children who run away from a group care facility may be making a statement that stress on them is too great or that the program is not meeting their needs or that they haven't heard from their parents, friends, or those people who are significant in their life. At such times it is crucial not only to find runaway youths and bring them back to a safe setting, but also to involve their families and referral sources (as appropriate) in determining whether the plan is working for each youth.

The child's running away to avoid home visits may be symbolic of his/her fear of going home or a message that not enough has been done to change the family. A child who runs away from the agency between home visits may be trying to get the agency to work faster on getting him/her home or reflecting that the placement is not meeting his/her needs and may in fact be harmful. Studies have documented that abuse/neglect in placement is 20 percent higher than that found in the community (Fontana, 1988).

If a child is worried that his parents will not take him back as he approaches discharge, running can be viewed as a protective measure for maintaining the stability of the child's situation and helping the parents to avoid making a decision. The parents may need more support in taking a strong position that they will indeed take the child back or in facing the reality of their child's needing to grow up outside the family.

Often children are so enmeshed with their parents that their behaviors closely correspond to their parents' behaviors. For instance, the same afternoon that a youth's mother was attempting suicide, the youth fell off a high swingset and broke his arm. The family worker missed the mother's increasing depression; the child did not.

Fire-setting, the scourge of all placements, is closely associated with a child's feeling of abandonment and total annihilation. The child's despair is so great that a conflagration is needed. The child symbolically is setting a fire under all involved to get them to move. Yet, fire-setting has often been seen as a contraindication to moving a child into a family environment. This in turn reinforces the child's hopelessness. At the same time, setting fires becomes addictive because fire is exciting, warm, mesmerizing, and brings an immediate response with much excitement. A fire represents energy and power for a child with little hope.

A fire tells us that we had better work faster on getting the child connected. We need to work on the reality of abandonment and help the child to find out if his/her parents can be a resource. It's also useful to involve fire fighters to work with the group care staff as volunteers and with the child as Big Brothers. Fire fighters can teach safe ways of handling fire and become appropriate role models. By directly addressing the child's fire-setting and the underlying fears of abandonment, we can help a family that may seem paralyzed by the child's behaviors and locked into a cycle of repeated rejections and evictions. We can show the family and the child that we hear their fears and can support them in looking at painful issues, especially the question: Can the child live at home?

When a child gets into trouble, staff often feel compelled to physically restrain the child. Psychotropic medications are often used as a means of controlling the child and protecting the child and the milieu. Despite the intentions of staff, physical restraint and medication often symbolize or reenact what the child perceives as abuse. Use of restraint needs to be supervised carefully to ensure that it is not abusive and is not used in the place of more appropriate interventions. When a child is out of control, we need to look at what led up to this incident and what needs to be done to avoid further incidents. Our goal is to help the child develop inner controls rather than to depend on outer controls. It is crucial to involve the parents as soon as possible. Involving parents in all important issues affecting the child is a way of engaging parents and stressing that we need their help in order to help their child (after Ausloos, 1981).

The existing family or the family imagined by a child is a vital resource for understanding and managing behaviors. When the child has no parents involved, we need to bring in whomever the child identifies as a resource. If the child cannot identify a resource, the agency must find a person in the community as a resource for the child. In short, we cannot ignore the child's need for a family.

DISCHARGE: PLANNED AND UNPLANNED

By maintaining a focus on the clients' goals and what must change so that a child can return and stay home, practitioners can help the youth and family succeed with a "planned discharge." A planned discharge symbolizes that critical issues have been addressed and that family members have made progress in improving their lives.

It is important that practitioners realize that change is a difficult and long-term process. In addition, the family worker must be aware of his/her own issues and be able to differentiate them from client problems and to understand how these intersect. Practitioners have their own "triggers" which elicit uncomfortable feelings. Often these are connected with feelings of being too pressured, being too close, feeling engulfed by client demands, or fearing rejection by clients. Regularly scheduled consultations and supervision are essential in maintaining an objective perspective on the process of change and the family worker's role with the family.

Sometimes, despite all the efforts of group care staff, consultants, and county workers, an unplanned discharge occurs. At times, the youth may return to his/her family even though staff expect everything to "blow." At other times the youth may end up in a more restrictive level of care. After a certain age (16–21), the next placement is likely to be in a detention center, jail, or a mental hospital. Older youths may end up discharged to the community at large with minimal realistic planning on how they are to survive.

Youths who disrupt are typically moved from one placement to another, i.e., "foster care drift." It is our belief that when a child "blows" at home or in the community after discharge, the most appropriate placement is in the same residential program. Staff at the agency know the child, the family, and the pattern of events which led up to the "unplanned discharge." Staff can put the youth's most recent disruption into perspective.

Disruption does not have to be a failure. If a child returns, staff can work with an understanding of what led to past unplanned discharges and disruptions at home. In contrast, moving the child to a new agency (or program within the agency) reinforces the family's pattern of multiple losses and acquisitions. This in turn prevents resolution of painful issues and growth.

CRISIS WORK WITH ACTING-OUT YOUTH

Crises do not represent the failure of staff or the family; crises represent the avoidance of painful or frightening issues. This realization can help staff to continue with their work to help a child have a family despite crises. Some children must finally face the fact that they cannot return to their family. This happens less often with the implementation of permanency work. Yet, despite all efforts, some youths cannot go home and continue to struggle with this reality throughout adolesence. These youths need help with facing this reality and developing other possible family connections. Planning for the future needs to occur, not only at discharge but also from the time of admission.

The extreme and sometimes dangerous behaviors of acting-out youth and the often frantic and inadequate responses of their parents and community establish *over and over* that the youth is in charge. In such cases, the youth is often acting out his/her feelings of depression, and in the process playing a critical role in acting out the family's pain. Such youth have often grown up with abuse, neglect, and little or no parental supervision. They have learned to take on immense control of their families and communities through extremely provocative behaviors which almost seem to beg community authorities to step in and manage the youth. This is done at great cost to the youths themselves in terms of constricted and often dangerous behaviors. Over and over, such youth demonstrate that when they are controlling everyone with their behaviors, they are out of control. They are trapped in dysfunctional roles and cannot develop their potential as young adults.

In group care we need to expect and look for crises to occur after placement. Often crises occur as a youth begins to form close relationships with staff. This closeness elicits the youth's fear of abandonment or betrayal of his/her family. Just as in working with families in crisis (see Chapter 3), we go with the youth's crisis. In the first few incidents, we examine the patterns of the youth's behaviors. What was going on in the youth's milieu in group care, in the family, and in the community? We work to understand the youth's behavior before the youth gets into a pattern of repeated acting-out and the need for restraints. By understanding how a youth acted out before and after placement, we can help the youth to anticipate what he/she will be feeling and how he/she can channel these feelings more effectively in family sessions and group sessions in the milieu.

After two months of placement, Benny, age 12, was in crisis. He refused to follow cottage rules and he had broken over a thousand dollars worth of stereo equipment in the recreation room. Staff met as a group after putting Benny in the time-out room. The team examined the reason Benny was originally placed and how this related to the present crisis. The following was noted:

- *Benny was beginning to get close to two childcare staff.*
- *Benny had begun to share a little about his life in his family.*
- *At the last family visit, Benny's mother (who was being monitored by child protective services) said that she was going to court in two weeks on an abuse petition alleging sexual abuse by both herself and her boyfriend.*
- *Benny had been originally placed as a result of the alleged sex abuse of himself and his sisters. Benny, who was the closest to his mother of his siblings, fought the police and then became withdrawn and immobilized — almost catatonic. Repeated efforts to place him with his sisters in foster care ended with Benny physically fighting with the foster mother in bursts of rage and then becoming withdrawn. This necessitated his separation from his sisters and placement in group care.*

The team recognized that Benny was in an untenable position. He understood that his mother could go to jail if he shared what had happened in court. Benny's on-going denial ("My mom didn't do anything") served to protect his family. When Benny began to get closer to childcare staff he felt a conflict of loyalty between these caring adults and his mother. Benny's destruction of the stereo and defiance of staff was his way of letting staff know that he was cutting off communication. The stereo was a metaphor for sound and what could not be said. Benny's acting-out served to maintain the family's denial.

With this understanding, the team told Benny that no one could force him to share what had happened. The team understood that Benny's crises would recur whenever Benny felt caught in the middle between the need to protect his mother and his own need to face the reality of what occurred. The team needed to work with Benny's family to accept the reality of what did happen and to understand how sex abuse can occur in a family, and what needs to happen to make it safe for everyone.

Our challenge in family-centered group care is to understand the youth's dilemma within his/her family. The youth's crises symbolize both the youth's and family's pain as well as their need to avoid. Family-centered group care can provide respite for the family and an opportunity to engage family members to work on getting a child beyond a powerful but self-defeating role as the "bad kid."

Society has a responsibility to provide an alternate legal and permanent family for those children who cannot be safely and healthfully raised by their families. . . .Society has a responsibility to provide support and resources to assist families formed by adoption in raising their children.

—Child Welfare League of America, 1987a, p. 4

The child who must be placed in substitute care at any age, and regardless of the reason, is torn from the biological and symbolic context of his identity. No matter how nurturing the substitute care, the child's ongoing task will always be to reweave the jagged tear in the fabric of his identity, to make himself whole again.

—C. B. Germain, 1979, pp. 175–176

CHAPTER 9

Building Family Connections for the Child Who Cannot Go Home

RECOGNIZING FAILURE

SURRENDER IS A FAILURE that cannot be minimized. It is a catastrophic loss; at the same time, it can be the beginning of an opportunity to build new connections. If work has been done well to help parents and children in placement to reunite (see Chapters 6–8), then parents and children will have learned whether they can live together. Parents make a plan for their child to be adopted based on recognition that they have tried but cannot parent the child at home. The parents make a painful decision in the best interests of both themselves and their child.

We begin by recognizing and dealing with the grief from this failure within the context of the parents' ethnic culture and multigenerational histo-

Portions of this chapter are reprinted from Kagan (1986) and Kagan (1982).

ry. For some ethnic groups, surrender and adoption are unforgivable and may lead to the parents' and/or child's being ostracized from the rest of the family. In such families, making an adoption plan may be resisted at all costs and the child may receive no permission to attach to another family. For other families surrender and adoption have been a way of life for generations so that another surrender evokes little emotion. In yet other families, a matriarch will step in to parent a neglected child and a cycle of close grandmother-grandchild relationships will continue, with the mother in a dependent, criticized role and the father absent.

Work with the parents and child to reunite must provide the parents with every possible resource to help them to succeed. The parents' failure then becomes concrete and can be recognized by the child. Without this effort, the child will always find excuses for the parents. For instance, it is tempting to say that the parents are simply too poor. Children do not accept such explanations, which leave them with the burden of feeling that they have caused too much strain for their parents to raise them. They often have a fantasy that once their parents can save enough money or get a big enough house, then they can go back home (see Fraiberg, 1962). Children know that, "You can live with your mother in a tent."

Similarly, we would never tell a child that your mother "loves you very much but cannot raise you." This contributes to a distorted sense of "love" for the child. Instead (after Gardner, 1970), we define love as what a parent actually does for a child on a concrete level from morning to night, day by day over the child's life. Love means being there for one's children, being responsive to their needs, caring and doing from breakfast through bedtime, through illnesses, cultural events, family crises, and holidays. We tell a child simply that his/her mother and father have realized that they "just can't take care of you" and help the child to see that this is based on the parents' history.

Since surrender leaves such intolerable feelings, we arrange for it to take place in a neutral setting, such as a courthouse, legal office, or department of social services. We would not want to have parents sign "surrender" papers in their home or near a holiday, which would then serve to reactivate feelings of loss on a daily or annual basis.

Ideally, surrenders should include a plan for open adoption, allowing the parent and child to maintain a connection and relationship. This does not obviate the message that the biological parent cannot raise the child and has made a painful decision to have the child raised by another family. The parents can more easily give permission to the child to grow up in another family if they know that they can from time to time make contact with their child. This is often crucial to facilitate a positive adoption plan. Otherwise, the child is forced to be totally disconnected from his/her past and the biological parent feels deprived of the ability to make the choice of ever seeing his/her child again. Most biological parents would react to this by in turn depriving the child of permission to be adopted. Of course, many children surrendered for adoption have been neglected and severely abused. Under these circumstances visits to the child's biological family need to be based on the child's need to reconnect.

DISENGAGEMENT AND REATTACHMENT:
A DEVELOPMENTAL PERSPECTIVE

All involved in adoption can get a better understanding of what it means to be adopted by asking themselves to imagine discovering that they were adopted—as a two-year-old, as an eight-year-old, as a 15-year-old. How would they feel? What would be their first reaction? What would they do? At the same time, consider how it would feel to surrender your own infant, two-year-old, five-year-old, etc.

Kay Donley (1984) has defined disengagement as the process of giving a child permission to make new attachments—to develop emotional bonds with an adult upon whom the child is dependent. For the clinician this process involves: (1) mastering the placement history of the child; (2) identifying the child's main attachment figures; (3) obtaining the permission of the child's past attachment figures (biological parents, relatives, foster parents) for the child to love and be loved by others; (4) giving the message to the child convincingly; and (5) reinforcing or repeating the message over time. Interventions to facilitate this process must be based on the child's developmental stage and unique characteristics.

Surrender of an infant involves a grief process for the whole family system, including grandparents of the baby. Since this grief will be reactivated time and again, the individuals involved must be given the chance to express their anguish, despair, and anger. We urge the parents to see their baby and to keep a picture of their baby, because "they can't give up and grieve something until they have had it." We also ask the parents to make a gift, e.g., some clothing, a bunting, for the child so that when the child is older he/she can be told "this is what your mother made for you." With this gift, the parent writes a message that can be read by the child.

The intent here is to make the loss real and provide a means for grieving. Making the loss real for both parent and child, e.g., with photographs, helps to prevent denial and repetition of the surrender with another pregnancy and surrender. Dealing with the reality of the baby also helps to lessen the extent of fantasies, images or ghosts which may haunt the mother through her life. It is also helpful for the mother surrendering a baby to make a choice from several selected families of which one she would prefer for her baby.

The preschool child who is being surrendered has most likely experienced prior separations from his/her mother, father, relatives (most often grandparents), and foster parents. These children often lack the secure attachment needed for positive growth and development.

Whatever the child's age, it is important to identify and address past losses and attachments and ability to bond. We need to learn what has happened and when it happened, especially in infancy and the preschool years. Events leading to unresolved losses are all too often replayed at a later date.

A two-year-old child, Maggie, was adopted after living for most of her life with foster parents. The adoptive parents were told only that the foster parents had refused to adopt Maggie. Maggie was simply moved one day from her foster parents to her new adoptive parents, with little or no preparation and no opportunity for the adoptive parents or Maggie to understand why her attachment to her foster parents had to be broken. From the time of adoptive placement, Maggie needed constant medical attention and as a teenager was extremely defiant to her adoptive parents. At age 13 Maggie began to act out sexually and by 15 was pregnant and moved out of her adoptive family. Her own daughter was placed at age three following sexual abuse by her boyfriend. Maggie's daughter was taken away at nearly the same age as Maggie herself had been traumatically separated from the foster parents who had raised her from birth. A multigenerational cycle of teenage pregnancy and traumatic separations continued despite the best intentions of the adoptive parents and adoption agency.

Our approach is to help the child learn about past separations and attachments. We work to avoid total cutoffs and recommend open adoptions, with a stress on the children's need to know their past. Biological parents, extended family members, institutional staff, and foster parents can leave a concrete message for their children through photographs, life books, written messages, recorded messages, or videotapes. Sometimes the number of possible connections and losses is staggering. For instance, nine-year-old Ralph needed to check out 19 different relatives and learn if he could live with them before he could begin to attach and develop a bond to his adoptive parents.

These connections can give the child at least a minimal sense of roots. Research has shown that positive support figures (relatives, friends) can help to compensate for negative influences a child experiences (Farber & Egeland, 1987; Fisher, Kokes, Cole, Perkins, & Wynne, 1987).

Our goal is to help a parent surrender without leaving the message that the child is bad or worthless or the parent is bad or inadequate. Parents must be able to take care of themselves and address their own needs as well as those of their child. In many cases, the development of a strong affectionate bond between parent and child never occurred, leading eventually to surrender and placement of the child in another family. When there is no bond, both parent and child can be given the message that "sometimes the chemistry between them just doesn't work." This can help to decrease the parent's guilt and focus on the interactional problems in the larger context of the family's conflicts, socioeconomic problems, and external stresses, rather than placing blame on either the parent or child.

A mother had been severely depressed right before the conception of her second child, Anthony. She had suffered the death of her older son and remembered Anthony as being difficult to handle from birth and "things not working out right."

Anthony was placed at age seven in a foster home and stayed there two years. The foster family also found Anthony very disturbed and disturbing. Everyone involved felt blamed for the failure of this placement and Anthony was moved to another foster home. In this case, Anthony had been sensing that he could not return home and both mother and child felt blamed by the foster parents for lack of progress on reuniting. Conflict between the mother and foster parents replaced and prevented any significant progress on getting the child home.

For progress to be made we had to focus on the relationship between Anthony and his mother and to give the biological parents permission to recognize that "the chemistry didn't seem to be right." Anthony's mother needed permission to distance herself and to face the reality that she and her son did not have (and never had) a positive bond and that this was not going to work out. Only by confronting the loss, experiencing the pain, and having the hope of further attachments could both mother and child move on with their lives.

Many surrendered children search for a special "chemistry" between parent and child. Children who were nurtured as infants by a foster parent, relative, babysitter, or family friend can often develop a close and warm relationship with an adoptive parent even though they had little or no nurturing from their biological parent. Such children have usually been bonded to someone in infancy and will search for another parent with whom they can bond. Parsons Child and Family Center's Regional Adoption Program has provided picnics and parties in which prospective adoptive parents and children mingle. This often facilitates matching as parents tend to gravitate toward one special child and parents and children have the opportunity to begin to form the special "chemistry" needed for attachment.

All children (even preschool children) need to be involved in the work of reuniting with their parents, as we observe how separations and visits affect the children. All children who can comprehend *need to hear* concretely that: (1) It is not their decision about whether their parents will take them back; (2) only the parent or the judge can make the decision; (3) their parent has had every opportunity and help to make things work out so that each child can return home; and (4) children cannot take care of their parents.

The older the child, the more guilt the child typically feels about not being home. For many children this guilt involves: (1) feeling angry and hateful at one's parents when society teaches children to always honor, respect, and love their parents; (2) feeling pleasure by escaping from a previously painful situation in their biological family; (3) being separated from their parent and not being able to care for the parent as they had in the past; (4) not fulfilling the responsibility they had in the past to protect their siblings from abuse or neglect; and (5) having received more material benefits as a result of placement. Poor children are often placed in middle-class homes and institutions and experience a more comfortable lifestyle in placement than they (or their parents and siblings) could get at home. Moreover, the adolescent who has the goal of independent living often cannot replicate the middle-class lifestyle he/she became accustomed to in placement, leading to increased frustration and resentment.

Children need to be given a strong message that, even though the biological parent cannot raise them, he/she wants them to be raised in another family and they can still have another family. Ideally this message is given directly by the biological parents (see Chapter 6). If this is not possible, children can be helped to see that their parents' actions over time have led to their surrender and opportunity for adoption.

HELPING THE EXTENDED FAMILY

Extended family members can be helpful or interfering in giving a child permission to move on to an adoptive family. Active support by extended family members prevents the child and parent from being left with negative messages that could hinder the child's attachment to a new family and block the parents and the child from fully grieving their loss. Not uncommonly, a parent surrendering a child has been in a dependent and weak position in his/her family or has intellectual and/or physical handicaps that make it impossible for him/her to raise the child. Grandparents, aunts, and uncles may be involved and dealing with their own feelings of guilt about not being able or willing to raise the child. This guilt may be expressed directly or covertly through chronic attacks on the biological parent, with underlying messages that the parent or child has failed and/or that the parent must keep on trying to regain custody regardless of how many failures have already occurred. Consequently, extended family members and significant others who may influence a decision-making process (or who may be competing for a child) need to be included in the diligent efforts to reunite and in the decision to surrender.

Donna's children were placed in foster care after the oldest daughters were found to have been sexually abused by Donna's boyfriend and also by Donna. Donna was placed on probation and diligent efforts were provided to help her work on her goal of getting her children back. Donna was a very likable woman who expressed a desire to improve her life and get her children back but was handicapped by great difficulties in perceptual-motor coordination, general knowledge, vocabulary, and verbal reasoning skills (verbal IQ of 67). Donna was very dependent on others and had frequently associated with abusive men.

Donna's mother and siblings were angry at Donna for letting her children be sexually abused. They criticized Donna and berated her for her poor parenting. At the same time, no one in Donna's extended family was able to care for Donna's children.

To work with Donna and her family, treatment review meetings were held monthly with Donna and her extended family to review progress. The family worker aligned with Donna and helped her to see that she could be a "good mother" by surrendering and giving her children a home that she had never been able to provide. The county worker set conditions for the return of the children, including Donna's compliance with rules of her probation and work on getting the children back.

The children's foster mother expressed a willingness to become an adoptive mother if diligent efforts failed and said that she would be willing to allow Donna and her extended family to continue to see the children even after adoption. The foster mother allowed Donna's mother and sisters to see the children in her home, so that they could see that the children were doing well and that the children could have continued contacts with their aunts and maternal grandmother.

At the treatment review meetings, the supervisor of the program, the county supervisor, and the consultant stressed the realities of Donna's past and present difficulties in providing the protection, care, and nurturance the children needed. With this combined effort, Donna's mother and siblings supported an adoption plan and Donna signed a surrender for her children to be adopted.

In some cases, continued visitation with extended family following adoption may not be possible because of past traumatic experiences and threats experienced by the children.

Two siblings placed in an adoptive home at ages four and seven soiled their pants after every visit from extended family members. The biological parents and extended family had voluntarily surrendered the children, with an understanding that they could continue to visit following adoption. These children had been sexually abused by their biological mother's boyfriend. It was important to help the adoptive parents to see how the visits brought out scary feelings in the children and how they might give the children permission and support to share these feelings. At the same time the extended biological family had to understand how the visits were af-

fecting the children. A decision was made that contact with the biological family would be only at the children's request until they were better able developmentally to handle their fear. The children also needed to receive messages that the adoptive family would keep them safe. Messages from the biological parent on how she had signed a surrender in order that the children could be adopted and raised in another family had to be repeated.

THE CHILD WHO SAYS "I DON'T WANT A FAMILY."

Most older children with long histories of multiple placements will say that they don't need or want another family. Adolescents tend to deny problems and are focused on developing their independence (Muuss, 1968). Teenagers often have an exaggerated view of their own strengths and resources as autonomous individuals and look forward to making their own way in the world.

Adolescents who are surrendered and are over 14 can legally decide in many states whether or not they want to be adopted. Such youth are typically torn between their own thrust towards independence and the implicit requirement of an adopted child to become dependent on another family. For adolescents caught in this dilemma, becoming adopted is often perceived as giving up the control they seek. An adoptive family is an unknown and a possible threat; it could rekindle the pain of a committed relationship, which could then fail again, leaving the youth feeling empty and vulnerable.

Adolescence is probably the hardest time for a youth to reconnect to a new family and yet a time when the youth desperately needs a family. Accordingly, we help adolescents to look carefully at what it would be like to grow up and eventually live outside the institution or foster family *without* a family of their own as a resource. It must be emphasized to the children/adolescents who have been freed and yet do not want to go on to another family that their biological family (and past foster families) made a choice, i.e., for them to be adopted by another family. For children to know their alternatives, they must experience concretely what it means to grow up in a family versus a community residence or an institutional program. They need to be told that an adoptive family is for life and that they will become part of the inheritance of the family, including receiving social security benefits and having grandparents for their own children, etc.

We tell these adolescents that they can keep their "roots" with their biological or past foster families and still add other resources. The difference between an adoptive and foster family or group care facility is highlighted in terms of who will optimally be there for the youth at different ages, e.g., 18, 21, 26, 35. We also point out the possibility of staff leaving a group care facility or foster parents terminating their foster care contracts because of illness, employment changes, or moves to another area.

Chronological age is not the key factor in determining whether a child should go to an adoptive home. Believing that a child is never too old for a home, we look primarily at the emotional age of the youth. Our challenge is to match a youth with a family that is willing and able to deal with the youth's paradoxical needs for security within a family and protection from getting too close due to normal adolescent development and a long history of disrupted attachments, family conflict, and often unresolved grief.

The process of mourning and reattachment is gradual and discontinuous (Steinhauer, 1974). We seek to match children with parents who can respect their pace in giving up fantasies of reunion with their previous families or their fantasy of independence from all families. Adoption of an older child means recognizing the adolescent's need for distance, yet at the same time offering to be there emotionally and physically.

FINDING UNCLE JOHN AND AUNT JOAN: THE AGENCY AND CHILD AS DETECTIVES

In some cases, a child in placement will appear to have no possible links to extended family members. If the child has been seen as extremely disturbed and is over age 14, work in such cases will typically focus on the child's behaviors and preparation for "independent living." These are often sad and angry youth who get into serious trouble with drugs, thefts, or other criminal behaviors, eventually ending up in jail or prison. These behaviors reflect their sense of having *nothing* to lose and their desperate search for immediate sources of gratification, excitement, and escape from feelings of emptiness. For such youth the goal of "independent living" confirms their sense of an empty future with no connections; even the caring and concern of foster parents or childcare staff will be restricted once the youth is too old to remain in the foster home or group care program, i.e., "after the child ages out."

It is important to explore the youth's fantasies about who could come and rescue him, as well as the attachments that he/she has experienced. For many such youth, a careful search through referral materials and contacts with referral sources will reveal that cousins, aunts, uncles, and even parents do exist. The youth can be engaged to help in the search for these relatives. This can involve visits to neighborhoods where the youth grew up, taking photographs of old homes, and requesting photos and other information from relatives. This process focuses the work on both helping the youth find out where he or she has come from and finding out what potentially positive connections can be rebuilt to end the youth's sense of isolation.

Often in such cases the youth's behaviors may be found to be very similar to those of relatives.

An adolescent boy who had been in group care facilities for eight years was repeatedly accused of petty thefts and breaking and entering neighbor-

hood houses. He had been referred to the agency as a child who had no family ties, and his behavioral problems were treated as isolated incidents. When a search was done to locate his relatives, it was found that he had uncles in a nearby county who had been serving time in jail for burglaries. This boy had received messages about men in his family prior to place-ment. He needed help to learn about the positives as well as the negatives in his family so that he could search for a home in a positive way.

Detective work focuses the staff and youth on the need to learn about the youth's past before he/she can move on to new attachments.

A 13-year-old boy, Robbie, was placed for the fourth time in group care following the failures of multiple foster home placements and two adoptive placements. Robbie's biological parents were unknown, and he appeared to have no positive attachments. He was seen as aggressive and impulsive with no friends or any close relationships with adults. In play therapy, however, Robbie repeatedly played out interactions with a maternal figure whom he called "Barbara." When asked about Barbara, he would say nothing.

A group care staff member and the boy went to the county department of social services offices to research any past connections. At the county offices, a child protective services worker recognized Robbie and offered to help in the search. This worker had been involved in the removal of Robbie at age four from the home of his babysitter, whom he identified as Barbara. In a short time, he and Robbie were able to locate the address and phone number of Barbara through the agency computer. The group care worker wrote to Barbara, met with her privately, and finally arranged for a session in her apartment with the boy.

For Robbie, like many other children in group care, new attachments were impossible until past losses could be grieved. Visits between Robbie and Barbara were arranged and led to his moving in with her as a foster child. With Barbara, it became possible to find out what the boy had experienced as a young child and why he had remained so attached to her after multiple placements. Robbie was not able to be adopted by Barbara, but he was at least able to rebuild a connection to her and improve his behaviors sufficiently to move from a residential treatment center into a foster home in the community.

Children need to know that every possible effort has been made to find, locate, and re-engage missing parents. We ask children who have been placed to name who they think could be a possible resource for them if their mother or father could not care for them. One boy listed 11 relatives as possible resources. This list later became the guide for helping to build connections for this boy after his mother and father surrendered him. Since the need for connections is so great, we explore any possible link for a child.

Fathers of many children in placement are often listed as unknown or missing. Many children with missing fathers end up with a negative stereotype of adult males and learn that the need for a father cannot be addressed directly in the family. Some children take on the task of looking for their fathers; failing in this endeavor, they may join an antisocial group or a cult or find an older boy who can be a "father figure" to them and at least temporarily make up for their loss. It is important that we *never minimize the loss of a father*, despite the mother's contention that the father was unimportant or disinterested. Legally every effort must be made to reunite a child in placement with both parents. Often the custodial parent may object, but there is no choice. If permanency work progresses with only one parent, the second parent will then have to be involved in diligent efforts at a later date if the custodial parent decides to surrender the child. This only prolongs a child's waiting for a family.

A teenage mother and father separated shortly after the second birthday of their daughter, Dorothy. The father surrendered the child with the understanding that he was not to contact his daughter until she was 18. For the next ten years the mother tried but failed to provide a home for her daughter. Dorothy moved from placement to placement, in and out of adoptive homes after her mother surrendered her, and back into a residential treatment center where she resumed contacts with her mother. Dorothy's mother saw Dorothy's father's brother one day and gave him the name of Dorothy's social worker. Within two days, Dorothy's father contacted his daughter after a 15-year absence and began to work on bringing Dorothy to his home.

The search for missing parents may have to go beyond the legal requirements to include relatives who have had a relationship with the child. Many times a parent or agency will cut off a child's relationship with a stepparent and not recognize the importance of that relationship. The child then suffers the loss of yet another parent; the remaining parent reinforces this loss by insisting that the stepparent was "bad" or unavailable.

PERMISSION TO HAVE A PAST

Children who have had an attachment to their biological parents cannot be expected simply to give that up because the judge has signed an adoption paper. Emotional bonds are much stronger than legal documents. Denial of the child's past simply does not work and the past will often be replayed.

Working on a life story is a concrete method of addressing past attachments, losses, and a child's roots (Jewett, 1978). By helping the child to develop his/her own life story we give permission to the child to have and to keep a past. Since adoption records are usually closed, it takes a great deal of work to make the past real. Visiting the courtroom, talking to the judge, visiting the child's former caseworker, etc., lend reality to why the child entered placement and was surrendered by his/her parents. By collecting photos, contacting relatives, going to old neighborhoods, schools, and friends, we enable the child to face the reality of his past.

Johnny thought he was evil and unadoptable. He was referred by family court after running away from his mother's home, not attending school, and sleeping in the streets. After Johnny was placed in a foster home, diligent efforts were made to reunite Johnny with his mother. Johnny's mother surrendered him, saying that it was the best thing because he always reminded the family of what her father did to her. When Johnny was placed into an adoptive home he began once again to roam the streets wearing pajamas under his clothes.

The family worker working with the adoptive mother began to help Johnny with his life book. His initial story of his biological family was of an idyllic home life with a mother who never beat him and a grandfather who loved him. Slowly, as the adoptive parent demonstrated her commitment to Johnny, he was able to share other memories. Using a genogram, Johnny was able to show that his grandfather was his father. He could then talk about being an "evil seed." Johnny could remember good times with his grandfather/father and bad times with his mother. Reality was painful; however, only after he addressed reality was he able to grieve and begin to express himself. Through the life story work Johnny learned to express his feelings and understood that he was not evil.

With adolescents, past bonding and identity are so important that we recommend that adoptive parents and courts permit a hyphenated last name. The acceptance of this name by the adoptive parents signifies acceptance of the child's total identity. This gives the child freedom to share with his/her adoptive parents what has happened in his/her life and who he/she is.

A child without a past is a child in limbo. We cannot ask a child to grieve losses if past attachments are not recognized. If we as practitioners ignore a child's past, we in effect help the child deny losses. This is why the life story is so essential for surrendered children. A child needs to have a past before he/she can have a future.

GAME THERAPY FOR CHILDREN IN LIMBO

Therapeutic games are an effective means of engaging otherwise resistant children (Gardner, 1975) who are not ready to do a life book. With proper training family workers can use the games conjointly with adoptive parents. Through games one can identify in a concrete visual format some of the covert behavior patterns repeated by a child who can't seem to attach to a family. Games such as Gardner's "Talking, Feeling and Doing Game" (1973) and Kagan's "Children Cast Adrift" (1982, 1986) can be utilized to provide permission and safety to experience and express feelings of rage, abandonment, fear, and grief. "Cast Adrift" (see Figure 9.1) can also reveal the cycles of behaviors that keep children trapped in their own rage and denial of their losses and unable to reattach. Belief and Feeling cards (see Figures 9.2 and 9.3) help a child to experiment with a variety of adaptive and maladaptive beliefs and to see the results of different ways of handling feelings.

After "Cast Adrift" is played a few times, we encourage children to develop their own personal game. This can be done on blank game grids (see Figure 9.4). We help children to highlight important goals for themselves, such as adoption, and to put these in key places, such as the corners of the game board. Side trails and special cards to be drawn can then be developed. The child's "own game" (Kagan, 1986) can provide significant clues to important attachments, e.g., to past foster parents, and messages the child has received that may continue to have a great impact on the child's behaviors. For instance, many children have received the message from biological or foster parents that they should grow up in a specific institution, just as the parent once did. Children's "own games" typically reveal relationships which are causing them a great deal of trouble and visually dramatize their difficulties in working through feelings of grief and loss. Personal games can also be used to identify a child's goals, e.g., to be adopted, and his/her assessment of whether this is really possible.

Games can give children permission to deal openly with some of the painful, covert issues, e.g., loss, grief, rejection, abuse, that have led to ongoing aggressive or self-destructive behaviors that prevent any adoptive placement. With identification of these issues, a family worker can deal more effectively with the child's need to explore significant relationships with parents or foster parents, etc.

Games can also prepare prospective adoptive parents for a child's tendency to repeat cycles of misbehavior and end up rejected. Painful conflicts can be dealt with through the game format. As conflicts are addressed on a less toxic level by the adoptive family and the child, the child can be freed of his/her role as a "bad" or "crazy" youth. Dysfunctional roles can be highlighted and parents engaged to help a child develop competence in coping with the past and in choosing among options for the future. In short, games can be used with a child to make covert beliefs, feelings, and behavior cycles with a child and his family overt.

WORKING WITH ADOPTIVE PARENTS

Adoptive parents need to begin with an honest look at their own situation. We highly recommend working with adoptive parents through use of an ecogram and genogram (after Hartman, 1984) and helping them make their own life story. Adoptive parents need to know that children come with past experiences and conflictual relationships. The child's life book should be integrated into the adoptive parents' life book.

An adoptive family must accept a child's past in order to integrate the child into the family. This can be facilitated by having prospective adoptive parents work in the child's placement setting to help the child to understand his/her past. It must be predicted to adoptive parents that children will reenact the crises and conflicts they experienced in their earlier families. In fact, adoptive families can easily end up becoming crisis-oriented and replay the child's earlier traumas of neglect, abuse, or rejection.

A home-based family assessment is highly recommended in working with prospective adoptive families (see Chapter 2). The intent here is not to diagnose dysfunctions but rather to work with the adoptive family to determine how an adopted child might fit in. The family's wishes and intents must be recognized and supported. A careful match is then made to the needs of prospective adoptive children.

The need for respecting the needs of adoptive parents was highlighted in the Lawrence family. Mr. and Mrs. Lawrence were unable to have children and wished to adopt the youngest of three boys who were siblings and a girl from another family. The county department of social services told the family that they must take all three boys. The family reluctantly agreed and a placement was carried out.

The oldest child soon left the family by acting out aggressively and was replaced in another family. The middle child, who had also been unwanted by the Lawrence family, quickly became scapegoated as the family problem. In family therapy sessions, the parents would sit stiffly, with their two youngest, adopted children running around, pulling each other's hair, scratching, poking, jabbing the adoptive parents, and destroying furniture. The older of the remaining two brothers sat still on a couch while his parents complained bitterly about his faults and problems. Meanwhile the parents ignored the physical abuse to their bodies and the room by the younger children. Eventually this family had the scapegoated brother placed and ended up with their initial request of the youngest of the three brothers and the adoption of another daughter.

We need to hear the adoptive parents' needs. Do they want a girl when we are trying to place a boy? We also need to help adoptive parents recognize the difference between adopted and biological children. The older adopted child cannot become as bonded as a biological child or a child adopted as an infant. Nevertheless, the older adopted child can develop attachments and become a part of the family.

Figure 9.1

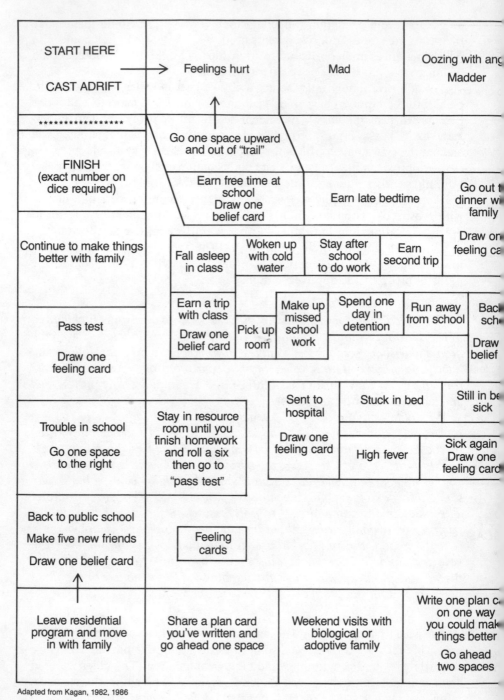

Adapted from Kagan, 1982, 1986

Figure 9.1 *(continued)*

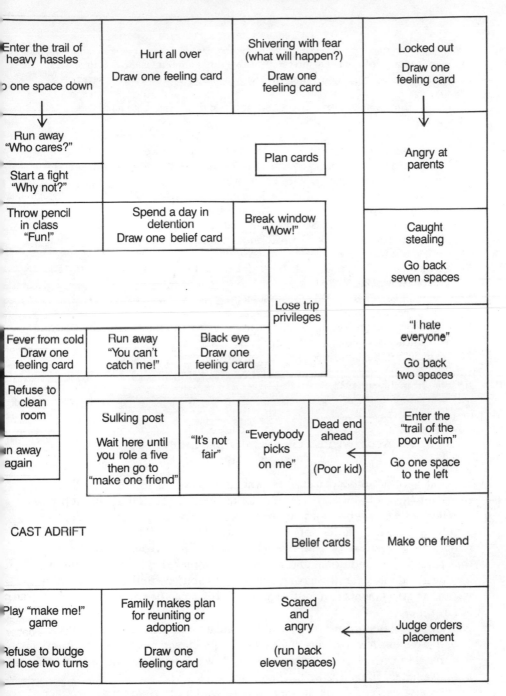

Figure 9.2

BELIEF CARDS

---

1. I am in charge of my behaviors. Repeat two times and move ahead four spaces.
2. I am a bad kid. Everybody hates me. Repeat two times and go back seven spaces.
3. Life is crummy and always will be! Say this two times as you go back two spaces.
4. I don't have to be perfect; I will just do my best. Move ahead four spaces.
5. I can be good or bad. It's up to me. Move ahead three spaces.
6. I don't need to get people to hate me. I can make friends and make it in a new family. Say this as you move ahead four spaces.
7. I can figure this game out! Keep thinking ahead as you move ahead four spaces.
8. I can't trust anybody! Repeat two times and go back four spaces.
9. It's everybody else's fault! Say this again and move back three spaces.
10. I know two good things that I am able to do. Name two things you can do and move ahead five spaces.
11. I am a mean kid and always will be! Think about this as you go directly to "The Trail of Heavy Hassles."
12. I am proud of what I can do. Share something that you are proud of with another person and move ahead four spaces.
13. I know two good things that I am able to do. Name two things you can do and move ahead four spaces.
14. I can make it! Say this three times as you move ahead three spaces.

Adapted from Kagan, 1982.

ADOPTIVE PLACEMENTS OF OLDER EMOTIONALLY DISTURBED YOUTH

Studies of adoptive placements (Kagan & Reid, 1986) have highlighted the significance of abuse, anger, and depression for youth in their adoptive families. As a youth becomes older and reaches adolescence in an adoptive family, it becomes harder for a previously abused youth to develop and maintain the intensity of adoptive relationships. Such youths have learned that parents are conditional and temporary (Donley, 1983). Acting-out and leaving an adoptive family may appear safer to abused youth than maintaining strong attachments to adoptive parents, which can be painfully shattered at any time.

Adoptive parents must be able to tolerate a youth's anger. The ability of adoptive parents to experience their own fears and rage has been significantly correlated with whether or not the youth was able to remain within the adoptive family (Kagan & Reid, 1986).

It is also useful to look at the adults to whom the child tends to attach while in group care and educational settings. The profile of these key adults in terms of ethnic background, occupation, race, and other characteristics can be guides to the type of person with whom the child could develop some form of connection.

The adoption of older children has been described as a "time of family crisis" (Katz, 1977). After an initial transition period, a new equilibrium is established in the family which may tend to be dysfunctional. Katz suggested that a major factor in adoption outcome is the family's ability to accept the child's different roots, conflictual family allegiances, and the legacy of the child's experiences. Other studies (Reid, Kagan, Kaminsky, & Helmer, 1987) have highlighted the importance of parental expectations in making adoptions work. Especially poignant is the often unrealized expectations of reciprocal love that an adoptive parent hopes will be established after the child bonds. Parents who have adopted older, abused/neglected children

Figure 9.3
FEELING CARDS

---

1. Feel scared but don't tell anyone. Instead "run away" and go back three spaces.
2. Feel sad but keep it all to yourself. Go for a long, lonely walk and miss your next turn.
3. Share with someone the saddest thing that had happened in your life and as you do move ahead four spaces. What happened?
4. "I can let myself feel scared without running away from my feelings." Instead of running away, move ahead three spaces.
5. Tell someone about one of the angriest times in your life and move ahead three spaces. What happened?
6. Tell someone about one of the happiest times in your life and move ahead three spaces. What happened?
7. Tell someone about one of the scariest times in your life and move ahead three spaces. What happened? What did you do?
8. Feel sad and tell someone something that makes you feel sad. Say it softly. Move ahead three spaces.
9. Feel scared and share something that scares you with one person. Move ahead three spaces.
10. Feel angry and show everybody by smashing your radio! Go directly to "The Trail of Heavy Hassles."
11. Feel angry and tell someone, "I feel mad because _____." Move ahead four spaces.
12. Feel happy but don't let anyone know. Keep a straight face. Don't laugh and get ready to feel angry as you move back three spaces.
13. Feel angry and show everybody by setting someone else up to get angry at you. And as they get angry, move back two spaces.
14. "It's okay to feel sad. I can let myself be sad and still be okay." Think of one thing that makes you feel sad as you move ahead two spaces.

Adapted from Kagan, 1982.

Figure 9.4

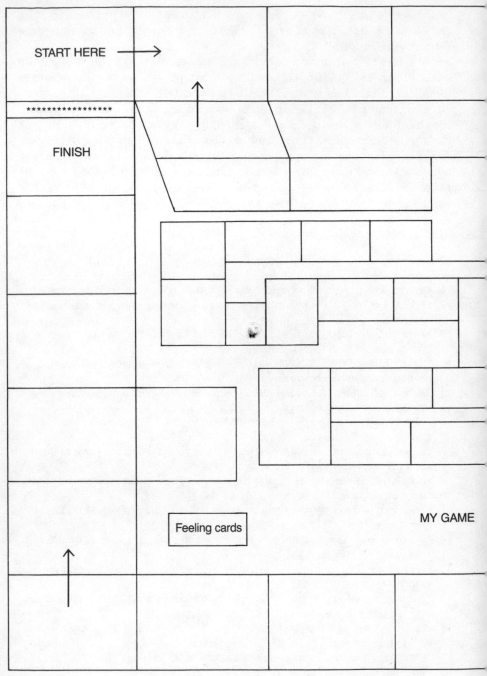

START HERE →

****

FINISH

Feeling cards

MY GAME

From Kagan, 1986

Figure 9.4 (continued)

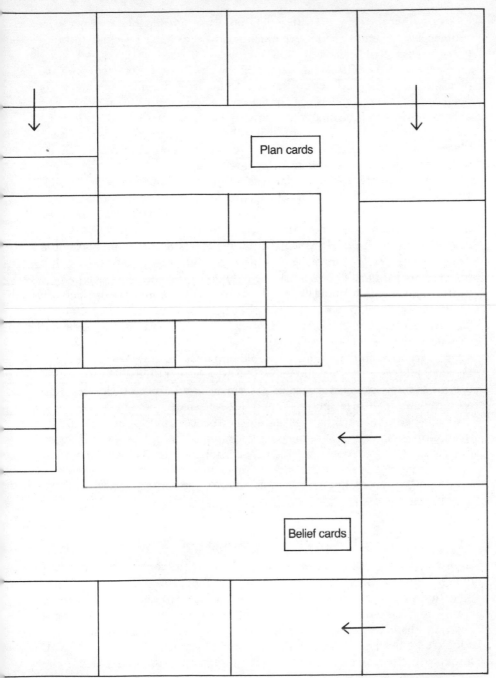

often feel that they end up with much more severe behavioral or emotional problems in the child and receive much less of the child's love and devotion than they expected (Reid et al., 1987).

Paul Steinhauer (1974) has described the child who experiences multiple placements in the first few years as a child who becomes "permanently detached." A child who has not bonded in the first years of life may never be able to develop an attachment to a parent. These children may go through a series of placements, each shorter than the one before. At the end of each placement, they experience another rejection so that they often end up feeling that they cannot tolerate family life.

Studies on adoptions of older institutionalized youth (Kagan & Reid, 1986; Reid et al., 1987) have challenged the "reversibility hypothesis" (Kadushin, 1970) that the effects of early childhood deprivation can be reversed through adoptive experience. Instead, it appears that many children who have suffered multiple placements, multiple losses and chronic abuse and neglect in their early years may not be able to form strong and positive child-parent relationships. The goal for such children is to find adoptive parents whose needs match with the child's ability to attach. Despite the difficulty in finding adoptive placements for such children, it is important to continue to look for families that can provide homes. Large families that won't demand closeness work especially well for children/adolescents who have learned never to trust. Such parents must be able to parent the child without expecting the child to attach emotionally. This model of professional parenting may be the only possible means of placement in a family for children who must manage intense feelings of abandonment, anxiety, and rage.

We believe that such parents should not be expected to raise a child by themselves and need to have ongoing coordinated help through post-adoption services. Such services provide support for the parents, including assistance in finding weekly relief, babysitting, and childcare in their homes. Post-adoption counseling services for children and parents also need to be available and funded.

THE MYTH OF INDEPENDENT LIVING

Many adolescents who can't go home have stated goals of "independent living." This is a misnomer. No youth can live independently in the community. To discharge a youth to "independent living" is to send the youth to an empty and intolerable situation of homelessness, joblessness, and loneliness. Youths who cannot return to their biological families or move into adoptive homes need help in building survival skills and connections with resources in the community. At the time of admission, we need to determine what skills and programs the youth will need after discharge from group care and begin to work on helping him/her to meet the criteria for those programs and to build connections with them. Resources must be obtained for these youths in the community as soon as it is established that family living is not a possibility. This may mean supervised living programs, sheltered workshops, outreach programs, and employer-sponsored programs in the community.

Adolescents need to be prepared for the real world. Youth who cannot return to their families or be adopted must be all the more prepared. They need to learn how to survive — how to get a job, how to be at work on time, how to follow directions in a job, how to open a bank account, how to begin to save, how to cook, how to shop, how to pay bills, etc. They need to learn a trade and to build relationships in the community, e.g., through half-time employment for youths over 15. Work should also lead to spendable money and should follow prevocational training. There is much merit in the old adage that youths build self-esteem through work.

At the same time that the youth works on building survival skills, he/she must also continue to work on feelings and fantasies connected with his/her family. Wherever possible, we strengthen positive relationships with extended family members. However, many such youth were brutally abused and abandoned. They live in a state of rage which has been internalized and may never go away. These youths need help to learn to control themselves rather than to be controlled — to anticipate what will lead them to explode and to learn alternate behaviors. Something as simple as sitting on one's hands or taking a walk must be learned and practiced as a necessary response to stress.

Each youth needs permission to grow up and reinforcement for doing so. This means giving up fantasies and recognizing the reality of having to take care of oneself. Group care staff need to avoid feeding into the youth's dependency needs and to insist that the youth learn how to work and survive with relationships built up over time in the community.

What is society's role in alleviating the situation of the multi-problem underclass? . . . Perhaps we must address the ultimate question of all: can a society moving towards greater instability in all its aspects provide permanence and stability for its children?

—A. Maluccio et al., 1986, p. 301

Nobody wants me.

—Statement by a child about to be evicted from his foster home after placement for three years because of chronic neglect, physical and sexual abuse in his biological family.

CHAPTER 10

When All Else Fails: Minimizing Foster Care Drift

ALL TOO OFTEN CHILDREN drift from home to foster home or home to institutional placement and back again during the critical years when they need a consistent attachment to a parent (Fanshel, 1971; Maas & Engler, 1959). And with each successive placement, the child's ability to relate and rebuild attachments decreases.

Bobby was born when his mother was 14 years old and his father, an alcoholic, was 20. In his first year, he was cared for by a succession of five relatives—all trying to help his mother for short periods of time. Bobby drifted from one relative to another due to his mother's inability to be a mother and a teenager at the same time. By age 11, Bobby had had 15 placements with his relatives, the longest being for two years. With each placement Bobby helped to evict himself by running away.

Bobby and his aunt were referred to the Parsons' Prevention Program to help Bobby's aunt maintain him in her home, since Bobby's mother had moved out of state. Bobby was anxious and often ran away from his aunt to the many relatives who had cared for him. He would stay for an hour or two and then run on. He was forever searching for his parents, grandparents, aunts, and uncles. Each visit abruptly ended with Bobby battling for control with the adult in the house. He seemed to say by his behaviors, "No one is in charge of me. I can't trust anyone."

It soon became apparent that Bobby couldn't stay with his aunt, who said he was "out of control," jumping out of cars, and running away from school and the home. Bobby couldn't talk about his feelings. With each successive placement, Bobby had become more untrusting, aggressive, and hopeless. At the same time he developed a myth about family members who had rejected him. He became more desperate to control the people around him, and as a result was "out of control." At the time of referral, a recommendation was made that, if Bobby could not remain with his aunt, he should be moved to a neutral setting where permanency work could take place. Bobby needed help to reconnect with his family members in a positive way. He needed to face the reality and pain of his past losses so he could begin to grieve and go on to rebuild attachments. By the time of referral, Bobby's dangerous behaviors had escalated to the point where residential treatment was needed.

Many children have had Bobby's experience replicated through the foster care system. As Steinhauer (1974) has pointed out, our systems of foster care and institutional placement have in many ways fostered the multiple losses and trauma which in turn have led to the development of psychopathic personality disorders. Children have become permanently detached or locked into a state of persistent, diffuse rage when the energy and love cut off from their original parent cannot be mourned and reconnected to the original or a substitute parent within a critical period of time. This time period is based upon the child's developmental level, with younger children moving into acute grief sooner (e.g., in as little as two days for one-year-olds).

Legislation in recent years, e.g., the Child Welfare Reform Act of New York State and the Federal Adoption Assistance and Child Welfare Act, was intended to minimize the length of time children remain in placement. These statutes provide standards for "diligent efforts" by parents and social services workers within a defined time frame in which parents must decide whether or not they can parent their children.

In line with this legislation the objective of our work with children at risk of placement is to minimize the number of losses, separations, and traumas experienced by these children and to help each child become a part of a "stable home" as soon as possible. We provide services to the biological family and when necessary help parents to make an adoption plan for their child in the best interests of the child and family.

Foster care drift can be minimized by taking strong stands and risks. Ann Hartman (1987) has challenged practitioners to consider placing babies and young children removed from their biological families because of abuse/ neglect into potential adoptive families. At the same time, all possible resources are to be provided to the biological parents to help them to change and provide the nurturance and safety their children need. This approach poses the risk of the potential adoptive parent forming an attachment that will later be broken. Yet for those infants and toddlers in foster placement, bonding to a primary parent figure is essential to facilitate reattachment to the biological parent or attachment to an adoptive parent. Moreover, this bonding often occurs naturally between a young child and a foster parent who provides love and security. If a child does require successive placements, it is better for the child to return to the same foster home so that at least one connection can be maintained.

For those children who cannot return to their biological parents, the number of losses and separations is minimized if the child can continue in his or her first placement rather than having to move from the first foster home into a second foster or potential adoptive home. The importance of minimizing unnecessary moves and placements is even greater for the child who has already been moved many times in his or her life — from Mommy to Grandma to Aunt Joan to . . .

Infants in foster care should be visited by their biological parents at least three times a week in order to build up a bond between the biological parents and their children. Foster parents can serve as primary caregivers to the biological parent *and* the child. Frequent visits can help the foster parent understand the needs of the biological parent and how to help her get her child back. If this fails, then the foster parent is in a good position to consider a plan of open adoption, which would permit the child to maintain connections with the biological parents. This in turn makes it easier for the biological parents to make an adoption plan for their child, since they do not have to give up all contact with their child and, it is hoped, feel that the foster/adoptive parents genuinely tried to help both them and their child.

Jimmy's earliest placement was at age six months, when his mother was in a psychiatric hospital for two months. Jimmy's mother, Rose, was diagnosed as schizophrenic. Jimmy was placed in a foster home where he quickly formed an attachment to the foster mother. When Rose was discharged from the hospital she visited Jimmy in the foster home. The foster mother nurtured Jimmy and Rose. Over time she became a resource to the family. Before Jimmy reached age seven, Rose was hospitalized three more times; each time Jimmy returned to the same foster home. Rose was able to express a desire to have the foster mother adopt Jimmy if Rose at some time could not care for him. The foster parents became a supportive extended family for this isolated mother and son. Like many children of parents who are hospitalized, Jimmy was very concerned about his mother. The foster parent understood that Jimmy needed to care for his mother. Helping Jimmy meant helping to take care of the biological mother.

Biological parents need to feel that they are truly being helped in order to avoid getting into battles. In most cases, biological parents will *not surrender* a child when they are battling the foster parents, an agency, and the court over custody of the child. Children of parents who are fighting the system often end up bouncing in and out of placement; their parents may appear more attached to the "battle" than to their child.

THE CRITICAL YEARS

The first five years are critical for the child's healthy development. During the first year, the child must bond securely to a caretaker who gives the child a sense of security and trust. In the following four years, the child must work on exploring the world. Individuation can only be accomplished within the safety of a nurturing and enduring relationship.

The child who experiences multiple placements or minimal care in the first year of life has little basis for trust and sees the world as a terrifying place. The child who is physically, sexually, emotionally abused or neglected after the first year has often learned that he/she must care for his/her parent or be rejected. Developing personal autonomy without provoking abandonment is often not possible for these children (see Masterson, 1976).

The first five years are the foundation of the child's future. The phrase "minimal care" often arises in regard to parents who can barely parent their children. Minimal care is not enough. We need to provide resources to help parents so that children can grow physically, cognitively, and emotionally within a safe and nurturing relationship.

"At risk" families should be identified early and offered services; for example, single women having babies could be visited following delivery and offered support services in the home. Quality daycare services need to be available to all families as a preventive measure and not just limited to families of working parents and parents involved in the child protective system. And most important, families must have a roof over their heads, i.e., adequate housing. Children of the poor have little chance to learn middle-class values (the mainstream values of our society) when they grow up in battered, dingy, vermin and insect infested housing, and communities with little or no resources for families.

If placement is necessary, permanency decisions need to be made in a timely fashion. Children under the age of five have little sense of time and can't afford to lose these precious years while waiting for their parents to change. Years can easily go by with a child remaining "in limbo." Bonding remains interrupted and the child lives in a world of temporary relationships. During these critical years, it is essential that permanency work be time-limited. When difficult decisions cannot be made by parents, judges need to understand and act on the child's behalf for resolution and permanency.

GETTING LEVERAGE

Court orders are often effective in providing the necessary leverage for families with chronic and severe problems to make difficult transitions. Someone needs to be the "heavy" in making firm orders that will stick. Someone also needs to monitor the family to ensure compliance. This is the mandate of departments of social services, mental health, and mental retardation. Otherwise the family will continue to revolve in cycles of perpetual crisis and trauma.

When social services agencies refer a family for counseling, "good guy–bad guy" roles can be established. The child protective worker can be the "bad guy" and monitor compliance with the court order. At the same time, the family worker can help family members to prepare for change, predict crises, empathize with the family's dilemma, and encourage growth and accomplishment. For the family worker, a firm and strong court order with monitoring by child protective services offers an opportunity to engage the family. When referrals to agencies are not possible, social services staff can take on both roles. This can be done most effectively where there is a court order in place. In some cases, the supervisor can be the "bad guy" and the worker "the helper."

Children need the backing of laws and court rulings which take final stands in their best interests. "Diligence of efforts" to reunite children in placement with their parents means work done by parents and family workers. "Diligence of efforts" must take place over time — within one year — and must be so convincing that all family members (children and parents), the lawyers, the legal guardian, and the judge involved are truly convinced that no more can be done to help children and parents safely reunite. The older the child, the more he or she needs to be involved in "diligent efforts."

Joey and Ellie were first placed in foster care at ages two and five and then replaced with a different family at ages nine and twelve, respectively. Their mother was described as "very child-like" and diagnosed as borderline retarded; she repeatedly brought young men into her home. Joey and Ellie's father had a long history of alcoholism and allegedly sexually abused his daughter from another relationship which led to the children's second placement. The prevention family worker and county department of social services worker became aware that Joey was very attached to his father and very concerned about his mother's well-being. Joey was brighter than either of his parents and very aware that if he and his sister were to go home, his parents had to make many changes.

Visits to the home were conducted weekly with family sessions after each visit. Often Joey would cry out, "There is no room for me in the house." Joey's room was being used as a clothes closet by family members. Social workers brought boxes to the home and helped Joey's mother and father pack up things in order to convince Joey that his parents were getting the help they needed to get him home. It took the reality of his parents' messing up his room again and again for Joey to realize that he could never go home. He decided it was all right for his parents to surrender him or for the judge to make a decision to terminate parental rights.

Allowing children to bounce back and forth from placement to placement simply cannot be tolerated. The cost for the child, the family, and the community is too high. Eventually the court must make final decisions when all else has failed and parents cannot decide in the best interests of their children and themselves. Too often, the court fails to make a decision in a timely manner. Years go by, with efforts to reunite the family becoming increasingly destructive to the children. A parent who is incarcerated or hospitalized is unable to care for the child. A parent who cannot find an appropriate living space, beds, furniture, and food within a realistic time frame (e.g., one year), even with all possible help, is again demonstrating that he or she cannot care for the child. No placement should exceed one year.

WORKING WITH THE COURT

To work effectively with crisis-oriented families, it is important to develop a strong relationship with family court judges. This means taking the time and making the effort to meet with judges, sharing concerns and program goals, and asking judges what they want and need from public and private practitioners. Most judges appreciate a thorough family assessment, which includes a clear picture of how the family has come to the point of requiring family court intervention (i.e., history), dynamics, and concise recommendations. A consultant (a social worker, psychologist, psychiatrist) speaking as a neutral expert can be one of the most effective and valuable assets to child protective investigatory, foster care, and adoption units. Assessments by the consultant add to knowledge about the family and strengthen recommendations.

Reports need to come from authorities recognized by the court and available to testify if needed. The signature of a Ph.D., M.D., or C.S.W. is often required. The court also needs well-documented reports from those working most closely with the family. Impressions need to be substantiated by observations. It is crucial that the information given to judges be sufficient in detail and clarity, as well as timely, to assist in critical decisions.

BUYING TIME

One of our goals is to teach crisis-oriented families to better utilize time. For youths referred for probation cases, it is often essential to convince the family court judge to give family workers more time and to avoid making statements such as, "If I see your face back in my courtroom, you will be placed." Crisis-oriented family members are typically very reactive and will tend to defy such orders. As a result, the youth will soon be placed. If John is told that the next time he takes something from the store he will be placed, this may very well happen. John has a responsibility to get help for his family and will act out again unless he sees his family getting help in a short period of time. The threat by the judge becomes a script for the future.

Our own research on families referred for services to Parsons' Prevention Program (Reid et al., 1988) has highlighted the need for more time to engage families, to help families to take effective control of their children, and to address difficult family dilemmas.

Tony was accused by his mother of trying to sexually molest his younger sister and had been placed on probation for physically attacking two girls in the community. Tony's mother was frightened by Tony's behavior and expressed intense anger at him. Tony, a large but anxious 14-year-old boy, had been extremely close to his mother until puberty. Tony's mother had had relationships with abusive men and when Tony was a young child she had been hospitalized because of a suicide attempt. Tony had gone into placements with relatives and then returned to his mother.

Tony's mother was initially extremely defensive, blaming Tony entirely for all problems and displaying an intense sense of fragility, with angry rebukes to any probes about herself. A family worker saw mother individually once a week and involved Tony in daily activities and tutoring. This provided a great deal of support to Tony's mother and after time she began to share her fears and to learn how better to manage her own life and children. With counseling, she began to relax and rebuild connections for herself in the community.

Tony initially did better but then was accused of again physically threatening a girl in the community. Placement was recommended by the probation department. The family worker, however, advocated that more time and more structured activities could help Tony and his mother work things out. The judge gave the family worker, Tony's mother, and Tony a second chance. Tony was enrolled in an after-school vocational training program and a specialized day treatment program. The family worker continued to support Tony's mother, while another social worker from the day treatment program brought up the need for change in order to keep Tony from being institutionalized in a detention center. Tony did extremely well in the day treatment and after-school vocational training program. His mother became more secure in her life and able to manage her son without fear, violence, or blame.

FINDING HOPE IN A SEA OF DESPAIR

We want to leave family sessions with a sense of hope—a sense that things can get better no matter how difficult they may be. If we continue to feel hopeless, the family will feel that as well. Expressing the hopelessness, getting it out into the open, can lead to work on what's lacking in the family and what needs to be done to make it better.

Finding hope is especially important at intake and review conferences. Our task at these conferences is to ensure that we have a workable contract, which includes an opportunity for change. If we accept constraints on our work and "things as they are," we will quickly find ourselves as depressed or agitated as our clients.

Elizabeth, 7 1/2, was one of five children who had been removed from her mother's home and placed into foster care following allegations of sexual abuse involving several of the children, including Elizabeth. Elizabeth reportedly had moved back and forth between her mother and her aunt, with her aunt having legal custody from age one month until age 5 1/2. She then lived with her mother for several months, until her removal to foster care following allegations of abuse.

Elizabeth was living in a foster home at the time of referral. Elizabeth's aunt still had custody but expressed no interest in caring for Elizabeth; however, Elizabeth's mother had been working with the county to bring her children home. At the time of referral, Elizabeth had been enuretic (days and nights) following the initiation of unsupervised visits to her biological mother's home. Elizabeth and another girl also began fighting in the foster home.

A psychological evaluation found that Elizabeth was developmentally more like a two-year-old in terms of emotional and social development than her chronological age of 7 1/2. Because of the lack of consistent parenting in her life, Elizabeth had tremendous needs for nurturance and sought affection inappropriately from adults. Elizabeth's foster mother had just given birth to her own baby, who was taking all of her attention and time. Elizabeth's needs became increasingly difficult for the foster parents to deal with. On several occasions the foster parents disciplined Elizabeth with screaming and physical punishment to such a degree that neighbors called the child abuse hotline. Elizabeth was not able to get her needs met in the foster home since she was competing for the same supplies as the foster parents' baby. Elizabeth felt much anger toward her foster parents and acted it out by regressed behavior, including urinating in a clothes basket.

At the time of the psychological evaluation Elizabeth appeared to be acting out feelings of chaos, abandonment, and fears stemming from her extremely uncertain position in her foster family, as well as fears about returning to her biological mother's home. She was cut off from important people in her life, including her aunt. Elizabeth continued to say that she wanted to return to her mother. At the same time, given the long history of placements before and after reports of sexual abuse in her biological mother's home, Elizabeth's attachments to her biological mother appeared to be primarily a hope for some kind of family rather than the reality that her biological mother could provide the safety and nurturance she needed. Elizabeth acted out her extreme insecurity and impermanence through her regressed behavior. Her enuresis represented regression and fears of renewed sexual abuse in the biological mother's home during home visits, fears about further abuse, and resentments about not getting her needs met in the foster home.

Elizabeth was stuck with little or no support from either her foster home or her biological mother. A family worker was helping the biological mother to work diligently to reunite with her children; yet, little attachment was seen between this girl and her mother. The biological mother continued to be involved with men who had histories of sexual abuse. Meanwhile the girl remained in a foster home where she clearly was not wanted and could not be cared for. Elizabeth was becoming a "lost cause."

It was crucial that the consultant and family worker take a clear stand that this was a girl who had nobody and nothing. We needed to begin work on building attachments for the girl. This included recontacting the aunt with whom she had lived on and off for several years as a young child to find out whether her aunt could raise her. It was also important to reinvolve Elizabeth with her siblings and to set a clear and definite time frame of no more than one year in which the biological mother needed to meet specific requirements in order for her daughter to return. These requirements included a safe home with no violence and security for the girl from further abuse.

To begin to carry this out, it was essential to coordinate "permanency" work with all service providers and ensure continued diligent efforts within a clear time frame with contingencies. Supervision of the mother's home by the county department of social services was essential. Furthermore, a consultant and family worker worked to provide individual therapy and the best possible school placement. The consultant and family worker also called for a careful evaluation of Elizabeth's foster home placement. A strong stand was taken that Elizabeth needed a home where she could feel wanted and cared for—a foster mother who could take a strong but warm position and accept Elizabeth's stated desire to return to her biological mother and at the same time understand how Elizabeth's behavior was related to her fears and experiences.

If we feel that we or other family workers are becoming exhausted and about to "burn out" with a case, it is almost certain that the contract is unworkable and that there is little or no hope of productive work with a family.

A family worker was bringing four children from two different foster homes to visit their biological mother, Mary, who wanted them back after several placements over the last five years. Foster placements for all the children were temporary, and in one case the foster parent was asking the county to remove the children from her care as soon as possible. At the same time, little attachment was seen between the children and Mary. Little or no change had occurred in Mary's life over the last four years.

Ted, age seven, appeared to be especially vulnerable to repeated abuse. He had had a different father than the other three children and had been sexually abused by the father of the other three children. Mary consistently left Ted and the other children unprotected, with little guidance and nurturance. Mary appeared to be an extremely empty woman, who had herself experienced long years of physical abuse and neglect.

The county department of social services repeatedly extended the time frame for working with this family, as they felt that the biological mother was doing the minimum necessary to avoid a ruling of "permanent neglect." She began to receive alcohol counseling on an outpatient basis and kept most visits with her children, with transportation provided by the family worker. Diligent efforts had been provided by the county worker for a year, followed by two years of work by a family worker. During consultation on the case, the family worker appeared extremely depressed about the lack of progress and risks for the children. She was concerned about Ted in particular since he appeared to have little chance of becoming attached to his biological mother or for that matter to any parent.

In this case, as Elizabeth's, it was essential that the consultant, supervisor, and family worker take a strong position that something needed to be changed. The children, and in particular Ted, appeared to get little in either their foster homes or in the home visits with Mary. They appeared doomed to remain in temporary foster home care while Mary did just enough to prevent a ruling of "permanent neglect." The effect of this status on the children was heartrending.

Continuing with this contract was leading to exhaustion and burnout of the family worker and was a disservice to the family. Instead, the consultant and supervisor took the position that something needed to change. A *firm recommendation was made that the county file a permanent neglect petition.*

At the same time, Mary was helped to look at whether she could care for her children permanently. With the help and nurturance of the family worker, Mary was able to respond to the permanent neglect petition by making a decision. Mary decided to surrender her children.

In permanency cases, parents choose by their actions whether they will (or can) provide the parenting a child needs. Our assessments and recommendations need to spell out what specifically parents must do to regain custody. Just recommending "family counseling" gives the court and social services workers little basis to measure a family's progress and essentially transfers the task of assessing what needs to be done to the family worker involved.

We as workers often find our recommendations blocked by budgetary, policy, or court constraints.

Mr. and Mrs. H. angrily denounced the county department of social services for keeping their younger three children (ages eleven, nine, and six) in placement for the last four years. Neglect (filthy living conditions, lack of heat, lack of supervision) and allegations of physical and sexual abuse had led to the initial placement. Mrs. H. appeared sincere in wanting her children back, but was easily overwhelmed and in the past had often left them in the care of an older sibling. Mr. H. also expressed a strong interest in his children's return but had worked weekdays in a distant community for the last eight years and was only home on weekends. Reports of past sex abuse by relatives and older siblings with the children were denied by family members.

Mr. H. only had sporadic contact with his children due to his work schedule, and Mr. and Mrs. H. had not participated in counseling for themselves or arranged counseling for an older son who had been diagnosed as extremely depressed and suicidal. The children said they wanted to return home but showed only minimal attachment to their parents, e.g., only asking to increase weekly supervised visitation by perhaps an hour.

In this case, the consultant recommended that return of the children be approached with great caution, since little had changed in the family over the last four years. A gradually increasing series of visits and eventual return home needed to be contingent upon: (1) Mr. and Mrs. H. participating in family counseling sessions; (2) Mr. H.'s being available during visitation to help his wife and maintaining contacts with his children during the week; (3) the parents and other family members acknowledging past sex abuse and implementing a plan for protecting the children; and (4) the children's being able to talk about violence and sex abuse with their parents. The consultant also recommended that the older son receive counseling and that the department of social services monitor the family, with periodic individual sessions with the younger children to assess whether any violence or sex abuse was recurring. In short, the consultant's plan called for addressing the issues that had led to the children's placement four years earlier and provided a basis for the county social services department to monitor the family's efforts to provide a safe home for their children. Nevertheless, the court sent the children home with only a month of monitoring because of the length of time the children were in placement, the failure of the court to rule earlier on neglect, and the court's subsequent loss of legal jurisdiction over the case.

Jane was a 25-year-old woman who had returned to her home community after living for a few years in another state. She became involved with a boyfriend and began work to have her children, ages six and seven, brought back to her. Jane, however, had done very little in the three years since separating from her husband to maintain contacts, to protect her children, or to secure their return. Instead, she had consistently taken the position of being powerless and escaped from her troubles by leaving the state where she and her husband had been living with their children. The two children had been placed because of neglect and separated with placement in different foster homes.

An evaluation session was set up and the children were flown to the mother's community for this meeting and a reunion with their mother. Jane had found an apartment for her children and was seeking custody with the assistance of Legal Aid. She had little information about her children, e.g., their performance in school, health, and had to depend on them to tell her what she needed to do. Jane denied problems and blamed others, particularly authorities, for not providing her with the assistance she needed and even for lack of permission to telephone her children in their foster homes.

Both children held onto the fantasy of reuniting with their mother; both had experienced multiple moves and the oldest child had been sexually abused by her biological father. Lately, she was doing well and showing signs of attachment to her foster parents. Her younger brother, on the other hand, was extremely anxious and had been stereotyped as "bad" and harshly punished in his foster home. While the older daughter was ambivalent about returning to her biological mother, her younger brother was clear that moving was the answer to his wishes to escape from his foster home.

Jane and her boyfriend's efforts to recover her children gave them an all-consuming cause and meaning to their relationship. Jane appeared to have limited ability to handle stresses and limited connections that she could rely on for help. Jane's ability to provide the consistent parenting needed by these children after years of multiple moves, neglect, and lack of contact was highly questionable. On the other hand, she was determined to pursue her legal rights to bring her children back to her home.

The children, after three years of placement and previous years of reported neglect, had little attachment to Jane. The state which had custody of the children requested an evaluation to determine one of two actions: immediate return of the children to their mother or denial of her request and continued foster placement. The consultants recommended that a series of extended visits be arranged for the children with their mother— both in her home and in the state where the children lived—and that these visits take place before the children were returned to their mother's home. This recommendation contrasted sharply with the options advanced at the time of referral by both states involved. No one wanted to pay for the cost of enabling these children to say good-bye to their foster parents or to give Jane the opportunity to gradually rebuild attachments to her children with help for all family members as they made this transition. The consultants also recommended that the state where the children lived assess the appropriateness of the son's placement in his current foster home and keep the children together if at all possible.

In this case, the state where the children were living was unwilling to pay for the costs of a series of visits and simply sent the two children to live with their mother. Little or no work was done on saying good-bye to the foster parents or providing a transition period for the family. On the positive side, the mother's county worker in her community continued to visit the family twice a month over the next year and provided assistance and support.

These two cases are examples of the pain workers, consultants, county administrators, and other service providers frequently feel with difficult cases. The consultants stressed the needs of family members for developing attachments, permanence, and safety in the best way possible despite limitations expressed by the court or county authorities. However, the court in the first case and the county authorities in the second case did not go along with these recommendations.

WORKING WITH PAIN

When workers are asked what they like or dislike most about doing prevention or permanency work, they typically identify two lists (see Table 10.1). If we were to ask our clients, foster parents, and family court judges what they like/dislike about their work, the very same issues would be identified with only slight variations. For example, clients dislike workers who don't change and repeat messages/approaches which clients find inappropriate, demeaning, or insensitive to their needs.

Dislikes reflect anger, exhaustion, and eventually burnout. These feelings result when the pain in the system is not identified and addressed. Pain is the

Table 10.1

LIKES AND DISLIKES OF FAMILY WORKERS

LIKES	DISLIKES
Agencies all working with the same goals.	Coordination of multiple services with different orientations, models of intervention, and goals.
Working with families who welcome me and make changes.	Working with families that don't change.
Helping children who return home from placement when the family has improved.	Sending children home before family has improved relationships with children.
Working with foster parents who help both children and parents with the pain of separation — foster parents who teach parents good parenting skills.	Working with foster parents who "sabotage" attempts to reunite children with families — foster parents who refuse to work with and help biological parents.
Keeping children safe within their family of origin or in a foster home or adoptive family.	Removing children from families.
When children return home or go to an adoptive home within a short period of time.	Extended lengths of time required to achieve permanency.
Parents who make decisions.	Going to court.
Judges who make decisions to terminate rights when no decisions can be reached by parents.	Judges who don't make decisions.
	Paperwork.

common denominator that both clients and service providers feel. If a family worker, client, county worker, or judge is angry or exhausted, the people involved in the family-service provider system are not dealing with painful issues. Problems arise when only one part of the system is feeling pain.

Jane, age 12, ran away from home, stayed out late with a gang of boys, and was not attending school. Jane's mother worked ten hours a day, played bingo every evening, and expressed resentment about Jane's problems leading to school complaints and calls. Jane's school eventually filed a court complaint against Jane as a Person in Need of Supervision (PINS).

One person cannot carry the pain without symptoms. If one person bears too much of the pain, he or she will act it out, just as Jane did in the case above. In that case, Jane and the school carried most of the pain. In contrast, if everyone shares part of the pain, change can begin to take place. Issues can be identified and responsibilities shared.

Too often, we perceive pain as something negative leading to irritability, anger, and exhaustion. However, pain also serves as a catalyst for change. "Without pain, there is no gain."

ASSESSMENT OF PAIN

We need to get in touch with our own pain from our first session through discharge. Workers need to validate their own feelings and then find out who's feeling the pain. What is mom, dad, etc., feeling? Why is everybody in some cases so angry, upset, or scared? What gets family members and service providers going when acting-out occurs? Who is doing the work? What is not being addressed?

We also check on who's not sharing the pain, e.g., the court, the parent, older siblings, grandparents, etc. How does this fit in the family service provider system? Who will be feeling pain when family members have to go to court . . . when Johnny has to be placed, etc.? Who should be worrying about a boy's safety or whether or not a child is in placement too long? Who should be upset about delays? These questions help us to identify who should be sharing the pain.

SHARING THE PAIN

The need to share the pain leads to effective strategies for stimulating change. When a worker feels exhausted and at his/her wits' end in family sessions, the worker needs to share this pain and ask the family members, "Who else is exhausted? I'm feeling tremendous tension and stress here. Is anyone else feeling this stress? Am I the only one?" This is a genuine expression of pain by the worker and allows family members to express their own pain.

To not share our discomfort would be in effect to discount family members as not being capable or willing to care or feel. Not sharing would also mean accepting a family rule that pain cannot be addressed and therefore change cannot occur. The worker/consultant/supervisor who only shares his/her feelings in closed staff meetings is discounting family members' potential for making changes. Workers may get some relief by sharing their own feelings of pain with one another; however, change may be blocked. The pain is not being shared by all members of the system.

Becoming too comfortable with pain is dangerous. Difficult decisions have to be made when work with the family has become too painful or exhausting for everyone involved. To accept pain in our work as a perpetual given is to again discount positive forces for change and to stabilize a family-service provider system with chronic crises.

With families who deny feelings, we continue to identify our own feelings and model that feelings can be owned and expressed. Most people are afraid of painful feelings, especially anger. We model that people can express feelings without abandonment.

Working with pain means confronting what is not being addressed, getting others to feel the pain, getting the individual who has pain to share the pain, using time limits which create pain, involving agencies, lawyers, judges, etc., in feeling some of the pain, and telling clients the "hard stuff." For example, "You don't have to agree with me, but I think there is a serious risk of. . . ."

This can only be done by sharing information on a regular basis with all family members and service providers. For instance, frequent reports to the judge about permanency work and regularly scheduled court appearances help judges know and understand progress in the case. In contrast, waiting until a year of diligent efforts is over before a court appearance or a report is made to the judge leaves the judge outside the painful work that is going on. The judge who sees a family for the first time after 12 months of diligent efforts is likely to see him or herself just *beginning* to work with the pain in the family. In such cases, the judge may extend work over another six months to a year in order to make his/her own interventions and to avoid the painful task of making a decision.

When pain has been shared, everyone concerned with the family becomes energized and feels effective; guilt about failure is avoided. If workers can share the pain with family members and others involved in the family, they don't have to take the pain home. Addressing painful issues is the best antidote to feeling overwhelmed, client-worker anger, exhaustion, and burnout.

As soon as I get one fire out, another building is burning down.

—Billy Joel, *Running on Ice*

It is not the things themselves which trouble us but the opinions
that we have about these things.

—Epictetus

If I am not for myself, who will be for me?
If I am only for myself, what am I?
And, if not now, when?

—Hillel

CHAPTER 11

Staying Alive When the Going Gets Tough

Most of us coming into the child welfare field arrive with expectations that *we* can help children and families to change and live better lives. We come armed with powerful new interventions we have seen performed by famous family therapists or read about in their books. Our urge to rescue propels us headlong into a desperate "dance" with families in perpetual crisis. As family workers we feel a tremendous need to induce change in the family. Soon, however, we are trapped in the mire of the family's chronic crises and depression. The crises of the family become our crises. We begin to feel frustrated, anxious, helpless, and hopeless.

To avoid feeling despair, workers may increase their efforts and soon find themselves running around in extremely tight circles, having one "crisis" after another and feeling tremendously overloaded. Each night they lie awake troubled by what they forgot to do that day and what needs to be done the coming day. In short, the client's feelings are absorbed by the family worker (after Long, 1986). Eventually the worker will act out these feelings of despair, hopelessness, and helplessness. Denying his/her own feelings, the worker will look for someone to blame: the family, specific family members, the referral source, the supervisors, the agency, etc. Or the worker will find ways to avoid visiting families or taking on new cases. Eventually staff will leave, feeling frustrated and exhausted.

Work with crisis-oriented and chronically troubled families is extremely difficult and requires a clear perspective on how these families function. In many ways, working with crisis-oriented families is like treating chronically ill patients (after Steinhauer, 1985). Family workers must avoid looking for cures and maintain appropriate expectations for their work. Success with these families is not "self-actualization" or even the ability to share personal pain in a traditional human growth group. Instead, we consider our work a success when a family is able to avoid repeating the traumas of previous generations. A family that can maintain itself, provide basic nurturance and supervision for their children, and avoid abuse and neglect is a tremendous success story. If the same family calls seeking help from our agency or another at the next developmental shift or point of stress, we have made tremendous strides. Rather than being referred or mandated for services by an outside authority, family members are taking responsibility for getting the assistance they need. This is a very positive outcome.

As family workers, we must realize that we can change only ourselves (Bowen, 1978) and must deal with our own discomfort. If we cannot do this, we probably will end up doing the family's work and feeling the family's pain. The worker's feelings, e.g., exhaustion, anticipation, and dread can be used as clues to the process in the family and the family's primary issues. By remaining sensitive and addressing our own feelings, we can deal with the many hazards of work with families referred for chronic and severe problems.

HAZARD 1. LACK OF CLINICAL SUPERVISION AND CONSULTATION

Structured time for supervision is needed by both new and experienced staff. This is not crisis-oriented supervision or "supervision on the fly." It means going over cases on a regularly scheduled basis. If workers come into the supervisors' offices all the time and supervisors quickly become part of ongoing crises, the agency ends up acting out the family systems they are trying to help. Regular structured supervision is not a matter of emergency calls. We believe that "crises" can wait, except in cases of genuine emergency where a child or other family member is felt to be at imminent risk of harm.

Asking staff members to stick with a regularly scheduled supervision time helps the worker to sort out what is important.

The supervisor helps the family worker to focus on the paramount issues of the case, to pull back and look at what is going on in the cycle of interaction involving the family, the family worker, and community. The supervisor can help identify the pain in the family, the patterns of interaction, the underlying meaning of events, and how crises maintain the family's balance.

The supervisor helps the worker to understand the family "dance," to avoid becoming mired in the family's rage, helplessness, and despair, to remain aware of his/her separateness from the family, and to address difficult issues that would otherwise be easily ignored. The supervisor's broad perspective on the needs of family members over time enables the worker to avoid becoming fixated on one critical aspect of the family and neglecting other issues.

The V. family (as described in Chapter 4) was referred because of concerns about the 11-year-old son's distractibility and refusal to do work at school. Mrs. V. had been seeing a psychiatrist for many years. At the time of referral she was looking for counseling for her son. Mr. V. and his four children were preoccupied with Mrs. V.'s fragility and the possibility that she could become suicidal at any moment.

The family worker engaged Mrs. V. in family counseling and the family stabilized, with the mother avoiding hospitalization for a significant period of time — one year. The family appeared to be making progress and the boy was doing better at school. The worker, however, missed some critical changes in the family at the start of the next school year, as the youngest daughter entered kindergarten and the oldest son developed physically as an adolescent. Both events seemed minuscule in comparison to the mother's ever-present fragility and past history of suicide attempts. These two events, however, brought up critical issues in the family concerning sexuality, past sex abuse, and abandonment. Mrs. V. took an overdose of a tranquilizer, resulting in a psychiatric hospitalization.

This time, in contrast to past suicide attempts, she took the pills and then quickly asked her husband to drive her to the hospital. This in itself was progress; however, the family worker was surprised by this seemingly unforeseen suicide gesture after a time of relative improvement. In consultation, the worker was able to see the significance of other changes in the family, e.g., the social and sexual development of the children, and how both these stages of development were life cycle changes which created "real" crises. At that point, the worker needed to understand that the family would revert to previous patterns and act out through suicide and/or sex abuse under stress.

As supervisors or consultants, we cannot just empathize or take care of the worker. We need to pull back and focus on the dynamics of the family-worker interactions. Who or what is missing? What patterns help avoid change? How are feelings and conflicts acted out by the worker? What can we predict?

The supervisor supports the worker but must not simply collude with the worker in labeling the family as "difficult" or "bad." When others become frustrated or angry, it is often too easy to protect them. The supervisor must not join the worker in acting out his or her frustration and anger toward family members. Real help for the worker means addressing the painful issues in the case and the painful issues for the worker. Growth is painful.

HAZARD 2. LACK OF SUPPORT FROM REFERRAL SOURCES AND FAMILY COURTS

We as family workers must recognize our position, including our lack of power to force families to change. We need to consider who has power to create leverage for change with the family. In many cases, only the family court can create the leverage needed to stimulate change and the greatest hazard for families is a judge who fails to make timely decisions. We begin by acknowledging our lack of control, as well as the value of not having control at the beginning of work with a family. By recognizing our lack of power we avoid the trap of attempting to take control of the family. This realization encourages us to work very hard to set up a contract supported by referral sources and agencies actively involved with the family. Most importantly, we need the support of family court judges.

In families with chronic problems where children are at risk, it is important to have a clear plan (see Chapter 10) to deal with predictable problems "when all else fails." A time line, monitoring, clear decision-making, and coordination among agencies are needed. Otherwise the worker is likely to end up angry at other systems that do not share the worker's systemic view of the family.

We need to address the needs of our referral source and to avoid becoming locked into adversarial relationships or symmetrical escalations of the family's problems. At the time of referral, the only true "client" is likely to be the referral source. We need to know what the referral sources want, what they need, and what they expect from services, as well as the laws and regulations that govern their work and ours. Together we must address pertinent issues. For instance, a mother working on getting her children back from foster care may need to have the children transported to and from her home. The distance of placement is often impossible for a poor family to conquer. Transporting clients can be therapeutic and needs to be validated; the family worker who transports has a captive client in the car. Transportation becomes part of the family worker's contract with the referring agency and part of the treatment plan.

HAZARD 3. WORKING WITHOUT A HYPOTHESIS

A sensitive family worker will quickly absorb the pain of the family; without regular supervision he/she will react more to these feelings than to the dynamics of the case. Feelings quickly become predominant over attempts to hypothesize and understand. The family worker who moves from crisis to crisis acting on immediate hunches is reacting to immediate pressures without taking the time to consider what he/she is feeling. Just like the families served, the family worker becomes embroiled in crisis after crisis, often not recognizing his/her role in the family or what issues the crises are helping to avoid.

A hypothesis about how a particular family is functioning helps the practitioner to step back and check out what is going on and what needs to change. Without a hypothesis the worker will likely react to immediate problems and become entangled in a series of "crises." We caution workers never to work without a hypothesis when dealing with the intricacies and complexity of real families. The art of the family worker is to assess and pull together feelings, observations, and facts into a hypothesis that accurately reflects the family's unique situation. The family worker can use this hypothesis to develop appropriate interventions and avoid pressures to rescue or criticize family members.

HAZARD 4. FORGETTING THE CLIENT

The essence of outreach work is to go to the family, to recognize family members' special needs and strengths, and to help them, beginning "where they are." This is the opposite of taking an orthodox "one-model" approach to families, in which the family worker utilizes a particular family systems treatment. For instance, we do not insist that we must work on a genogram or that "everybody including grandparents must come." We do invite critical members of the family and then work with those present in an effort to eventually involve other family members. This does not mean ignoring basic family systems principles, such as, "More is always better" (Whitaker, 1976), that eight to ten generations (and more) may be involved in schizophrenia (after Bowen, 1978), or the importance of working within a multigenerational context (Bowen, 1978). In fact, we would add that multiple generations (three or more) are needed to create and maintain sexual abuse, child abuse and neglect, and incest. However, our task is to engage family members and whomever we work with, to keep in mind the larger (multigenerational) family and ecosystem.

Bergman (1985) has written about barracuda families who will bite on his creative and powerful interventions. Our challenge is to engage families who are often forgotten and who will not "bite." By going out to families and recognizing the dilemmas that keep them from becoming "clients," we avoid taking only those clients who fit a particular model of therapy and ignoring the rest.

HAZARD 5. BECOMING PART OF THE FAMILY

Once the family worker is engaged in work with a family, it is very easy to become simply another stabilizing force who remains with family members as they go through repeated crises. The family worker may have succeeded in getting the family to allow him or her to visit and even to talk about critical issues. The family worker senses the extreme anger, fear, pain, and shame in the family and may choose not to confront problems for fear of losing the family and being abandoned. In essence, the family worker may give up on working for change and settle for being loved. The worker becomes an accepted supporter of a family system which cyclically appears to be on the brink of disaster.

The supervisor and consultant play a critical role in helping the worker to see how he/she may have become stuck in working with the family and in addressing painful issues for both the family worker and the family. As both "outsiders" and yet team members, the supervisor and consultant can address a cycle or pattern seen in the family and set limits on the family worker's work. This may involve a supervisor's taking a position that "This is it! We can't watch anymore!" In cases where a child or other family member is suffering, we must intervene and acknowledge our pain to the family.

An eight-year-old girl was referred because of school behavior problems which had led to suspension and the probability of expulsion. She was living with her maternal grandparents after being neglected and then abandoned by her teenage mother and father. The history revealed that the grandmother's son had been placed at age eight. When the grandmother and grandfather fought, the girl would go over to each one saying, "I love you, I love you. . . ." The grandmother would complain incessantly about the eight-year-old girl, yet defend her against the grandfather.

The grandmother gained a lot of weight. The grandfather became impotent and would not take care of a prostate problem. As both grandparents' complaints about their relationship and the girl escalated, the girl increased her acting-out in school. The family worker was regularly welcomed into the family for sessions but came back to the office frustrated, tired, and in pain.

With this family it was important for the supervisor to bring up the pattern that was emerging and to address in a review conference the proba-

bility of the girl's being expelled from school and placed outside the home — a repetition of what had happened to her uncle. In addition, we had to point out the lack of pleasure and exhaustion in the family and the fact that the worker was taking these feelings back to the office with him. Recognizing this helped to free the worker to address critical issues concerning the girl and the grandparents' need to take care of themselves and have pleasure. The grandfather went in for prostate surgery and the grandmother lost weight. The worker was also able to use the supervisor's message to help free the girl from the conflicts between her grandparents.

Hazard 6. Expecting a Miracle

Working with chronically troubled families means not getting the quick reinforcement of miracle cures. Instead we look for small changes. In the case cited above, the grandfather's going in for surgery and the grandmother's weight loss were positive signs of their addressing their own needs — small but significant changes after longstanding neglect of both their own needs and those of their grandaughter.

Human beings are not static entities or blocks of granite to be chiseled into a fixed form by the artistic family worker. Life means movement and change. For family members who have not received the security and nurturance that most of us take for granted, each developmental stage and transition may bring on stress. It is crucial that we not look for cures and that we see a client's call for help from the perspective of the family's evolution over time. A client who asks for help instead of being hotlined for abuse or neglect is a success.

Hazard 7. Ignoring Our Own and the Family's Need for Safety

Just as families cannot work on problems without a roof over their heads, workers cannot engage and work with families if they or family members fear harm to themselves or others. Workers observing guns, knives, threatening animals, etc., must recognize their own discomfort and fear and set ground rules for their own safety. "It's your choice to have a good watchdog, but I am not comfortable coming into your house unless he is placed safely in another room."

Our feelings, including our need for safety, must be shared with the family. This is illustrated in the three following cases.

A worker visiting a family in their isolated farmhouse became aware that the father, who worked for the sheriff's department, was sitting at the table with his guns still in their holsters on his belt. The family was talking about how to get closer and eliminate any future violence. The very fact that guns were present during this discussion created a feeling of fear and powerlessness in the worker. The family worker expressed her discomfort and asked that the guns be locked away during meetings. The father laughingly complied; by doing so, he showed that he was willing to work in family sessions.

In another case, a woman repeatedly threatened to hurt her spouse. The family worker asked if she really meant to do this. The woman responded "no."

Emily W. a 39-year-old mother of three, greeted her family worker and supervisor by saying that she expected her boy friend, Bill, to storm into her apartment at any moment with a loaded gun. The supervisor told Emily that if this was true, it wasn't safe for her staff or herself to remain and also wasn't safe for Emily and her children. In fact, she, under the child protective laws, would have to report Emily for neglect if Emily stayed in the apartment with her children. Emily decided to leave the apartment with her children and sessions were resumed in another location without the threat of violence. In the next session, Emily worked on providing a safer environment for her family.

In each of these examples, the family worker needed to address violent threats in order for the family worker to have sufficient comfort—to feel safe enough—to remain in the room with the necessary perspective and ability to work with family members. The family worker demonstrated that even violent threats could be addressed and by so doing helped parents to provide safety for their children. In addition, the family worker was also able to assess whether the family members involved were serious about their threats and in control of their behaviors.

Safety also includes the family, neighborhood, and home. We tell workers, "If you're not safe, you can't help a family." Going into a neighborhood known for drugs, gangs, and violent shootings is dangerous for the worker and also a dangerous environment for the family. Many poor families have had little or no choice as to where they can live. They often must learn how to cope and survive as safely as possible. The worker can share his/her fears (the dark hallway, the broken stairs, the elevator), and ask someone in the family to accompany him/her to and from the apartment. If that is not possible, the family worker may need to have another worker or supervisor come along.

HAZARD 8. DISCOUNTING FORMER WORKERS AND INFORMATION: THE EGOCENTRIC FAMILY WORKER

Many families will list a long string of professionals who have tried and failed to help them. The family may refer to these workers with disdain or anger and appeal to the new family worker to help them and do better than other family workers. The family worker may be tempted to feel that he/she has special skills or knowledge that will allow success where all others have failed. It is crucial for the worker to find out as much as possible about what has happened in the past and in no way to discount past workers.

For the family, each therapist may represent another challenge to its integrity. The egocentric worker operates from an isolated position. Rather than learning from what has happened in the past (what helped, what didn't help), the worker is left to fail again—most likely repeating what has happened before.

HAZARD 9. GIVING UP ON CRISIS-ORIENTED FAMILIES

Clients remember family workers who don't give up. Many professionals who have experienced work with crisis-oriented families would maintain that "You can't work with these families. Why bother? They won't change." Such statements ignore the strengths in these families: strengths that are often not seen without a home visit or the persistence to keep on going as the family tries to scare you away. They can and do make small changes— changes that can lead to larger systemic changes (Watzlawick et al., 1974) and can mean the difference between a child's growing up with chronic abuse and neglect versus a child's having a chance to build a positive relationship with someone who cares and will continue to be there for the child.

Being "where the client is" means recognizing the client's capacity. The worker needs to maintain realistic expectations: not too high and not too low.

A father who had been institutionalized as a child now worked long hours as a garbage collector. His children had been sexually abused while in the care of his wife, from whom he was separated. The father obtained custody of the children and was referred for services because he was yelling at the children and unable to provide the supervision needed. The worker tried to get the father to do more and to give more to the children. The man was asked to give what he had never received at a time when he was (and had been for many years) exhausted. For this father, maintaining his children in a safe environment was significant progress. Instead of insight-oriented services, he needed concrete services, such as after-school programming five days a week for his children and a homemaker.

If we operate from the assumption that a parent cannot parent, then we will give up in advance and feel hopeless. Even with the most depressed and helpless-looking clients, strengths may exist in the larger family system. We work to bring in other family members, to learn more about how the client's helplessness fits in, and where resources may lie that could be tapped to help the family. Helping families means building positive, supportive relationships for the parents as well as children.

The multigenerational family has been pictured as a tree with a stem and branches above ground and roots below. The tree in trouble is a tree that in many cases has damage to its roots or has sustained damage through the environment. With only a fragile hold in the soil, the family is vulnerable to every storm. Every gust of wind poses a crisis that could topple the tree.

In families, root damage is caused by bonding problems, cutoffs from relatives, enduring conflicts among family members, and distance based on a need to avoid painful issues. The practitioner needs to know where the root damage is and where connections can be rebuilt or strengthened.

HAZARD 10. NOT LIKING ANYTHING ABOUT YOUR CLIENT

Practitioners may have an immediate reaction to particular clients: "I don't want them." Other practitioners may feel that they don't want any crisis-oriented families; they should find a field where they can work with clients who have different kinds of problems, e.g., medical, developmental disabilities, etc. A practitioner working with a crisis-oriented family member needs to be able to see something positive in that person or family. With a difficult and often an unlikable client, we ask ourselves, "What does this client do to be unlovable? How did this client become this way, and how does being unlikable function to protect the client or his/her family?" We can address this directly, e.g., "You're working hard to keep me away or make me not like you." This often leads to denial by the family member. We can continue to work by saying, "Okay, then let's work together. And when you do something that I think is trying to keep me away, I'll let you know."

Work with crisis-oriented families means developing positive connections. This will be impossible if we see nothing positive in the client. Each of us has our own likes, dislikes, and special "triggers" which activate intense feelings. To like or not like a client is a judgment. While we can use our feelings as clues to family dynamics, we need to avoid becoming judgmental. Instead, we need to look at how and why a client keeps so many people away.

HAZARD 11. BECOMING ATTACHED TO ONE FAMILY MEMBER

Practitioners need to be sensitive to the needs of their clients without becoming tied into the needs of one particular family member and ending up as a combatant in family battles. If we work with a child blamed for family problems, it is extremely easy to empathize with the child's pain and to see the child as an innocent scapegoat for the family's problems. Professionals working with children are typically sensitive to the needs of a child because of their own family experiences. We quickly become locked into the role of a rescuer for a child and use our diagnostic skills to search for other family members (or sometimes other professionals) causing the child's pain. It is very easy to ignore (or excuse) the child's role in maintaining a troubled family or to get caught up in the rebellion of the child to his/her parents.

Losing perspective of the interactional cycle of family members, community authorities, and family workers occurs not only in individual work with scapegoated children but also in intensive efforts to help parents who have been neglectful or abusive. Once we experience the extreme pain and fragility of a parent, it is easy to become engaged in prolonged efforts to help that parent. As time goes on, it is very easy for the practitioner to ignore or simply not to see the pain experienced by the children in the family. The practitioner relentlessly pursues the goal of helping the parent to become a better parent and avoids addressing the extent of neglect or abuse that the children are living with on a day-to-day, month-to-month basis. The destructive impact of this abuse or neglect continues. The parent may after some years improve, but what about the children?

We need to address difficult issues in our work with crisis-oriented families. This means facing issues of neglect that may interfere with the current crisis or effort to mobilize a parent.

A teenager reported to a family worker that her mother went to bars, leaving the younger children alone. When the practitioner arrived at the parent's home to take her to an important meeting for the teenager, who was the "identified patient" in the family, she found that the six-year-old daughter had been left alone and that her mother had already gone to the meeting. The practitioner left the girl home alone and did not report this as another sign of neglect or take action to address the needs of the six-year-old. Instead she focused her energy on continuing to engage an angry parent and to help that parent take charge of a rebellious teenager. Neglect in the family remained a hidden but crucial issue.

Gradually the practitioner becomes identified with the individual he or she is trying to help. The pressure experienced by the practitioner to generate change in his or her client leads to a search for someone else to blame if change does not occur. The practitioner becomes seduced into identifying with one individual and missing the role that individual has chosen to play in the family. With different practitioners working with different members of the family, it is often possible for family battles to be played out between different practitioners, each representing the needs and desperation of his or her particular client. Each family worker becomes an ally of one family member or one generation, e.g., the children, the grandparents, and becomes embroiled in the family's chronic battles.

HAZARD 12. DOING THE FAMILY'S WORK

Practitioners can also get caught in the role of perpetually doing things for the family. This may stabilize the family but also discounts the ability and responsibility of family members to do what is needed. Initially in working with a crisis-oriented family we want to help family members take charge. After going through the first crisis with them, we pull back, putting our efforts into predicting and slowing down family crises.

The practitioner who cannot pull back will soon experience exhaustion and become a part of the family's repetitive crises. Ongoing work with crises provides a high level of excitement, which can help the worker to avoid his/her own depression and frustration with not seeing change. Crises make us feel active, needed, and powerful—if only on a temporary basis. Like an addiction, however, repetitive work with a family's crises has a down side—hopelessness, despair, and exhaustion.

We can easily take on the immense responsibilities of underresponsible clients and soon find ourselves carrying the exhaustion of the families we seek to help. Similarly, supervisors can take on the burdens of their staff. Exhaustion is transferred upwards from the family, with the professionals involved feeling more and more tired. As our personal support systems (spouse, friends, relatives) tire of hearing of our exhaustion, we will be told that we are working "too hard" and "are crazy" for working with these families. The family worker and supervisor soon come to feel both overwhelmed and isolated.

The key to avoiding an epidemic of exhaustion is to recognize our exhaustion and give this back to the client. In supervision sessions with an exhausted worker it is important to: (1) empathize with the worker; (2) assess what is exhausting about the work; (3) assess whether the family is engaged; and (4) help the worker to give the exhaustion back to the family.

We share how overwhelmed and tired we feel with the family, e.g., "We're exhausted, aren't you?" We also share our frustration. If the exhaustion comes from deep fears or concerns about what might happen, it is important for us to set realistic goals, including small changes, and for the supervisor to give a message that, if there is no change in crucial areas of the family's safety and well-being, we will need to leave. "When are you going to put a stop to it?" "We can't work if the children and you continue to live with threats of more abuse." We need honestly to say to the parents that unless things change we will not have enough energy to continue; in fact, we would be too tired to help. This is an approach that works only when the family worker has been engaged with a family. The supervisor's statement about the need for discharge serves as an intervention to free a family worker and to motivate a family which has been engaged with the family worker.

In permanency work, exhaustion usually means that it is necessary to reassess and develop a much tighter and stronger plan with county authorities. It may be important to "up the ante" with, for example, more visits in order to get some motion. For instance, a parent may be calling for return of her children but visit infrequently over a long period. County authorities and past workers may feel that the parent will never be able to take the child back. The child remains bouncing back and forth between the family and foster homes with little or no change. In such cases it is important to set a clear time frame and clarify what needs to happen by when and with what consequences.

If we feel exhausted at the beginning of the case, it may mean that we are getting fed up with crisis-oriented families. Or it may be a signal that a certain family is activating our own personal "triggers." It may also mean that we do not have sufficient agency or supervisor support. It is important that these issues be addressed in supervision and that cases be assigned so that staff can work with clients in a positive and productive manner. This may mean that a supervisor analyzes who on his/her staff works best with what kind of clients. It also means assistance to the family worker in developing skills and strengths to work with more types of clients. Often clients whom a family worker cannot stand represent difficult issues; the family worker who is willing to address those issues can often grow in his/her personal life.

If we feel exhausted in the middle phases of our work with a family, it is likely that we have become locked into an uncomfortable role. We need to carefully assess what is bothering us. For instance, we may "love" a family but ignore troubling issues. We may have become incorporated into the system without seeing change and still worry that things are not working, e.g., that abuse or neglect may be continuing.

If we feel exhausted at the end of our work with a family, we must consider the meaning of loss of the family for ourselves as well as the loss of the family worker for the family. Ending with a family involves elements of the grief process. As professionals we may try to deny or ignore our feelings of loss and anger. Here again, it is crucial to have a supervisor who will help the family worker to address these feelings and recognize the growth that has taken place.

HAZARD 13. KEEPING SECRETS

We as practitioners need to avoid keeping secrets and share our perceptions with clients. In this way, we avoid inadvertently colluding with a family member or with outside agencies in hiding an issue that needs to be addressed. For instance, in the case cited earlier, the practitioner who ignored the six-year-old child left home alone was in effect colluding with the parent in neglect.

A quick test as to the level of secrecy in our work is to ask ourselves whether we would be uncomfortable allowing clients to read our reports or the records. Unfounded or biased assumptions that can be damaging to a client should not be part of a record.

HAZARD 14. WORKING WITHOUT SUFFICIENT SUPPORT AND RECOGNITION

It is crucial that an agency recognize the extreme difficulty of working with crisis-oriented families. Often outreach workers are part of a larger agency working in many fields or programs ranging from private adoptions to traditional outpatient clinics where clients come in seeking and willing to pay for help. Outreach workers may feel discounted if the agency operates under the premise that "Everyone works the same; everyone faces the same issues." This ignores the necessary skills and competence required of outreach workers. The extreme difficulty of this work needs to be addressed in contracts between the agency and funding source. Funding is needed for both monetary recognition and support (supervision and consultation).

Effective work with crisis-oriented families requires the full backing and support of the agency. This means recognizing the value and skills inherent in outreach work and giving credit to the workers who provide this service. It also means providing a rich and stimulating professional development program. Workers need to learn the skills of outreach work and to experience the value of this effort.

Respecting clients also means learning from them what helps and what doesn't help. Asking for client feedback through brief surveys provides a rich source of information to family workers about what is useful, as well as reinforcement to workers. Clients may be able to indicate on a survey how helpful services have been and yet not be able to share this appreciation directly. Evaluation programs are a critical part of an effective program because staff need to see that the work they are doing is useful.

Recognizing the value of outreach is essential if the agency wants to begin where the family "is at." If a "resistant" family does not get outreach, problems will likely escalate until the family is court-ordered to come in for treatment or somebody is placed. Then, when work begins, families see workers as part of a larger institution which is their adversary. Outreach is a way to get families to see practitioners as helpful—a tremendous accomplishment in itself. Outreach is also a way of providing a much needed service to referral agencies, who often resent going to an institution for help and then being asked to provide outreach work while the "professionals" wait in nicely appointed clinics for the referral source to bring in the "client."

The agency needs to recognize staff efforts by compensating them appropriately for their skills and the difficulty of their jobs. Salary scales need to reflect the responsibility of coordination with referral sources (schools, medical centers, etc.) and the competence needed by a worker going out alone to a family which has been described as being "resistant" to past services and at high risk of violence or neglect. Outreach workers are giving up the comforts, security, and control of the clinic to go out on their own using themselves as their primary resource.

THE NEED FOR OUTREACH AND PERMANENCY PLANNING FOR FAMILIES

Our greatest concern is that families are not getting the support they need and that fewer professionals are willing to reach out and help those families whose needs are the greatest. In both popular and professional literature there is a tremendous focus on developing and caring for oneself. Outreach was once an integral part of health care and the core of social work in the United States. Over the past few decades physicians have, by and large, stopped making house calls and social workers have come to often feel demeaned by both the image of social work presented in the media and the low compensation typically provided for social work positions. In reaction to this feeling of being demeaned, many social workers in the 1980s have moved into private practices and out of child welfare work.

Outreach work is for people who have a fascination with the human condition—professionals who are both sensitive and eager to understand more about the hows and whys of human behavior and have a curiosity about what makes people tick (after Friedman, 1987). Outcomes in work with crisis-oriented families are seen by those who know how to look. Small changes in a family's day-to-day life can eventually lead to an end of placement, an end of abuse, and a home for the child "in limbo."

In a world with less resources, it has become more fashionable to avoid those who are described as "resistant," "bad," or "crazy" (especially the poor). Professionals can simply say "you're not ready" for therapy. "Come see me when you are ready to work on my terms." In contrast, we are advocating that human services agencies provide programs in which professionals work to engage "hard-to-reach" families. The cost of perpetual crisis is simply too high—for family members and the community.

Initial Home-Based Family Assessment

Date of visit: _____

Name of referred child: _____

Family members present during visit: _____

_____

Family members absent from visit: _____

_____

Reasons given for absence of family members: _____

_____

_____

Parsons' workers participating: _____
_____

Description of house, furnishings, and neighborhood: _____
_____
_____
_____

Family's understanding of what the problems are and why Parsons was asked to visit: _____
_____
_____

How long have the problems been building up? _____
_____
_____

What resources has the family used to deal with problems: _____
_____
_____

Have they been of help? Yes _____ No _____. In what way? _____
_____
_____

What help/service the family wants now: _____
_____
_____

Family roles as observed during visit. Who makes the decisions?
_____
_____

Who does the talking? _____
_____

Who keeps the pressure on? _____
_____

Who takes the pressure off (peacemaker)? _____
_____

Who sets the rules? _____
_____

Who disciplines? _____
_____
_____

Family seating arrangements (diagram showing who relates to whom and whether positive/negative): _____

_____

_____

_____

Who are the extended family and/or friends available to the family in the community? _____

_____

Are they positive or negative influences? _____

_____

Are finances a family concern? _____

_____

Observation of family strengths: _____

_____

_____

Observation of family weaknesses: _____

_____

Unresolved assessment questions based on this visit: _____

_____

Recommended direction for the next step in the assessment process: _____

_____

Treatment needs which were clarified by home visit assessment: _____

_____

Permanency Work: An Outline

The following outline provides a framework for coordinating permanency work.

I. Review of referral material and case records
   A. The original crises bringing the family into care are reviewed. Events which led to the first placement (even several placements ago) provide important clues to family strengths and vulnerabilities.
   B. Court orders and placement conditions are clarified. Copies of the court order are obtained for both the family worker and the family of the child. Many families have appeared in court but have little idea what the judge said in the formal order. The court order is concrete and helpful in bringing reality to the family and to the child.
   C. It is important to determine who are the legal parents.
   D. Ongoing consultation with legal staff begins at this point.
II. Preparation for the permanency meeting

A. Home visits are arranged to engage the family, the child, and foster parents and to set up a meeting in which the family and helping professionals can be present to plan for the children. Parents need to be engaged by the helping worker and asked to identify any significant family members they may want to be present.

B. A chairperson is assigned. In counties in which the agency has an ongoing contract, the agency's consultant may co-chair the meeting. If there is one agency involved, we suggest that the chairperson be the family worker's supervisor. If more than one agency is involved with either the family or the child, a foster care supervisor from the department of social services should chair the meeting.

III. The permanency meeting

A. All present need to review the past and what brought the children into foster care and how parents and children have been handling separations.

B. All present need to discuss their concerns and to discuss the court order. Children need to be involved in every step, helped to express their questions, and to understand what will be happening.

C. We like to have all children present at the meeting. The meeting may be the only time that siblings get to see each other. It is also a time to observe attachments. Who holds the baby—mother, father, siblings? Which children are in foster care? Where do the children sit—beside their biological parents, next to the foster mother, or next to the department of social services worker? Do the parents take charge of their children? Do the parents help their children? Or do the parents demand attention for themselves?

D. The permanency meeting is an opportunity for children to hear two critical messages: (1) that the parents need to do some specific things before they can go home, and (2) that the children cannot influence how soon they can go home.

E. The parents, children, and all helping agencies need to agree on the goals that are established for the family. Children over five years of age with behavior problems while in foster care need to have goals to improve behaviors. We need to stress that we will help parents reunite with their children as quickly as possible.

F. Despite their children being in foster care, parents are urged to become involved in their health and school needs. In cases of medical or educational needs, it is important that foster parents accept the parents' involvement and support the parents' going with their children to school meetings and doctor's appointments.

G. Time limits are established and the next review meeting is scheduled. The family worker or coordinator saves time and energy by scheduling later sessions while everyone is assembled at this meeting.

H. Progress review conferences are scheduled frequently since these meetings both create and help maintain anxiety needed for change. We find it helpful to review and clarify all professionals' roles at the review conference. What will they be doing with family members during and between conferences? We also need to be sure that the parents have one primary helper working on reuniting them with their children.

IV. Transportation and Concrete Services

    A. Transporting children to and from visits is an important therapeutic task and we want to involve the family if at all possible. Time in the car is time with the child at the height of his or her anxiety. If county social services and agency family workers are to share the task of transporting a child, the family worker should be the one who brings the child to the family. The family worker needs to be seen as helping the family to reunite.

    B. It is also very important that the family worker be involved with all ancillary agencies to help the family secure the concrete services necessary to reunite a child with his/her family. No child should be deprived of his or her family because the family cannot get such necessities as a bed, additional food in the home during visits, etc. At the same time, children must see their parents' success or failure realistically. They can be aided in this process by seeing that their parents are receiving as much concrete help as possible.

V. Predicting crises as anxiety grows

    A. In order to predict crises that will likely recur as visits increase, it is *most* important to involve the foster parents in the reunion process. They can share their input as to predictable crises occurring once visits gain momentum. They will also be able to hear what children may or may not do to try to take charge, i.e., act out to get themselves evicted and returned home sooner.

    B. The parents need to be involved in counseling so that they too will hear about what their child might do. They also need to hear the family worker's predictions as to what crises will occur to avoid change, decisions, and reunion.

    C. All helpers need to agree that changes in the treatment plan will be discussed with the family and children at progress meetings. Helpers need to understand and be part of predicting crises.

    D. Meetings need to address the pressures, the pace, and the pain experienced as well as the progress or lack of progress the family is making. Meetings are essential so that all those involved with the family can deal with events between meetings therapeutically.

REFERENCES

Angelou, Maya (1985). Introduction. In A. Norman, *Keeping families together: The case for family preseveration*. New York: The Edna McConnell Clark Foundation.

Ausloos, G. (1978, October). *Delinquency and family dynamics*. Paper presented at the International Psycho-Education Seminar, Paris.

Ausloos, G. (1981, October). *Acting out adolescents: Systems in conflict*. Keynote address presented at the Second Annual Parsons/Sage Fall Institute, Albany, New York.

Ausloos, G. (1985, April). *Systemic approach to acting-out youth in and out of placement*. Symposium conducted at Parsons Child and Family Center, Albany, New York.

Ausloos, G. (1986). The march of time: Rigid or chaotic transactions, two different ways of living time, *Family Process*, *25*(4), 549–557.

Bateson, G. (1979). *Mind and nature: A necessary unity*. New York: Dutton.

Beck, A. J., Kline, S. A., & Greenfield, L. A. (1988). Survey of youth in custody, 1987. Washington, D.C.: Bureau of Justice Statistics, U.S. Department of Justice.

Bell, J. E. (1963). A theoretical position for family group therapy, *Family Process*, *2*(1), 1–14.

Bepko, C. & Krestan, J. (1985). *The responsibility trap: A blueprint for treating the alcoholic family*. New York: The Free Press.

193

Bergman, J. S. (1985). *Fishing for barracuda: Pragmatics of brief systemic therapy*. New York: W. W. Norton & Company.

Bergman, J. S. (1986, March 6, 7). *Fishing for barracuda: Pragmatics of brief systemic therapy*. Special Conference for Parsons/Sage Winter-Spring Programs, Albany, New York.

Berman, C. (1987, December). No place to call home, *Redbook*, p. 156.

Block, N. M. & Libowitz, A. S. (1983). *Recidivism in foster care*. New York: Child Welfare League of America.

Boszormenyi-Nagy, I. & Spark, G. (1984). *Invisible loyalties*. New York: Brunner/Mazel.

Bowen, M. (1978). *Family therapy in clinical practice*. New York: Jason Aronson.

Bowlby, J. (1960). Grief and mourning in infancy and early childhood. In R. S. Eissler, A. Freud, H. Hartman, & M. Kris (Eds.). *Psychoanalytic Study of the Child*, Vol. 15. New York: International Universities Press.

Bowlby, J. (1973). Separation: Anxiety and anger. (*Attachment and loss: Vol. 2.*). New York: Basic Books.

Bowlby, J. (1983). Attachment. (*Attachment and loss: Vol. 1*) (2nd ed.). New York: Basic Books.

Breit, M., Im, W., & Wilner, R. S. (1983). Strategic approaches with resistant families, *The American Journal of Family Therapy*, *11*(1), 51–58.

Cecchin, G. (1987). Hypothesizing, circularity, and neutrality revisited: An invitation to curiosity. *Family Process*, *26*(4), 405–413.

Child Welfare League of America (1987a). *Report of the Child Welfare League of America National Adoption Task Force*. (p. 4). New York: Author.

Child Welfare League of America. (1987b). Study finds child welfare workers earn less than trash collectors. *Children's Voice, Vol. 3*, p. 4.

Claburn, W. E., Magura, S., & Chizeck, S. P. (1977, December). Case reopening: An emerging issue in child welfare services, *Child Welfare*, *56*, 655–663.

Cole, E. S., (1985). Permanency planning—A better definition, *Permanency Report*, *3*(3), p. 4. New York: Child Welfare League of America.

Compton, B. (1979, May). *The family-centered project revisited*. School of Social Work, University of Minnesota, photocopy.

Council of Family and Child Caring Agencies (1987, May). *Child abuse alert: A desk reference*. (pp. 1–6). New York: Author.

Donley, K. S. (1983, April). *Adoption disruptions before and after legalization*. Presentation at "Think Tank" Symposium. Cornell University Cooperative Extension, New York, New York.

Donley, K. S. (1984). *Post placement service analysis*. New York Spaulding for Children. Unpublished manuscript.

Dulberger, J. A. (1988). *Refuge or repressor: The role of the orphan asylum in the lives of poor children and their families in late-nineteenth-century America*. Unpublished doctoral dissertation, Carnegie-Mellon University, Pittsburgh, PA.

Erikson, E. (1986). *Childhood and society*. 35th anniversary edition. New York: W. W. Norton & Company.

Fanshel, D. (1971, February). The exit of children from foster care: An interim report, *Child Welfare*, *50*, 65–81.

Fanshel, D. & Shinn, E. B. (1978). *Children in foster care: A longitudinal investigation*. New York: Columbia University Press.

Farber, E. A. & Egeland, B. (1987). Invulnerability among abused and neglected children. In E. J. Anthony & B. J. Cohler (Eds.). *The invulnerable child*, (pp. 253–288). New York: Guilford Press.

Fein, E., Maluccio, A. N., Hamilton, V. J., & Ward, D. E. (1983, November/December). After foster care: outcomes of permanency planning for children. *Child Welfare, 62*, 485–558.

Fein, E., Maluccio, A. N., & Kulger, M. (1986, August). *Psychology and permanency planning—who me?* Presented at the 94th Annual convention of the American Psychological Association, Washington, DC.

Festinger, Trudy. (1983). *No one ever asked us: A postscript to foster care.* New York: Columbia University Press.

Finkelstein, N. E. (1980). Children in limbo, *Social Work, 25*(2), 100–105.

Finkelstein, N. E. (1981). Family-centered group care—The children's institution, from a living center to a center for change. In A. Maluccio & P. Sinanoglu (Eds.). *The challenge of partnership: Working with parents of children in foster care.* New York: Child Welfare League of America.

Finkelstein, N. E. (1988). The role of residential care. In C. Gorman & R. Small (Eds.). *Permanence and family support: Changing practice for group child care.* Washington, DC: Child Welfare League of America, Inc.

Fisch, R., Weakland, J. H. & Segal, L. (1982). *The tactics of change: Doing therapy briefly.* San Francisco, CA: Jossey-Bass Publishers.

Fisher, L., Kokes, R. F., Cole, R. E., Perkins, P. M. and Wynne, L. C. (1987). Competent children at risk: A study of well-functioning offspring of disturbed parents. In E. J. Anthony & B. J. Cohler (Eds.). *The invulnerable child* (pp. 211–228). New York: Guilford Press.

Fontana, V. (1988). Keynote Address Presented at Symposium on Abuse and Neglect: Prevention and Intervention. New York State Commission on Quality Care, Bolton Landing, New York, March 9, 1988.

Fossum, M. A. & Mason, M. J. (1986). *Facing shame: Families in recovery.* New York: W. W. Norton & Company.

Fraiberg, S. H. (1962, January). A therapeutic approach to reactive ego disturbances in children in placement, *American Journal of Orthopsychiatry, 32*, 18–31.

Frawley, R. (1986). Preventive services evaluation report: Parsons Child and Family Center Prevention Program. Albany, New York: New York State Council on Families (photocopy).

Friedman, Edwin. (1987). How to succeed in therapy without really trying, *Family Therapy Networker, 11*(3), 27–31 & 68.

Frommer, E. (1979, March). Preventive Work in Vulnerable Families with Young Children, *Child Abuse and Neglect III*, p. 778.

Gardner, R. A. (1970). *The boys and girls book about divorce.* New York: Jason Aronson.

Gardner, R. A. (1973). The talking, feeling and doing game. Cresskill, New Jersey: Creative Therapeutics.

Gardner, R. A. (1975). *Psychotherapeutic approaches to the resistant child.* New York: Jason Aronson.

Germain, C. B. (1979). Ecology and social work. In C. B. Germain (Ed.). *Social work practice: People and environments.* New York: Columbia University Press.

Goldstein, J., Freud, A., & Solnit, A. (1973). *Beyond the best interests of the child.* New York: Free Press.

Gruber, A. (1978). *Children in foster care.* New York: Human Sciences Press.

Guerin, P. (1976). *Family therapy: Theory and practice.* New York: Gardner Press.

Gurman, A. & Kniskern, D. (1978). Research of marital and family therapy: Progress, perspective and prospect. In S. Garfield & A. Bergin (Eds.), *Hand-*

book of psychotherapy and behavior change (pp. XX, 2nd ed.). New York: John Wiley & Sons.

Hartman, A. (1978). Diagrammatic assessment of family relationships, *Social Casework*, *59*(8), 465–476.

Hartman, A. (1984). *Working with adoptive families beyond placement*. New York: Child Welfare League of America.

Hartman, A. (1987, March). *Innovations in Social Work Practice*. State University of New York at Albany, Social Work Conference.

Henley, H. C. & Plumer, E. H. (Eds.). (1978). *The residential child care worker: Concepts and functions*. Chapel Hill, NC: University of North Carolina Press.

Horowitz, M. J. (1976). *Stress response syndromes*. New York: Jason Aronson.

Jewett, C. L. (1978). *Adopting the older child*. Harvard, MA: The Harvard Common Press.

Joel, B. (1986). *Running on ice* (Bridge Album), OCT 40402. Columbia Records: CBS Inc.

Kadushin, A. (1970). *Adopting older children*. New York: Columbia University Press.

Kagan, R. M. (1982). Storytelling and game therapy for children in placement, *Child Care Quarterly*, *11*(4), 280–290.

Kagan, R. M. (1983). Engaging family competence to prevent repetitive and lengthy institutionalization of acting-out youth. *Residential Group Care & Treatment*, *1*(3), 55–70.

Kagan, R. M. (1986). Game therapy for children in placement. In C. E. Schaefer & S. E. Reid. (Eds). *Game play: Therapeutic uses of childhood games*. New York: John Wiley & Sons.

Kagan, R. M. & Reid, W. J. (1986). Critical factors in the adoption of emotionally disturbed youths. *Child Welfare*, *65*(1), 63–73.

Kagan, R. M., Reid, W. J., Roberts, S. E. & Silverman-Pollow, J. (1987). Engaging families of court-mandated youths in an alternative to institutional placement. *Child Welfare*, *66*(4), 365–376.

Kagan, R. M. & Schlosberg, S. B. (1988). When love is not enough: Creating a context for change. In C. Gorman & R. Small (Eds.), *Permanence and family support: Changing practice for group child care*. Washington, DC: Child Welfare League of America.

Kaplan, L. (1986). *Working with multiproblem families*. Lexington, MA.: D. C. Heath & Company.

Karpman, S. (1968). Script drama analysis. *Transactional Analysis Bulletin*, *26*, 39–43.

Katz, L. (1977, March). Older child adoptive placement: A time of family crisis. *Child Welfare*, *61*, 165–171.

Keith, A. (1975). The place of families in treatment. In *The professional child care worker: A guide to skills, knowledge, techniques and attitudes*. New York: Association Press.

Keith-Lucas, A. & Sanford, C. (1977). *Group child care as a family service*. Chapel Hill, NC: University of North Carolina Press.

Klein, A. F. (1975). *The professional child care worker: A guide to skills, knowledge, techniques and attitudes*. New York: Association Press.

Krystal, H. (Ed.) (1976). *Massive psychic trauma*. New York: International Universities Press.

Krystal, H. (1978). Trauma and affects. In A. Solnit (Ed.), *Psychoanalytic study of the child, Vol. 33*. New Haven, CT: Yale University Press.

Krystal, H. (1984). Psychoanalytic views on human emotional damages. In B. A.

van der Kolk (Ed.), *Post-traumatic stress disorder: Psychological and biological sequelae*. Washington, DC: American Psychiatric Press.

Kushner, H. S. (1981). *When bad things happen to good people*. New York: Avon Books.

Lahti, J., Green, K., Emlen, A., Zendry, J., Clarkson, Q., Kuehnel, M., & Casciato, J. (1978). *A followup study of the Oregon project*. Portland, OR.: Regional Research Institute for Human Services, Portland State University.

Littauer, C. (1980, April). Working with families of children in residential treatment. *Child Welfare, 59*, 225–234.

Long, N. (1986, March 19) *Psychotic and acting-out youth in the classroom*. Workshop presented at Parsons Child and Family Center, Albany, New York.

Maas, H. S. & Engler, R. E. (1959). *Children in need of parents*. New York: Columbia Univerity Press.

Mahler, M. S., Pine, F. & Bergman, A. (1975). *The psychological birth of the human infant: Symbiosis and individuation*. New York: Basic Books.

Maltsberger, J. (1985, September) *The borderline patient: Dynamics and treatment*. Symposium conducted at Capital District Psychiatric Center, Albany, New York.

Maluccio, A. (1979). *Learning from Clients*. New York: The Free Press.

Maluccio, A. N., Fein, E., & Olmstead, K. A. (1986). *Permanency planning for children*. New York: Tavistock Publications.

Maslow, A. (1962). *Toward a psychology of being*. Princeton, New Jersey: D. Van Nostrand Co.

Masterson, J. F. (1976). *Psychotherapy of the borderline adult*. New York: Brunner/ Mazel, Inc.

McGoldrick, M. & Carter, E. (1982). The family life cycle. In F. Walsh (Ed.) *Normal family processes*. New York: The Guilford Press.

McGoldrick, M. & Gerson, R. (1985). *Genograms in family assessment*. New York: W. W. Norton & Company.

Minuchin, S. & Fishman, H. C. (1981). *Family therapy techniques*. Cambridge, MA: Harvard University Press.

Morawetz, A. & Walker, G. (1984). *Brief therapy with single-parent families*. New York: Brunner/Mazel.

Moss, S. Z. & Moss, M. S. (1984). Threat to place a child. *American Journal of Orthopsychiatry, 54*(1), 168–173.

Murdock, G. P. (Ed.) (1965). *Social Structure*. New York: Free Press.

Murray, H. & Bellak, L. (1973). Thematic Apperception Test. Cambridge, MA: Harvard University Press.

Muuss, R. E. (1968). *Theories of adolescence* (2nd ed.). New York: Random House.

Norman, A. (1985). *Keeping families together: The case for family preseveration*. New York: The Edna McConnell Clark Foundation.

Oliver, J. (1977). Some studies of families in which children suffer maltreatment, *Challenge of child abuse*, A. Franklin (Ed.) (New York: Grune & Stratton, 1977), 16–37.

Papp, P. (1983). *The process of change*. New York: Guilford Press.

Parad, H. (Ed.) (1965). *Crisis intervention: selected readings*. New York: Family Service Association.

Pittman, F. S. (1984, March). Wet cocker spaniel therapy: An essay on technique in family therapy, *Family Process, 23*, 1–9, p. 5.

Pittman, F. (1987). *Turning points: Treating families in transition and crisis*. New York: W. W. Norton & Company.

Reid, W. J., Kagan, R. M., Kaminsky, A., & Helmer, K. (1987). Adoptions of older institutionalized youth, *Social Casework, 68*(3), 140–149.

Reid, W. J., Kagan, R. M., & Schlosberg, S. B. (1988). Prevention of placement:

Critical factors in program success, *Child Welfare, 67*(1), 25–36.

Rieker, P. R, & Carmen, E. H. (1986). The victim-to-patient process: The disconfirmation and transformation of abuse. *American Journal of Orthopsychiatry, 56,*(3), 360–370.

Riessman, F. (1973). New approaches to mental health treatment for low income people. In J. Fischer (Ed.), *Interpersonal helping: Emerging approaches for social work practice.* Springfield, Il: Child C. Thomas.

Roberts, G. E. (1982). Roberts Apperception Test for Children. Los Angeles, CA.: Western Psychological Services.

Rutter, M. (1981). *Maternal deprivation reassessed.* Harmondsworth, England: Penguin Books.

Sacco, F. (1987). *A field training manual.* Agawam, MA.: Outreach Specialists, Incorporated.

Schlosberg, S. (1987, October). Permanency training. New York State Sanction — Funding Training Classes. Binghamton, New York.

Schlosberg, S. B. & Kagan, R. M. (1988, January). Practice strategies for engaging chronic multiproblem families. *Social Casework, 69,* 3–9.

Seligson, T., (1988, July 31). Wanted: A permanent home. *Parade Magazine,* pp. 4–7. New York: Parade.

Seltzer, M. M. & Bloksberg, L. M. (1987). Permanency planning and its effects on foster children: A review of the literature *Social Work, 32*(1), 65–68.

Selvini Palazzoli, M., Boscolo, L., Cecchin, G., & Prata, G. (1978). *Paradox and counterparadox: A new model in the therapy of the family in schizophrenic transaction* (E. V. Burt, Trans.). New York: Jason Aronson.

Selvini Palazzoli, M., Boscolo, L., Cecchin, G., & Prata, G. (1980). Hypothesizing, circularity, neutrality: Three guidelines for the conductor of the session. *Family Process, 19*(1), 3–12.

Sherman, E., Neuman, R., & Shyne, W. (1973). *Children adrift in foster care: A study of alternative approaches.* New York: Child Welfare League of America.

Simon, R. (1987). Good-bye paradox, hello invariant prescription: An interview with Mara Selvini Palazzoli, *Family Therapy Networker, 11*(5), 16–33.

Simpson, E. B. (1987). *Orphans: Real and imaginary* (1st ed.). New York: Weidenfeld & Nicolson.

Spinetta, J. & Rigler, D. (1972, April). The Child Abusing Parent, a Psychological Review, *Psychological Bulletin,* LXVII, pp. 296–304.

Spitz, R. A. (1945). Hospitalism. An inquiry into the genesis of psychiatric conditions in early childhood. In R. S. Eissler, A. Freud, H. Hartman, & M. Kris (Eds.). *The psychoanalytic study of the child,* Vol. 15., 1960. New York: International Universities Press.

Stark, F. H. (1985). Improving the lives of foster care and adopted children. Congressional Record. (June 19, 1985). E 2891–2892.

Steinhauer, P. (1974, April). *How to succeed in the business of creating psychopaths without even trying.* Unpublished manuscript. University of Toronto.

Steinhauer, P. (1985). *Permanence, placement and a child's developmental needs.* Workshop presented at Parsons-Sage Winter/Spring Program, Albany, New York, February 28, 1985.

Thomas, C. B. (1967, June). *The resolution of object loss following foster home placement.* Smith College Studies in Social Work, p. 179.

Tomm, K. (1987). Interventive interviewing: Part II. Reflexive questioning as a means to enable self-healing. *Family Process, 26*(2), 167–183.

Tomm, K. (1988). Interventive interviewing: Part III. Intending to ask lineal, circular, strategic, or reflexive questions? *Family Process, 27*(1), 1–15.

Treadway, David. (1987, September 18). *The wolf in sheep's clothing: Alcoholism in the family*. Keynote address presented at the Eighth Annual Parsons/Sage Fall Institute, Albany, New York.

Trieschman, A. E., Whittaker, J. K., & Brendtro, L. K. (1969). *The other 23 hours*. Chicago, Il: Aldine Publishing Company.

Uhlig, R. H., Plumer, E. H., Galasy, J. R., Ballard, G., & Henley, H. C. (1977). *Basic training course for residential child care workers*. Washington, DC: Children's Bureau, Office of Child Development, Department of Health, Education, and Welfare.

United States Department of Health and Human Services, Administration for Children, Youth and Families, Office of Human Development Services. (1983). *Child welfare research notes #1*. Washington, DC.

Vaillant, G. (1986, August). Attachment, loss and rediscovery. *The Psychiatric Times*, pp. 1, 10–15.

Walk, R. D. (1956). Self-ratings of fear in a fear-involving situation, *Journal of Abnormal and Social Psychology*, 52, 171–178.

Watzlawick, P., Weakland, J. H., & Fisch, R. (1974). *Change: Principles of problem formation and problem resolution*. New York: W. W. Norton & Company.

Wegscheider, S. (1981). *Another chance: Hope and health for the alcoholic family*. Palo Alto, CA: Science and Behavior Books.

Weitzman, J. (1985, December). Engaging the severely dysfunctional family in treatment: Basic considerations. *Family Process*, 24, 473–485.

Whitaker, C. (1976). A family is a four-dimensional relationship. In P. Guerin (Ed.). *Family therapy: Theory and practice*, (pp. 182–192). New York: Gardner Press.

Whittaker, J. K. (1981). Family involvement in residential treatment: A support system for biological parents. In A. Maluccio & P. Sinanoglu (Eds.). *The challenge of partnership: Working with parents of children in foster care*. New York: Child Welfare League of America.

Wynne, L. C., Ryckoff, I., Day, J., Hirsch, S. I. (1958). Pseudo-mutuality in the family relationships of schizophrenics. *Psychiatry*, 21, 205–220.

Zigler, E. F., Weiss, H. B., Kagan, S. L. (Undated). Programs to strengthen families. Chicago, Il: The Family Resource Coalition.

INDEX